Analyzing
Everyday Texts

RHETORIC & SOCIETY

edited by Herbert W. Simons
Temple University

EDITORIAL BOARD

This series will publish a broad-based collection of advanced texts and innovative works encompassing rhetoric in the civic arena, in the arts and media, in the academic disciplines, and in everyday cultural practices.

Books in this series:

Control and Consolation in American Culture and Politics: Rhetorics of Therapy
Dana L. Cloud

Communication Criticism: Developing Your Critical Powers
Jodi R. Cohen

Analyzing Everyday Texts: Discourse, Rhetoric, and Social Perspectives
Glenn F. Stillar

GLENN F. STILLAR

Analyzing Everyday Texts

Discourse, Rhetoric, and Social Perspectives

Rhetoric&Society

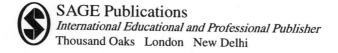

SAGE Publications
International Educational and Professional Publisher
Thousand Oaks   London   New Delhi

For information:

SAGE Publications, Inc.
2455 Teller Road
Thousand Oaks, California 91320
E-mail: order@sagepub.com

SAGE Publications Ltd.
6 Bonhill Street
London EC2A 4PU
United Kingdom

SAGE Publications India Pvt. Ltd.
M-32 Market
Greater Kailash I
New Delhi 110 048 India

Printed in the United States of America

Library of Congress Cataloging-in-Publication Data

Stillar, Glenn F.
    Analyzing everyday texts : discoursal, rhetorical, and social
perspectives / by Glenn F. Stillar.
      p. cm. — (Rhetoric & society ; v. 3)
    Includes bibliographical references (p.) and index.
    ISBN 0-7619-0060-8 (cloth : alk. paper). — ISBN 0-7619-0061-6
(pbk. : alk. paper)
    1. Discourse analysis. 2. Rhetoric. 3. Sociolinguistics.
I. Title. II. Series. III. Series: Rhetoric & society (Thousand
Oaks, Calif.) ; v. 3.
P302.S726 1998
420'.1'41—dc21
                                          97-33815

This book is printed on acid-free paper.

98 99 00 01 02 03 10 9 8 7 6 5 4 3 2 1

Acquiring Editor:	Margaret Seawell
Editorial Assistant:	Renée Piernot
Production Editor:	Sherrise M. Purdum
Production Assistant:	Denise Santoyo
Typesetter:	Christina M. Hill
Print Buyer:	Anna Chin

Contents

Foreword   vii

Acknowledgments   x

1. Everyday Texts   1

2. The Resources of Discourse Analysis   14

3. The Resources of Rhetorical Theory   58

4. The Resources of Social Theory   90

5. Text Instances and Critical Practices   107

6. Integrating Theoretical Resources and Critical Practices   179

References   197

Index   201

About the Author   206

For Rita and Elmer

Foreword

A student pleads for an extension of time on an already late paper. A famous artist is interviewed on British television by a friend and admirer. An automobile manufacturer "counter-advertises" by featuring a heavyset African-American woman purchasing its product. A Canadian bank makes a "gift" of its expertise in pamphlets offering to help customers in dealing with their financial problems. The promotional material on a box of cereal makes us feel better about ourselves in reinforcing our decision to purchase the product. A seemingly scientific report on a child's dysfluency problems offers the possibility of an ideological reading.

These are the ostensibly simple but multilayered texts that Glenn Stillar, an English professor at the University of Waterloo in Canada, subjects to uncommonly close analysis. In the process, Stillar teaches a system of textual analysis combining critical tools drawn from functional linguistics (Halliday), rhetoric à la Kenneth Burke, and the social theorizing of Pierre Bourdieu and Anthony Giddens. This is a heady mix, and before Professor Stillar sets to work on the more difficult cases, he provides chapters of introduction to the three subsystems comprising his framework for analysis.

Originally called "The Rhetoric of Discourse as Social Practice," *Analyzing Everyday Texts* should be of interest to rhetoricians in both English and Communication departments in North America and in programs of study across the Atlantic that feature the analysis of social texts under such headings as critical linguistics, discourse analysis, and cultural studies. So many fields have claimed property rights to the analysis of everyday texts, and under so many headings, that the beginning student must surely be mystified as to where and how to get the necessary preparation. Oftentimes, disciplinary programs in textual analysis compound their intellectual imperialism with blindness to what is going on across the hall in sister departments. If textual analysis is often "thin," as some of my colleagues complain, it may be because critics often rely exclusively on the narrow metalanguages of their respective disciplines.

Stillar's *Analyzing Everyday Texts* is not a survey of analytic techniques. Nor even is it a comprehensive introduction to the theorists featured in the book. For example, the Burkean scholar may be disappointed that Stillar says little or nothing about Burkean dialectics, or about cluster analysis, or about chart-prayer-dream, or about Burke's poetic categories. What Stillar does do extremely well is show how the critical tools he selects can be fitted consistently and insightfully to the cases he examines. Says Stillar:

Even the selections I make within the fields of discourse analysis, rhetorical theory, and social theory stand as a deflection of other concerns, inventories, and methods which have been pursued in these disciplines. It can only be so. Deflection—in this case, drawing attention to this approach rather than that approach—need not be read as an attempt to suppress an "other." Although I have not touched on narrative theory, poetics, conversational analysis, pragmatics, sociolinguistics, other types of discourse analysis, classical rhetoric, or other types of social theory, I acknowledge their relevance to this project and keep all doors open. However, by systematically outlining the inventories of theories I do use and showing how they may be applied, by presenting extended applications, and by presenting a model for both evaluating and understanding their complementarity, I am attempting to give you at least one explicit way to mark differences that make a difference in text and text practice.

I applaud Stillar's selection of critical terms. Although the many metalinguistic tools in Chapter 2 don't come alive until Chapter 5, they are demonstrated over and over again to have critical value in close analyses. Stillar's readings of Giddens, and especially of Bourdieu, a difficult writer, are clear and cogent; they provide a convincing demonstration of how culture is both a cause and an effect of our seemingly innocent textual practices.

As for Kenneth Burke, whose writings I know best, I am overawed at how well Stillar has woven together Burke on logology, on dramatism, and on rhetoric to produce a systematic method of analysis with which Burke, the least "disciplined" of theorists, would have been proud. When Trevor Melia and I sent around our prospectus for *The Legacy of Kenneth Burke* (1989), an astute acquisitions editor who had arranged for the republication of nearly the entire Burke corpus, advised us that the what the world needs now is not another assessment of where Burke fits in the pantheon of contemporary and postmodern theorists, but a methodologically self-conscious treatment that can teach would-be Burkeans how to read innovatively, as Burke did, and avoid cookie-cutter criticism. Glenn Stillar has taken us a long way in that direction.

—*Herbert W. Simons*

Acknowledgments

I would like to thank several people for helping me with this project. My friend and colleague, Dave Goodwin, helped me at every stage by listening to my plans and by discussing details patiently. His suggestions were often more elegant than I have been able to execute. I acknowledge my debt to colleagues in the systemic-functional linguistics community-particularly Jim Benson, Jay Lemke, and Michael Gregory. Three graduate students (who I have the pleasure of supervising) spotted errors and offered encouragement along the way-Rachel Nash, Cameron Reid, and Tracy Whalen. My thanks also to the anonymous reviewers who provided encouraging and thoughtful criticism of the book in manuscript form. At Sage, Margaret Seawell (acquisitions editor), Renée Piernot (editorial assistant), Jennifer Morgan (permissions editor), Sherrise Purdum (production editor), and A. J. Sobczak (copyeditor) were all excellent people to work with. Finally, I thank Lesley Falkner for her spirited companionship and support.

1 Everyday Texts

This book explores the discoursal, rhetorical, and social meanings of "everyday" written texts such as personal notes, brochures, advertisements, and reports. We interact with these sorts of texts all the time: We sort through junk mail, we correspond with coworkers, we flip through magazines and newspapers, we skim over promotional literature, we ponder legal and medical reports, we surf the Internet, and so on. Everyday written texts produce a variety of responses in us: We may be incensed by the language of an advertisement, puzzled by a colleague's memo, or amused by a bulletin-board posting; we may feel threatened by a medical report or suspicious of a brochure's promises; or we may quite simply ignore some texts—this, too, is a response. In each case, the text is an impetus for our active response.

Everyday written texts are ubiquitous and play a significant role in our exchanges with others in social life. Their complexity and their consequences, however, do not often receive close critical attention. No matter how mundane we may take these types of text to be, they all (a) exhibit complexity in terms of the linguistic resources we draw upon to make and understand them, (b) perform critical rhetorical functions for the participants involved, and (c) powerfully summon and propagate the social orders in which we live. To analyze these characteristics of texts, understand how these texts are constructed, and explore their implications, we need a requisitely comprehensive framework, one that enables us to identify and interpret text features as constituents of discoursal, rhetorical, and social practices. This book offers such a framework.

To introduce discoursal, rhetorical, and social analysis, I will begin with Text 1.1, an example of an everyday written text. Text 1.1 is a student note. I received it as a participant in a particular type of institutional context—an English department of a Canadian university. At the time I received the note, I had just finished teaching a senior-level undergraduate course called "Introduction to Semiotics." The requirements for the course included a final paper worth 30% of the student's grade. As the note explains, I had given the student extra time to complete the paper, but the student submitted the paper on a slightly later date than the one we had agreed on. I graded the paper and left it in our departmental mail room to be picked up by the student.

As a teacher in a large English department, I have received quite a few similar notes; many teachers have. They are a genre familiar to student and teacher alike. Sometimes these notes show a great rhetorical and linguistic sensitivity. I have received ones that have struck me as very clear and convincing; occasionally, they are quite clever. Often they demonstrate a keen sense of timing, face-saving deference, and sophisticated orchestration of role and responsibility—all packed in a few short lines. In short, notes of these kind are complex discoursal, rhetorical, and social *acts*.

From one point of view, the text is an active step in a sequence of related social goings-on. It *does* something in its social context. For those of us who have taken part in the university as students or teachers (or both), this text performs a recognizable role in a series of acts. For example, an assignment usually is given a particular due date. Students are expected to complete the work and hand it in by that date. Instructors expect that a student should explain (or some kind of penalty is imminent) if his or her work is late. Overdue work both requires and initiates some kind of discoursal and rhetorical response. The text is a part of a whole sequence of acts that surround what we might call "getting-permission-to-hand-in-late-work," which is itself part of other sequences of action such as taking a course, getting a university education, and so on.

The text is also a *symbolic* act. It uses language and accompanying resources such as a choice of medium—written, not spoken—to accomplish the act (the student doesn't draw a picture!). It is symbolic—or, more appropriately, linguistically semiotic—in that it draws upon linguistic signs for representing events as well as the people, things, and

---

TEXT 1.1
Handwritten note from student to teacher.

Professor Stillar, [date]

Thank you for giving me an extension on this paper, it was greatly appreciated. I'm sorry it is a little later than I had originally planned, but I had a great deal of difficulty getting back into semiotics mode.

Have a good summer.

Sincerely,
[signature]

---

circumstances involved in those events. It draws upon linguistic signs for constructing role relationships between the writer and the reader. It also draws on linguistic signs for creating a coherent and cohesive message in this particular medium—it uses signs that enable us to recognize it as text. In other words, the text has signs that construct content (it is about something), create relationships (it is addressed and exchanged), and produce texture (it is organized, it has structure). It also draws upon language resources to accomplish a rhetorical act; it results from an assessment of audience and of purpose, and it aims to bring about a change in a state of affairs. It is a social act that demonstrates the workings of institutional rules, relations, and resources: rules about late work and course completions, the relations between students and professors, and the different symbolic resources that go with these social roles.

"The symbolic act is the dancing of an attitude," Kenneth Burke tells us in *The Philosophy of Literary Form* (1941/1973, p. 9). This view provides us with a suggestive starting point for looking at the relations among the discoursal, rhetorical, and social conditions and consequences of the student note. That is, we can conceive of a symbolic act, such as that recorded in Text 1.1, as a "dance" by keeping in mind a simple definition of dance—"To move rhythmically, usually to music, using prescribed or improvised steps and gestures." We can say that a dance is

patterned in some way: It is not generally haphazard. This is certainly
the case with our text. Whether or not we decide that the text is made
according to convention (i.e., it is "prescribed") or is an act that is
executed by the writer's own "creativity" (i.e., it is "improvised"), we do
recognize that it has pattern: It creates "differences that make a difference" (Bateson, 1979) that make it a comprehensible discoursal, rhetorical, and social act in its context. It is not random, chaotic, or unstructured
as an act. Equally important, the act/dance is a display of some sort. It is
a performance that represents something to somebody. Just like dance,
the text makes "moves" that are intended to be recognized as meaningful in a particular type of situation. As a dance, it is also embodied: It
manifests both materially and semiotically some of our community's
ways of typically carrying oneself in such situation. In this case, a
handwritten note, on such-and-such paper size, delivered with such-and-
such timing, is a regular kind of practice in the university community.

Burke also says that what is being danced is "an attitude." The
attitudinal nature of dance is clear enough: The moves, steps, gestures,
types of contact, and so on of dance do not simply distinguish one kind
of dance from another (a jig from a reel from a waltz): They also declare
our attitudes and orientations to our partners, our audience, and other
dancers. The style of our dance may be oriented to seduction, to a sense
of community and participation, to an obligation, to instilling a sense of
longing, and so on.

Like dance, the student note is both an intersubjective event (it
transacts relations between interested parties) and an orientational act
(the transaction negotiates attitudes). Attitudes come out of and shape
the ways in which we would construct identification, that is, seek common ground or common substance. Attitude both signals and constructs
the forms of address the text takes—the social distance expressed, the
solidarity presumed or anticipated.

Attitude and orientation inhere in the text because the acts it both
records and initiates cannot be separated from the real human agents
who perform them in contexts always rife with real social conditions and
consequences. All symbolic acts articulate their participants' interests
in—their orientation toward—what is being represented and who is
being addressed. A symbolic act is not simply "about" something; it
indexes our position with regard to that something—whether we think
it desirable, possible, likely, good or bad, and so on—and with regard to
that "someone" we are addressing—whether we tell, ask, or command,

and whether we construct our addressee as "above," "below," or "equal." The symbolic act is the material with which we play out our motives, our interests, and our stance in relation to others and to ourselves.

Discoursal, Rhetorical, and Social Action

This book brings together three different, but complementary, perspectives on text as practice, or as *action:* discoursal, rhetorical, and social perspectives. Discourse is "action": It does things for social agents in the real contexts of their living. No discourse takes place outside the situated, embodied experiences and interests of the participants involved in an exchange. Discourse is an integral part of the complex goings-on that make up social life. "The role of discourse in society is active," Lemke writes. "It not only reconfirms and re-enacts existing social relationships and patterns of behavior, it also renegotiates social relationships and introduces new meanings and new behaviors" (1995, p. 20).

Discourse always draws on a variety of systems of meaning-making resources. It instantiates the resources of language codes (phonological and graphological, lexical and syntactic, and semantic resources). It instantiates various generic conventions for how different types of texts are constructed, exchanged, and received in recurring types of situations. In each of these relationships, discoursal practice is both constrained and enabled by past, present, and projected discourse; it is inserted in and productive of history. It peers, Janus-headed, at two dynamic and ever-evolving horizons: one way, toward the other actual discourses and discourse conventions it relies on for relevance; the other way, toward the multiple, only semi-stable systems of resources it draws on to construct relevance.

Discourse involves rhetorical action because it constitutes a major means through which we link ourselves to one another and to the social environments of which we are a part. The principal function of rhetoric

> is rooted in an essential function of language, a function that is wholly realistic, and is continually born anew; the use of language as a symbolic means of inducing cooperation in beings that by nature respond to symbols. (Burke, 1950/1969b, p. 43)

Text not only is "woven together" itself but also weaves us together. It is a fundamental means through which we create identification—what Burke sometimes calls "consubstantiation," whereby identification is achieved through a sharing of the "substance" (the terms, the meaning potentials) of text. As instantiated discourse, text is the "substance" that social agents share. It functions to bring together what is inherently divided, to bring about a transformation. Text is symbolic exchange between real social agents in situations bearing tangible consequences, and as such it always embodies motive and interest—not (simplistically) the motives and interests *of* the "individuals" involved, but those of the whole host of social systems and structures with their attendant resources "speaking through" social agents. The dynamism and tension inherent in this variety of motives and interests is created by and marked in textual practice. Rhetorical analysis, in general, seeks to understand the transformations in perspectives that the symbolic action of text initiates. Dale Bertelsen writes that:

> Transformation . . . is the process Burke relies on to explain the ineffable movement between subjective perception and social context, from biological to symbolic and vice versa: the redefinition or recontextualization of individuated perception in a socially recognizable form, or the influence of that form on human perception. (1993, p. 235)

Transformation is the central act of rhetoric. For identification to occur, a change in attitude and orientation must occur, and a change in attitude and orientation amounts to a change in the ways we are likely to act.

The act of participating in discourse is also, of course, a social act. We recognize that instances of discourse, by symbolically framing, enacting, and organizing experience, are linked inextricably with the social systems and structures through which we interact with one another. Anticipating a central theme of the rest of the book, I want to stress here that discourse bears a dual relation to social systems and structures. On one hand, it reflects the social. From this perspective, we recognize discourse as a product of social systems and structures: It is determined by them. On the other hand, discourse constructs the social. It is one of the major means and processes through which social relations are articulated and realized. It therefore is both a medium and an outcome of social practice (Giddens, 1984). We will consistently ask about the role of text in the social (and vice versa). This inquiry requires guidance from social theories that have conceptualized human agency in relation to both symbolic action and other forms of social action that are both constrained and enabled by a society's myriad systems and structures.

The Structure and Goals of This Book

This book outlines an integrated and comprehensive framework for the close critical analysis of everyday written texts, puts the theory into practice by providing extended analysis of three very different types of text, and reflects on this analytical practice in terms of its theoretical implications. Chapters 2 to 4 outline frameworks for analysis in these three perspectives. Chapter 2 covers the resources of discourse analysis; Chapter 3, the resources of rhetorical theory; and Chapter 4, the resources of social theory. Chapter 5 brings these resources to bear on three instances of text to exemplify and engage in the practice of critical analysis. The chapter consists of three cases. The first is an analysis of a print advertisement for Saturn automobiles; the second, an analysis of a series of financial advice booklets produced by a large bank; and the third, an analysis of a speech pathologist's progress report concerning a young boy's participation in a fluency program. Chapter 6 reflects on the consequences of bringing together the resources of discoursal, rhetorical, and social analysis. Specifically, it (a) summarizes the characteristics of text and text practices, (b) outlines the requirements of an integrated and comprehensive theory for the analysis of everyday written texts, and (c) identifies the analytical practices that are enabled by such a theory.

The book is structured, therefore, to realize what I see to be the principal goals for the critical analysis of everyday written texts. Critical analysis must be capable of identifying and interpreting the **systemic, functional,** and **social** characteristics of texts and text practices. It must be carried out with a theory that is requisitely **diverse, systematic,** and **applicable.** It must also enable researchers to produce explicit **critique, participate** in the textual practices they analyze, and provide a vocabulary with which to **communicate** their analyses.

My outline of discoursal, rhetorical, and social theory foregrounds the **systemic, functional,** and **social** characteristics of text. I will characterize **systems** as resources for making meaning in symbolic acts. Instances of text draw on (instantiate) the resources of a variety of systems: systems for linguistic meaning-making, for rhetorical acts, and for social practices. Systems represent the potentials for meaning-making acts—the available choices, combinations, and relational values of meaningful elements of symbolic action, whether they are linguistic, rhetorical, or social. The resources of linguistic, rhetorical, and social systems are interpreted as **functional** resources; that is, they are identified, organized, and interpreted with reference to what they "do" in instances of textual practice. I will also emphasize and illustrate symbolic acts as **social** acts. Because symbolic acts are social, we have cause and reason to inquire into their characteristics and functions. Everyday texts are an integral part of social life: In the day-to-day flow of social interaction, they record and construct the ways we are organized in terms of who we are and what we do, our visions of what is good and what is bad, who is powerful and who is not, and why.

To attend to the systemic, functional, and social characteristics of texts, we require a theory that is **diverse, systematic,** and **applicable.** It must be **diverse** to respond to the complexity of text structures and functions, text types, and situations of text exchange that accompany all discursive practice. It must be **systematic** by enabling us to organize statements produced by analysis consistently and explicitly both within each perspective (e.g., discoursal, rhetorical, and social) and among the perspectives in a complementary fashion. The theory also must be **applicable** in that it enables us to produce insights that go beyond a mere labeling of the text—that is, the theory must enable us to gain fresh insights into the conditions and consequences of textual practices in social contexts.

A theory of text analysis ought to enable researchers to develop defeasible **critique,** indicate ways to **participate** with the texts they analyze, and provide them with an appropriate and cogent vocabulary with which to **communicate** their analyses. **Critique** is enabled when the integrated theory allows researchers to both gather evidence and form arguments about the discoursal, rhetorical, and social functions of textual practices in some real context. Critique may take many forms and may have different purposes depending on who critiques what, on what occasions, and for what purposes. In any critical context, however, the types of evidence garnered and the scope of the arguments developed should be explicitly and systematically related to the principles of the theory. Analysis leads to new perspectives on texts and text practices. When we analyze, we produce new knowledge that shapes our own attitudes, which, in turn, are the locus of new ways to **participate** with texts and text practices—as critics, as teachers, as students, as writers, and as readers. Critical analysis and participation presuppose a consistent and coherent vocabulary with which to **communicate** arguments, evidence, and the products of our engagement with texts. An integrated theory of discoursal, rhetorical, and social analysis is a language variety that enables a public exchange of the processes and products of analysis.

Sources and Perspectives

This book integrates three theories that may help practitioners of discourse analysis to work toward what British linguist J. R. Firth (1968) called "renewal of connection." He says theory employs "abstractions which enable us to handle language in the interrelated processes of personal and social life in the flux of events" but adds shortly after that "Renewal of connection with the processes and patterns of life in the instances of experience is the final justification" (pp. 14, 24). By bringing together rhetorical, social, and discoursal theory, I hope to convey that analysis (which too often is construed as "objective") itself is a form of participation with the very practices it analyzes: Analysis produces reflexivity that affects and is affected by the acts it seeks to understand. This seems to me especially important when we consider that, in some of the major contexts in which discourse analysis is conducted, the analyst often is a practitioner of the type of text being analyzed (e.g., an academic studying the nature of academic genres), often teaching either how to analyze text or how to participate in some type of discourse or both (e.g., a writing teacher who blends analysis and practice in a course of instruction). The analyst also often has some critical and practical stake in the field(s) of which the object of analysis is a part (e.g., a forensic analysis of text as grounds for expert testimony in a legal proceeding). This list could, of course, be extended.

Bringing together rhetoric, social theory, and discourse analysis is a daunting task: In some ways, it necessitates touching on major trends in the complete intellectual history of the 20th century. My project here is much more modest. It stands as only a limited selection from theories and theorists that I hope to be able to show as making up a suitable, useful, and generative combination.

From rhetoric, I draw mainly from the work of Kenneth Burke—predominantly from his own writing, but also occasionally from the work of Burkean scholars. Burke's work spans almost eight decades. Within it, there are at least eight major books (composing the core of his work) that are still in print and widely taught, discussed, and written about.[1] Burke has contributed a considerable number of critical concepts to dialogues on language, rhetoric, and symbolic action. In the pages that follow, I attempt to get those concepts speaking together with aspects of social theory and discourse analysis to create new perspectives on discourse as social practice.

From social theory, I draw mainly from the works of Pierre Bourdieu and Anthony Giddens. Again, my use of these scholars constitutes a very small selection of key concepts from their theories; a full treatment of their theories is beyond my scope here, let alone a treatment of concepts from other social theorists whose work bears upon my subject. In Bourdieu's case, I focus on his theorizing of *habitus,* our propensity to act in the social world according to embodied systems of durable, generative, and transposable dispositions. Of particular interest is the nature and effect of differing types of linguistic *habitus*—those dispositions that affect our access to and exercise of symbolic power in particular social contexts. In Giddens's case, I focus on the concept of the duality of structure in analyzing the rhetoric of discourse as social practice. The duality of structure concerns the dual relation to social systems held by social agents and their practices. The theory of structuration, as Giddens labels his major contribution, does not analytically separate agency and structure: It posits that social systems are constituted by the actions of agents while at the same time, social systems enable and constrain agents' actions. Giddens (1984) says, "the structural properties of social systems are both the medium and outcome of the practices they recursively organize" (p. 25). Of course, the formations of practices that influence and come out of our discoursal practice are key properties of our social systems.

From the field of discourse analysis, I draw on work that, to a greater or lesser extent, has been influenced by the systemic-functional theory of M. A. K. Halliday. Systemic-functionalism is concerned with the social semiotic nature of text: It focuses on the social and functional origins, contexts, and consequences of linguistic semiosis. Particularly significant in this tradition is Halliday's metafunctional hypothesis, which focuses on the meaning potentials of linguistic signs as organized by and oriented toward three principal semiotic functions simultaneously: the ideational (texts construct content), the interpersonal (texts construct social relations), and the textual (texts exhibit internal organization and construct external contextual relevance).

By bringing these resources together, I emphasize the utility and relevance of analysis rather than the purity and pedigree of the theoretical tools. I am not interested in protecting the boundaries around disciplines and subdisciplines; however, I try to avoid an approach that simply pulls concepts out of their theoretical systems willy-nilly. In each case where I draw on theoretical resources from the fields of rhetoric, social theory, and discourse analysis, I provide definitions, criteria, and rationale for how the concepts fit into the overall project of this book. I try to do so in an explicit enough way for readers to understand the position the book advances and, more important, in a way that enables a response.

A Note on Text and Discourse

In discourse analysis, the term *text* has come to refer, most commonly, to the record of discoursal processes involving, but not limited to, language systems. It can occur in a written or spoken (often transcribed for analysis) mode. Text instantiates the phonological and/or graphological, lexical and syntactic, and semantic resources of a language. It also instantiates other resources for making linguistic messages, such as generic conventions and expectations (e.g., a written recipe's ingredients, method, and presentation sections) and other community expectations for the forms and functions of particular discourse types. In this sense, it is a meaningful unit, an instantiation of meaning-making resources, including such "material" resources as voice quality in spoken texts or font choice in written texts because these, too, are meaning-making resources. Texts exhibit some kind of unity or texture that enables them to be (socially) recognizable as a whole. The acts that go into "making" and "understanding" text are obviously implicated in recognizing (often differing) forms of unity. Who says what to whom in what situations affects our perceptions of the unity and relevance of text in relation to its social context.

The term *discourse* is most often used to refer to the social activity through which we make meanings with linguistic and other semiotic resources. This term emphasizes the forms of interpretation, interaction, and exchange that pattern text meaning potentials. Discourse concerns the participants involved, the particular kinds of situations in which text plays a part, and the social systems and structures that bear upon how and what text can mean to those involved. This has led many scholars to speak of "discourses" in the plural sense or the "discourse of X" in the classificatory sense. These terms are meant to distinguish characteristic ways of speaking, writing, and interpreting text in relation to recurrent social activities. For example, there are a number of different discourses of education. These are patterned ways of meaning and ways of doing that construct particular values, subjects, and activities that make up the complex social construction of education. When outlining a budget to Parliament, a finance minister speaks through a discourse of education different from that of an undergraduate student filling out a teacher evaluation form. Speeches made by parents at a PTA meeting instantiate a discourse of education different from those instantiated in talk around the staff room coffee machine. The texts produced on different occasions within these different discourses of education exhibit significant differences, but we may also see them as belonging to the same discourse of education when we focus on similarities in rhetorical functions (e.g., creating "common ground" among different interested groups), relationships to particular social practices (e.g., debates concerning prayer in classrooms), or instantiated linguistic and generic features (e.g., the registerial features of policy statements).

I will most often refer to "text" in the following pages because I want to emphasize its instantiality, its materiality, and its being a realization of discourse. The two terms are complementary, then, with particular texts realizing particular discourses. The text as record is always related to socially determined and socially determining discoursal practices: It is never simply a "thing." We meet discourse and discourse*s* through instances of text. In general, discourse analysis, as I am conceiving of it here, takes as its object the text's indices of specific social activities and relationships—its traces of "discourse." Similar treatments of text and discourse can be found in Fairclough (1989, 1992), Hodge and Kress (1988), Lemke (1995), and Thibault (1991).

Note

1. The eight books I refer to here are (with first publication date followed by revised edition date) *Counter Statement* (1931/1968a), *Permanence and Change: An Anatomy of Purpose* (1935/1984b), *Attitudes Towards History* (1937/1984a), *The Philosophy of Literary Form: Studies in Symbolic Action* (1941/1973), *A Grammar of Motives* (1945/1969a), *A Rhetoric of Motives* (1950/1969b), *The Rhetoric of Religion: Studies in Logology* (1961/1970), and *Language as Symbolic Action: Essays on Life, Literature, and Method* (1966).

2 The Resources of Discourse Analysis

This chapter develops a framework for analyzing discourse—for describing the linguistic structures and functions of text and exploring their relations with the social contexts of their use. The framework foregrounds the **systemic, functional,** and **social** characteristics of discoursal practice. When we make and exchange text, we instantiate the meaning-making potentials of language systems. **Systems** are organized sets of linguistic structures: the arrays of "what can be done" in terms of selections and combinations of linguistic units. The organization of the language system and the interpretation of its possible structures is conceived of in terms of **function.** The framework recognizes that linguistic structures simultaneously function to represent experiences of the world, construct social relationships among the participants in discourse, and create text that is internally cohesive (i.e., has some measure of recognizable unity distinguishing it as text) and coheres with its context (i.e., is relevant to its context of use). Finally, the framework understands both systems of linguistic resources and the functions they perform as social phenomena. They are social in terms of their origins, contexts, and effects: in origins because our linguistic meaning-making systems have evolved in relation to and have been shaped by socially situated discoursal practice over time (they have not sprung into existence as full-fledged resources out of nothing), in contexts because the meaning potentials of a linguistic system are realized in concrete instances of text in which the scope of its linguistic functions is bound by real social conditions ("meaning" is function in context), and in effects because the functions of text in context always have social consequences. The framework investigates how text constructs social activities and relations, that is, how text produces, reproduces, and occasionally challenges the social norms and expectations of particular communities and the distribution and exercise of power among groups and individuals.

A Discoursal View of Text 1.1: Choice and Effect

As the instantiation of the potential of a language "system," linguistic meaning-making (engaging with instances of text) can be characterized as "choice." Chosen linguistic signs do not have value simply in positive terms (i.e., for being what they are) because they get value, in part, from signs not chosen in particular subsystems of the language. For example, a statement is meaningful in terms of speech function because it contrasts with command or question speech function: It does not assign the same role possibilities for complying or responding to the reader or hearer. Making and understanding a text is a process of selecting or choosing from a host of systems of the language. Halliday (1978) comments, "Text represents choice. A text is 'what is meant,' selected from the total set of options that constitute what can be meant. In other words, text can be defined as actualized meaning potential" (p. 109).

When we engage with text, we use a particular register (or registers) to participate appropriately in the social activity at hand. We may think, for the moment, of registers as the typical, socially recognized and situationally relevant, linguistic forms that people draw upon to engage with the recurring social situations of the communities to which they belong. For example, a particular register is called upon in the situational context in which Text 1.1 arose. Seeking permission to submit (or giving explanation for) late work in this situation calls for the exchange of a particular type of text exhibiting linguistic patterns that befit the social activity, the social roles involved (i.e., student and professor), and the medium of exchange (in this case, written language). The exigencies of the situation call for the student to make some choices that affect the characteristics of the text to be exchanged. We could represent some of the choices informally. The student decides to produce a text or not (the negative option here is just as meaningful, of course). If the student does produce a text, it will have to be exchanged in some mode (spoken in person, over the phone, through a voicemail message, written in a note delivered on its own or with the late work, handwritten or typed, and so on). The student has to make choices about timing—when to exchange the text (before the due date, after, during office hours, after hours, and so on).

The student also faces choices about the language of the text itself. (Note that this description, being synoptic, suggests a consciousness, sequentiality, and linearity in the process that should not be taken to represent what is a dynamic process.) The text will reflect the student's choices for making the text cohesive as a whole and as a symbolic act that coheres with the situation. The text will reflect the student's choices about representing the participants, events, circumstances, times, and so on that surround the activity. It will reflect the student's choices of the appropriate language for the social relationship between student and professor. All these choices perform functions—organizing, representing, and interacting—in connection with the situation, and they do so simultaneously. I will deal with them individually before showing their place in the framework for discourse analysis.

ORGANIZING

Text draws on the resources of the language system (or more accurately, the resources of the register appropriate to the situation at risk) to create both internal cohesion (so the text "hangs together" as a whole) and to create coherent connections with its context. Cohesive structures help us distinguish text from "non-text": They function to show parts of a text as being related to other parts and function to provide greater or lesser saliency (prominence) of some parts of the text over others. Coherence structures help us build connections between the text and its context. These structures range from pointers in the text to the context— such as items like "these," "those," and "there" (cf. "this paper" in Text 1.1), through to the sequencing and structuring of larger spans of text that help us recognize it as being an instance of a particular register and thus related to particular types of situations (e.g., the sequencing and timing of turns used to end an informal telephone conversation). Patterns of cohesion and coherence in a text are greatly conditioned by its particular mode (written or spoken) and the range of material and semiotic resources of the mode (e.g., handwritten or typed, face-to-face or over the telephone, in person or delayed by voicemail, and so on).

The choice of mode is a particularly salient feature of Text 1.1. For example, certain forms of response are curtailed because the text is written and not exchanged in a face-to-face situation. It creates a delay that I think "favors" the student's chances: I cannot simply speak an immediate response. If I want to turn down the request, I have to contact the student. The text, at this point, is our only form of contact. Also, the note was written by hand—not surprising, but meaningful in the sense that this choice has enabled the student to combine personalization (the handwriting is an index of the student's direct involvement) and informality with the "impersonality" and formality of the written, nonpersonal contact mode.

Looking at the language of the text itself (rather than aspects of its mode affecting the meaning potentials of its exchange), we can see a thematic progression that is bounded by topics that are quite distant from the central "problem" (i.e., this is a later-than-late paper) at hand. Theme is an important element for building cohesion. It is a major means by which information is structured in text: It signals what is "given" and what is "new" information, what is prominent, and what the clause is about. We may gloss the function of theme along the lines of "What I want to tell you about is. . . ." For example, in the statement, "John broke his leg," I am telling you something about "John." In "His leg was broken," I am telling you something about "his leg": I have chosen a different point of departure, a different theme. The thematic progression in a text—what its themes are, how they stay the same, how they change, and so on, over the course of a text—is a part of how it creates cohesion but is also a way in which it sets an agenda by focusing our attention on certain things rather than others. For example, the themes in Text 1.1 are as follows: *Thank-you / it / I / but, I / (You)*. Notice that what the text begins with and ends with are what we might call, informally, "other-oriented" themes. They are not about the student, or the student's paper, or its lateness; they are about the addressee. The last theme, the "what I want to tell you about" that the reader is left with, is not about the paper or seeking permission at all. It is much better to end this way, I think, from the student's point of view, than to end with "I hope you like it [the paper]" or even "Thanks again" because these bring the focus back to the student and the lateness of the paper. *Have a good summer* does not just fulfil the generic expectation that a letter should have a complimentary closing; it improvises within this constraint by using a theme (the theme is an action "you" are asked to perform) that, though still a complimentary closing, leads attention to other matters—ones that are a good distance from the "thornier" issues at hand.

REPRESENTING

A text draws on the resources of the language system to construct content; it is "about" something in the sense that it names and arranges participants, processes, and circumstances. It constructs temporal and perspectival conditions for these through the linguistic resources of tense and aspect. In other words, it represents social experiences and activities. Just what the text is about in terms of content—what it selects as relevant things, persons, events, relations, times, places, manners, and so on—affects and is affected by its relation to the particular social activity or field of which it is a part. In this case, the text obviously needs to be about the paper, its being late, and the student's expressing regret. The institutional context "requires" that these things be represented, as it were, but the particular selection and arrangement of these as participants, processes, and circumstances affects the meaning potential for everyone involved. The situation certainly can be represented in more than one way.

When we consider "what is going on" in a text, we are focusing on the main processes. In the first instance, we can begin by looking at the main verbs of the text to see what is going on. Simplifying somewhat, we recognize that verbs will be one of three general types: They will be action processes ("hit," "run," "make"), mental processes ("think," "love," "see"), or relations ("be," "seem," "appear," "have"). On the whole, the situation the note constructs is a mental event in which the student expresses thanks (*Thank you*) and appreciation (*was . . . appreciated*)—both of which are mental processes—and in which relational processes link mental states (emotions) to the addresser (*I am sorry; I had a great deal of difficulty getting back into semiotics mode*). Mental processes with first-person singular subjects (*I*) are in some ways less "questionable" than action processes or relations; we cannot really call into question someone's being sorry or full of appreciation unless we are willing to challenge seriously his or her integrity.

INTERACTING

A text draws on the resources of the language system to construct forms of interaction between an addresser and an addressee in particular social roles. A text builds interaction by both indexing a particular subject position for the addresser and by construing exchange roles for the addresser and addressee. Text enables the construction of subjectivity through the selection and combination of resources that can signify a possible orientational and attitudinal role for the speaker/writer toward the content of the discourse and in relation to other socially constructed subject positions. At the same time, it signals the relations *between* participants by assigning addresser and addressee roles through resources such as mood (for example, we construct different roles for our addressees depending on whether we make statements, ask questions, or issue commands).

Text 1.1 consists almost exclusively of statements (grammatically, indicative declarative mood). I am being given information—told something—rather than being asked or commanded. This information constructs a particular role for me as a potential respondent; the giving of information does not explicitly signal what I should do in the same way a question or command does (a question calls for an answer, a command calls for some form of compliance). Significantly, the student does not question (e.g., "Will you please accept this late paper?") or (politely) command (e.g., "Please accept this paper") because each of these mood choices creates a responding role for me that may, in the eyes of the student, too explicitly bring up the possibility of refusing the request or not complying with the (polite) command. The one (grammatical) command in the text, *Have a good summer,* does not carry an expectation that the addressee is obliged to fulfill the command on behalf of the addresser. The "benefits" of compliance to these sorts of polite, formulaic commands (other examples include "Break a leg!" "Take care," and "Have a good time") accrue to the addressee rather than the addresser.

I have presented this informal analysis of Text 1.1 to preview the general organization and focus of a social and functional framework for discourse analysis. The linguistic patterns in the text are identified and interpreted in terms of the function that they perform in relation to the contexts of their use. The multiple functions I identified (i.e., organizing, representing, and interacting) in the text both (a) *respond to* the situation—the mode of communication, the social activity, and the social roles determine the presence and function of these functions—and (b) *shape* the situation in that our recognition and participation in such an event and our understanding of the roles involved are substantially determined by the characteristics of these functions in the text.

Discourse Analysis

There are many different ways to do discourse analysis, each informed by different linguistic theories, frameworks, inventories of concepts, and rationales for analysis (see Schiffrin, 1994, for a selected survey of approaches). The framework that I outline and exemplify here is one that I think will be useful for those who are interested in supporting rhetorical and social analysis with discourse analysis. It is a hybrid model that brings together theoretical concepts from systemic-functional linguistics, communication linguistics, and social semiotics.[1]

The object of analysis for a social and functional discourse analysis is language activity—actual texts occurring in real contexts. As the social exchange of meaning, text is the product of a number of meaning-making resources. It is the "output" of meaning-making systems, and its record is amenable to systematic analysis. It is also a dynamic process that consists of continuous selection from those resources (text as part of a communicative event) where choices at one stage affect choices that follow.

Language as Function

Following Halliday (1978, 1994), I will recognize that language resources are organized along the lines of three general functions. The **ideational** function concerns language's resources for constructing content. Language represents things, concepts, relations, and events and their circumstances: Text is always "about something." The **interpersonal** function concerns language's resources for shaping interaction. Language constructs social relations between participants in situations of its use. The interpersonal resources of the language enable users to assign roles to their addressees and to express their attitudes toward addressees and toward the content of their messages: Text is always "to and from somebody." Ideational and interpersonal meanings are realized in texts, in organized messages that are more or less internally cohesive and exhibit some kind of coherence with the contexts of their use. The **textual** function concerns those resources of the language that enable parts of a text to be linked with other parts to create cohesion, allow parts of a text to be foregrounded as prominent, and create coherence in relation to the text's situation: Text always exhibits structure and organization.

These functional labels are not meant to exhaust the possibilities for what language is "used" for or what it can "do." Halliday (1978) comments:

> On the one hand, "function" refers to the social meaning of speech acts, in contexts of language use; on the other hand, it refers to components of meaning in the language system, determining the internal organization of the system itself. But the two are related simply as actual to potential; the system is a potential for use. (p. 72)

Texts in use (real texts) realize the potential of all three types of function simultaneously. Although analyzing the linguistic patterns of texts requires us to speak about one function at a time, we must recognize that the three functions are interdependent. For specific analytical purposes, we may focus on a particular function in a text or part of a text, but all the message-carrying units of the language exhibit the three types of functional meaning.

I will be using semantic labels to describe realizations of the three metafunctions. A social-functional view of semantics focuses on meaning-in-use where "meaning" is understood as the function of the structure in some context of use. Halliday (1978) says that a "sociological semantics implies not so much a general description of the semantic system of a language but rather a set of context-specific semantic descriptions, each one characterizing the meaning potential that is typically associated with a given situation type" (p. 114). Semantic functions are closely related to the lexical, grammatical, and phonological forms that realize them. My main concern, however, in the analyses that follow in this chapter and in Chapter 5 is with the *functions* of linguistic patterns—that is, with the contribution of variations in patterns of form to the ideational, interpersonal, and textual meaning potentials of the text. To this end, I will use a set of semantic labels for classes of functions.

The following three sections outline some of the principal functional resources in English for constructing ideational, interpersonal, and textual meaning. The lexical and grammatical forms that realize these structures are numerous and complex. To make the functional interpretation of lexical and grammatical forms widely accessible to readers, I have—wherever possible—used well-known, "traditional" labels. To keep the grammatical vocabulary consistent, I use the terms found in *Collins Cobuild English Grammar* (1990). For semantic distinctions, I rely—with some modifications—on categories used in communication linguistics (Gregory, 1985, 1988, 1995). For clarity, semantic labels will occur in italics throughout. Readers may find it useful to consult Tables 2.1 and 2.6–2.8 (pp. 33, 49, 54) when reading through the following sections.

Ideational Resources

Halliday (1978) comments on the situational demands made upon the ideational resources of the language system:

> Language has to interpret the whole of our experience, reducing the indefinitely varied phenomena of the world around us, and also of the world inside us, the processes of our own consciousness, to a manageable number of classes of phenomena: types of processes, events and actions, classes of objects, people and institutions, and the like. (p. 21)

I will use the following categories to identify ideational structures in texts: **process** types and **participant** roles, **circumstantial** roles, **time** and **perspective,** and **concept** taxonomies.

PROCESS TYPES AND PARTICIPANT ROLES

To represent experience, language is called upon to construe events and relations that involve animate and inanimate participants. **Processes** (events and relations) are realized as one of three different types: **actional, mental,** or **relational.** These different classes of process are typically accompanied by different classes of **participants**—the entities involved in the events and relations. Within each class, we need to recognize subclasses to distinguish crucial differences in the way experience or content is constructed.

Table 2.1   Ideational Resources and Functions

Resource	Process Type and Participant Roles	Circumstantial Roles	Time and Perspective	Concept Taxonomies
Structures	• action, mental, and relational processes • typical participants	• time, place, manner, reason, purpose, contingency, role	• before-now, now, after-now • ongoing, com-completed	• reiteration, collocation
Representational functions	• represents events, states, and relations • represents participants (human, animate, inanimate, etc.)	• represents circumstances surrounding processes	• represents temporal and perspectival framing of processes	• constructs conceptual field

Action processes contain a central participant—"the **agent**"—who performs the action. The action normally extends to some goal, some "acted upon." Depending on the nature of the goal, the process will be subclassified as one of the following: **affective, motion, transfer, resultative,** or **designative.** Table 2.2 outlines these subclasses. The first column identifies the six subclasses of action process type. The middle column identifies the central participants involved in the different classes of action processes. The last column gives an example of the process type. Participants are labeled, and the process (realized grammatically by the verb) appears in italics.

Mental processes do not "act" on a goal in the way most action processes do. All mental processes have two central participants: a **processor** (the sentient being that does the "mentalizing") and a **phenomenon** (that which is "mentalized"). Depending on the particular verb realizing the mental event, the process will be one of five different subclasses: **perceptive, reactive, cognitive, verbal,** or **creative.** Table 2.3 displays these differences.

Relational processes are usually realized by a linking verb such as *be, have, seem, appear,* or *become.* Seven subclasses are recognized. The first five—**identification, attribution, classification, possession,** and **location**—are duo-relational; that is, they involve two participants. The last two—**existential** and **ambient**—are homo-relational, involving only one participant.

Table 2.2 Action Processes

Process Type	Central Participants		Example Sentence			
Affective	Agent		Felix	*cut*	the cake.	
	Patient		Agent		Patient	
Motion	Agent		Felix	*went*	to the store.	
	Location		Agent		Location	
Transfer:	Agent		Felix	*put*	the book	on the table.
locational	Item	Location	Agent		Item	Location
Transfer:	Agent		Felix	*gave*	a book	to Mary.
personal	Item	Recipient	Agent		Item	Recipient
Resultative	Agent		Felix	*built*	a house.	
	Resultant		Agent		Resultant	
Designative	Agent		Felix	*played*	tennis.	
	Range		Agent		Range	

Table 2.3 Mental Processes

Process Type	Central Participants	Example Sentence			
Perceptive	Processor	Felix	*saw*	the man.	
	Phenomenon	Processor		Phenomenon	
Reactive	Processor	Felix	*liked*	the movie.	
	Phenomenon	Processor		Phenomenon	
Cognitive	Processor	Felix	*understood*	the movie.	
	Phenomenon	Processor		Phenomenon	
Verbal	Processor	Felix	*said,*	"I like apples."	
	Phenomenon	Processor		Phenomenon	
Creative	Processor	Felix	*wrote*	a short story.	
	Phenomenon	Processor		Phenomenon	

A few comments on process type are necessary. First, when analyzing a text for process type, there are times when it is not necessary to give as detailed a classification of process type and participant as these inventories allow, while at other times it may be necessary to add to this

Table 2.4 Relational Processes

Process Type	Central Participants	Example Sentence		
Identification	Identified Identifier	Felix Identified	is	the gardner. Identifier
Attribution	Carrier Attribute	Felix Carrier	is/seems/appears	witty, Attribute
Classification	Classified Classifier	Felix Classified	is	a gardener. Classifier
Possession	Possessor Possessed	Felix Possessor	has/owns/possesses	a shovel. Possessed
Location	Located Locator	Felix	is/lives	in the garden. Locator
Existential	Existent	There	are	three gardeners. Existent
Ambient	Ambient	It	's	raining. Ambient

inventory. Minimally, we should distinguish among the three major classes of process type. Second, although the clause has been identified as the central grammatical structure that realizes processes (because it contains a verb), we should note that processes can be realized in nominal groups as well. This is especially important in the case of nominalization, in which events or processes are realized in nouns or nominal groups. For example, the nominal group "a government investigation" contains a **relational:classification** process (the "investigation" is classified as a "government" one) and a **mental:cognitive** process (where "investigate" is the process and "government" is either the **processor** or the **phenomenon** depending on whether we interpret the "government" as doing the investigation or being investigated).

Analyzing clauses and groups for process type focuses on how language constructs experience—what is "going on" in the text. The text consists of a series of processes of doing (i.e., **action** processes), sensing (i.e., **mental** processes), and being (i.e., **relations**), in the most general sense. Identifying patterns of process type in text enables the analyst to begin to get a picture of how the text constructs "reality," how it "slices

Table 2.5   Circumstantial Functions

Type	Example Sentence
Time	Felix exercised *at five o'clock.*
Place	Felix exercised *at the gym.*
Manner	Felix worked *quietly.*
Reason	Felix ate *because he was hungry.*
Purpose	Felix exercised *to get into shape.*
Contingency	Felix exercised *even though he was tired.*
Role	Felix worked *as a gardener.*

up" what is a continuum of phenomena into processes that reflect and construct particular perspectives on experience.

CIRCUMSTANCES

Processes that structure perspectives on events and relations are accompanied by **circumstances.** The lexical and grammatical resources of the language system provide a number of structures with which to construct circumstantial functions in relation to processes and participants. Processes and participants are set in relation to such circumstances as **time, place, manner,** and so on. Halliday (1994) identifies several circumstantial functions and their typical lexical and grammatical realizations. His list of the different classes of circumstantial functions represents a detailed set of distinctions for our purposes. Subclasses can be recognized within these general classes, but I will raise these distinctions only when they become necessary in detailed analysis of actual text. Table 2.5 (a modified version of Halliday's list) lists the different circumstantial functions that "attach" to processes and provides an example sentence of each with the circumstantial element appearing in italics.

The examples in Table 2.5 demonstrate that a variety of structures can realize a circumstantial function. Circumstances may be realized by single words (*quietly*), prepositional phrases (*at five o'clock, at the gym*), and dependent clauses (*because he was hungry*).

TIME AND PERSPECTIVE

A major part of a text's functioning ideationally to construe experience involves its relationship to **time** and **perspective.** Circumstantial elements help construct these relations, but grammatical tense and aspect are clearly involved as well. I will consider **time** and **perspective** as semantic relations constructed from the position of the text's point of writing or speaking. Process, participants, and circumstances are construed as being **before-now, now,** or **after-now** in terms of **time. Perspective** is construed as either **ongoing** or **completed.** Semantic time is clearly related to grammatical tense (past, present, and "future") but is realized by other structures such as adverbs and adverbial groups (e.g., "Tomorrow, I go to work"; "During the next three weeks, Jane is in charge"). These two examples demonstrate that temporal relations are not constructed solely through grammatical tense: They are present tense but realize an **after-now** temporal reference.

Perspective is also a semantic relation that cannot be reduced to a single grammatical form. It is most commonly and clearly realized by the contrast between perfect and continuous aspect in the verbal group (e.g., "She *has* climb*ed* the mountain"; "She *is* climb*ing* the mountain"), but we need to note that **perspective** is a factor even when it is not overtly realized grammatically in a text. For example, a sentence like "She climbed the mountain" can be interpreted only as **before-now** in terms of **time;** in terms of **perspective,** however, it could be interpreted as **ongoing** (as in, she "habitually" climbed the mountain in the past) or **completed** (as in, on a particular occasion or occasions, she finished climbing the mountain). The co-text (surrounding text) and context of such a sentence would most likely clarify the interpretation of perspective. To summarize: **Time** and **perspective** are semantic, discoursal relations that are typically, though not exclusively, realized by grammatical tense and aspect respectively.

CONCEPT TAXONOMIES

This aspect of ideational meaning concerns the clustering and arrangement of lexical items. Lexical items ("content" words and phrases) cluster in different ways in text depending on their relationship to the situation of which the text is a part (see the section titled "Register" below). Simply put, words keep different company given the particular register or registers being instantiated by the text. Lexical relations are often discussed as an aspect of the textual function because they contribute to the text's cohesion through repetition, synonymy, and so on, but lexical relations are also an important resource for constructing ideational content. The term **concept** is used to label the items realized by lexical items because in a particular instance of text, the significantly meaningful features of each lexical item are conditioned by the text and its context. In a particular text, we may recognize a set of **concepts** with a particular hierarchical arrangement. In another text, the same lexical items may realize **concepts** that belong to different sets and have a different hierarchical arrangement. For example, in weather reports "high," "low," and "temperature" all collocate (i.e., the presence of one of the terms creates a more than average expectation for the others to occur). Also, "temperature" is a superordinate term for the other two. In a personal letter describing one's mood, "high" and "low" would more likely collocate with concepts like "good" and "bad" and have a superordinate category different from "temperature."

AN ILLUSTRATION OF IDEATIONAL ANALYSIS

Texts 2.1 and 2.2 are the beginnings of two different prefaces to writing handbooks. I will use the two texts to illustrate the main components of the ideational function: **process type** and **participants, circumstances, time** and **perspective,** and **concept** taxonomies.

The ideational resources of language are called upon to structure experience, to represent a particular arrangement of "reality." As the opening lines of the preface to a writing handbook, each of these two texts creates a point of entry into its "world" by selecting and arranging participants, events, and circumstances. Each uses the resources of the ideational function differently to represent the authors as authorities in their fields. In the first, the author is represented as an authority because of the **roles** she has played in her career, whereas in the second, the authors construct authority predominantly through showing how their book responds positively to **circumstances** in their field.

In Text 2.1, we are presented with **mental** processes where the author is **processor.** Two types of mental processes dominate: **cognitive** (*reviewed, evaluated, seen*) and **reactive** (*appalled, distressed*). The pattern of events is constructed along the lines of mentally experiencing something about writing or writing instruction and then forming a mental reaction to it.

Circumstantial elements related to these mental events play an important part in this pattern. For each **cognition** and **reaction** that *I* is involved in, the circumstantial function of **role** is involved (see Table 2.5). *I*

TEXT 2.1

As a teacher of composition, linguistics, and literature for twenty years, and as a director of a large writing program for eight years, I have seen more handbooks than I could ever have imagined existing when I took my own freshman composition course in 1959. I have reviewed handbooks for other publishers, I have evaluated them for use in my own teaching, and I have debated with composition committees about the virtues and vices of various handbooks we have considered for use in our writing programs. As a teacher of linguistics, I have been appalled at the unrelieved prescriptivism of many handbooks, and as a teacher of literature and composition, I have been distressed at the unwillingness of many linguistically oriented texts to tell students how modern readers react to certain variations in style and grammatical usage (xiii).

SOURCE: From *The Confident Writer* (2nd ed., p. xiii), Gefvert, © copyright 1988 by Norton. Reprinted with permission.

---

constructs permission and authority to review, evaluate, debate, be appalled, and be distressed based on her **role**: *As a teacher of composition, linguistics, and literature for twenty years, as a director of a large writing program for eight years, As a teacher of linguistics.* These **roles** provide alibis for the subjective construction of the situation through **mental** processes: They authenticate reactions.

Text 2.2 demonstrates a similar abundance of **mental** processes, but they belong to a different subclass. Here the dominant experiences are constructed as **verbalizations** (*discussing, offers*) and **creations** (*wrote, provide*). A greater variety of **processors** engage in these **mental** events: We go from the book itself as **processor** to *we* (the authors) to *discussions of writing in other handbooks.* **Mental** processes are oriented in this text toward production—something comes out of the effort—whereas in Text 2.1, the mental processes were oriented toward **cognition** and **reaction**. Unlike Text 2.1, Text 2.2 has no realizations of the **circumstance** of role. Prefaces often deal with the occasions for writing a book—the author's reasons, motivations, and so on. In Text 2.1, we see that the various **roles** the author had played provided her motivation. In Text 2.2, motivation is realized by a circumstantial element (**reason**): *We wrote* The Scribner

TEXT 2.2

This is a handbook for writers. It begins by discussing what writing is and how to do it well. It goes on to offer suggestions about writing essays, papers, and reports in different disciplines and for taking essay exams. Throughout, it shows how an understanding of words and sentences, paragraphs and punctuation, grammar and usage helps writers with the actual work of writing.

We wrote *The Scribner Handbook for Writers* because we wished to create a college handbook that would be useful not only as a reference guide to grammar and language, but also as a guide to writing. We wanted to provide an accurate and comprehensive demonstration of how writers actually write. The discussions of writing we found in other handbooks seemed to oversimplify the often messy and complex process of writing. Instead of the realities of writing—and its intimate connections with reading and thinking—we found formulas and procedures that described a finished product rather than a method for showing students how to become involved successfully in the intricate and exciting process of writing college essays.

SOURCE: From *The Scribner Handbook for Writers* (p. xv), DiYanni and Hoy, © copyright 1988 by Allyn and Bacon. Reprinted with permission.

Handbook for Writers *because we wished to create a college handbook that would be useful not only as a reference guide to grammar and language, but also as a guide to writing.* Circumstantial elements create the exigency for writing in both cases: In Text 2.1, role motivates, and in Text 2.2, reason motivates.

The construction of time and perspective in the two texts also represents two very different takes on experience. Text 2.1 is framed in before-now time and completed perspective (*have seen, have reviewed, have evaluated, have debated, have been appalled, have been distressed*). This framing of time and perspective constructs all the events and circumstances as being ones that are done and gone, as it were. It creates the expectation that all those bad things about other handbooks are finished; they are in the past, and the future will be different. Text 2.2 frames time and perspective in two dimensions rather than one as Text

2.1 does. In the first paragraph, where they discuss the book itself, the authors construe **time** as **now,** and the **perspective** is that the events are **ongoing** rather than **completed.** In the second paragraph, where they discuss why they wrote the book, **time** is **before-now** (in the past they did things), but **perspective** is **ongoing:** The events they experienced (*we found*) and the things they did (*we wrote*) were before now, but what they found, wrote, provided, and so on still exists, still continues. Their perspective on the exigencies surrounding writing their book is one of continuity. Unlike Text 2.1, in which the events are **completed,** Text 2.2 constructs events as **ongoing.**

A brief look at the lexical patterning of the two texts reveals how each preface works to arrange **concepts** in ways that help promote the interests of the perspectives being put forth. A similar pattern occurs in both the texts: Each contains two clearly marked sets of **concepts** that we could label "us" and "them," or alternatively, "this" and "that." In Text 2.1, the first set comprises the different names for the circumstantial **role** that the author constructs for herself (*teacher of composition, linguistics, and literature, director of a large writing program, teacher of linguistics, teacher of literature and composition*). Additional items in this set include *composition committees* and *writing programs.* The roles or positions that the text's addresser can take up and participate in are made numerous and diverse by this set of concepts. Conversely, the set of **concepts** naming "them" or "that" are significantly less numerous and diverse. In this set we could include *handbooks* (used five times) and *texts*—a significantly less differentiated conceptual field. In addition, a set of negative qualities and attributes identifies this text's "other": *unrelieved prescriptivism, vices and virtues, unwillingness.* On one hand, then, the set naming "us" and "this" is explicitly ameliorated by differentiation and specification, while on the other hand, the set naming "them" and "that" is made implicitly pejorative by underdifferentiation and collocation with a set of predominantly negative attributes.

A similar pattern occurs in Text 2.2. Here, however, we have a set that differentiates and specifies numerous aspects of the writers' book (*a handbook for writers, a college handbook, a reference guide, a guide to writing, an accurate and comprehensive demonstration*). The set naming "them" is undifferentiated—named only once (*discussions of writing . . . in other handbooks*)—and is again accompanied by a negative attribute (*formulas and procedures*—considered negative attributes in the context of writing handbooks). In Text 2.2, as in Text 2.1, the clustering of concepts naming the significant participants in the field is arranged to condemn the "other" (i.e., other handbooks) by keeping them undifferentiated, simple, and unitary in contrast to the differentiated, complex, and multiple concepts used to name the addressers' roles and participation.

An analysis of the instantiation of ideational resources in a text focuses on language as representation. Process types, participants, circumstances, time and perspective, and concept taxonomies all contribute to a construction of particular versions of social activities—of how things are in the world—from particular perspectives. I will return to the ideational function below, when discussing register, to explore its relationship to contextual variables in language events.

Interpersonal Resources

Halliday (1978) describes the situational demands made upon the interpersonal resources of the language system:

> Language has to express our participation, as speakers, in the speech situation; the roles we take on ourselves and impose on others; our wishes, feelings, attitudes and judgements. (p. 21)

When looking at the interpersonal function of language, we focus on its role in interaction. Our rhetorical perspective sees all language as interpersonal to the extent that all of its resources are a part of how identification, addressivity, and transformation are effected through discourse. From the point of view of a functional interpretation of the resources of the linguistic system, however, we can identify certain linguistic resources as being organized by the necessarily interactive and interpersonal demands placed upon language. Interpersonal linguistic resources construct two main types of interactive meaning potential. One is associated with the constructed speaking/writing subject and concerns the expression of attitudes, intentions, and evaluations. The second type concerns the linguistic resources that construct relations between speakers/writers and listeners/readers. I will use two terms to identify these different dimensions of interpersonal meaning: **positional** and **relational.** In a social-semiotic perspective, we are not implying that the interpersonal function—which constructs both positional and relational interactive meanings—originates or emanates from an "individual" con-

Table 2.6   Interpersonal Resources and Functions

Resource	Speech Function	Modality	Attitudinal Lexis	Sentence Adjuncts
Structures	• statement, question, command, exclamation	• modal verbs (*can, could, may, might, must, ought to, shall, should, will, would*)	• qualitative and emphasizing adjectives • manner and degree adverbs, • linking verbs • reporting verbs • cognitive verbs	• attitudinal • vocative • tags
Positional functions	• assigns speech roles	• constructs speaker/writer orientation	• indexes speaker attitude	• indexes speaker attitude, assessment of possibility, certainty, etc.
Relational functions	• indexes authority, politeness, etc.	• assigns obligation, permission, etc., to addressee		• assigns speech roles (vocative, tags)

sciousness. It is not just a matter of "that is simply what so-and-so thinks." As Lemke (1992) points out:

> The [interpersonal] function could as easily be called the Social-constitutive function. Its essence is not simply the expression of the speaker attitudes but the construction, through the text, of the world of social diversity. What matters, then, is not so much that this speaker "has" this attitude, but that the text has meaning in a community where there is a system of specific, divergent possible attitudes, and that the text is constructed within that universe of attitudes even as it helps in turn to construct it. (p. 86)

For these reasons, I will refer to those resources that enable speakers/ writers to construct attitudes, evaluations, and so on as **positional** resources. No easy division can be made between those linguistic resources that construct a subject's **position** and those that construct **relations** between subjects. The resources of the language system for acting and *inter*-acting with language are spread across a number of lexical and grammatical structures. For example, grammatical mood (i.e., interrogative, declarative, imperative) contributes to interaction in that choice of mood places our listeners or readers in a particular speech role; it therefore performs a **relational** function. In certain contexts, we may also interpret mood choice as contributing significantly to the construction of attitude: To give a series of commands, for example, in a particular situation may indicate the speaker's assessment of his or her authority. In such a case, we may recognize the significant **positional** value of such mood choices. Context and co-text usually enable us to differentiate the two. For example, in a sentence like "John must do his homework," the modal verb "must" could construct a **positional** meaning for the speaker—that is, it expresses a hypothesis—in a context in which someone speculates on what John does with his time. In another context, the same modal verb, used in the same sentence, could construct **relational** meaning in that it could indicate an obligation that John has to fulfill. Although **positional** or **relational** meanings, and in some cases both, can be signaled in single structures, I will differentiate between the two in discussing a number of significant interpersonal resources.[2] The interpersonal functions of text are constructed through both dimensions. I will discuss interpersonal function resources under the following categories: **speech function, modality, attitudinal lexis,** and **sentence adjuncts.**

SPEECH FUNCTION

One of the principal forms of participation we have as speakers/writers and listeners/readers in discourse is the dialogic role we assign or are assigned by the speech function of sentences. The propositions and proposals we exchange in discourse set up basic interactive roles for us in the language event. A question makes the speaker a "questioner" and the hearer a potential "responder," and so on. I will work with four categories of speech function: **statement, question, command,** and **exclamation.** These are labels that characterize a semantic function identifying how sentences assign interactive roles to interactants in a particular discourse. Speech function is not always directly realized by grammatical mood. Grammatical mood is determined by the presence and ordering of the subject and the finite element of the verb or verbal group in an independent clause. Speech function is as much determined by the social relationship between the interactants, and the characteristics of the context, as it is by the grammatical structure of mood. We will need to consider speech function on a case-by-case basis because it is influenced by contextual and situational factors (such as "politeness," for example).

For instance, when we ask someone at the dinner table, "Could you pass the salt?" we have made a grammatical question (a yes/no interrogative), but the speech function of this sentence is most commonly interpreted as a **command.**

MODALITY

In general, the term **modality** has been used to identify the functions of those lexical and grammatical resources that construct a speaker's/ writer's attitude toward the ideational content (often called the propositional content) of the text. **Modality** has also been used to refer to those lexical and grammatical structures that are involved in constructing forms of interaction by assigning permission, obligation, and so on, to listeners and readers. These two uses closely correspond to the two dimensions of interpersonal meaning I have identified as **positional** and **relational.** I will use the term **modality** to refer specifically to the functions of modal verbs (i.e., *can, could, may, might, must, ought to, shall, should, will, would*) in realizing both **positional** and **relational** interpersonal meaning. Other resources that construct similar meanings (such as certain classes of adjectives and adverbs) will be discussed in the next section, which concerns attitudinal lexis.

The number of ways in which modal verbs are used to realize both **positional** and **relational** interpersonal meaning are too great to list here. *Collins Cobuild English Grammar* (1990), for example, divides modal verb functions initially into two categories: those used for "indicating possibility" and those used for "interacting with other people." Within each of these categories, many subcategories are identified. Rather than develop a detailed description for each of these subcategories here, I will adopt the principle that in analyzing the interpersonal functions of a given text, all instances of uses of modal verbs will be identified according to whether they function to construct **positional** or **relational** values. After doing so, it may be necessary to give a more detailed description of the instances or patterns of modal verb use according to their different subcategories.

ATTITUDINAL LEXIS

In this category of interpersonal resources, we are concerned with lexical and grammatical structures other than speech function and modality that do, nevertheless, construct both **positional** and **relational** meaning potentials. These resources include certain subclasses of adjectives and adverbs and certain subclasses of verbs that realize mental and relational processes.

Collins Cobuild English Grammar identifies five major subclasses of adjectives: qualitative, classifying, color, emphasizing, and postdeterminers. Of these, **qualitative** and **emphasizing** adjectives are most relevant to the interpersonal function. A **qualitative** adjective identifies a quality that, in the estimation of the speaker or writer, someone or something possesses. We may think of most qualifying adjectives as having a positional value because they assign qualities from some point of view. For example, the adjective *smart* in "She gave a smart answer" signals the speaker's assessment of the quality of the answer from some position. **Qualitative** adjectives are also generally gradable—meaning that they may be modified by *very* or *rather*—further signaling a subjective cline according to which the phenomenon is evaluated. Most **qualitative** adjectives can be used in superlative and comparative structures (e.g., "She gave the smartest answer," "She gave a smarter answer"), both of which signal the speaker's position. **Qualitative** adjectives contrast with **classifying** adjectives. **Classifying** adjectives, as the name implies, assign the things they modify to classes. Generally, they cannot be graded or used in superlative or comparative structures. We do not generally speak of "a very medical problem" or "a most medical problem," for example. A number of adjectives, however, can function as qualities or classifiers. With an adjective like *religious* in "He is a religious person," we would have to determine whether or not *religious* could be graded or used in the comparative or superlative structure to determine whether or not it is being used as a **qualitative** or **classifying** adjective. **Classifying** adjectives do not perform an interpersonal function, whereas most qualitative ones do because they indicate a speaker's assessment or evaluation.

The other subclass of adjectives that construct interpersonal meaning are **emphasizing** adjectives. This class includes items such as *absolute, complete, utter, perfect,* and so on, as in "He acted like an absolute fool at the meeting." They indicate a strong feeling or response on the part of the speaker and therefore construct **positional** value.

Two subclasses of adverbs exhibit an interpersonal function. Many adverbs of **degree**, which modify qualitative adjectives, index speaker evaluation (and hence have **positional** value). For example, *unbelievably* in "That was an unbelievably long class" gives information about the speaker's opinion. Other adverbs of **degree** include *absolutely, extra-*

ordinarily, somewhat, amazingly, positively, remarkably, and *wonderfully.* Many adverbs of **manner,** which give information about the way in which a process takes place, have a **positional** value. Normally, these adverbs realize the **circumstantial** function of **manner** (see "Circumstances," above) and are thus a part of the ideational structure of sentences. When we consider, however, that acts, events, and relations do not necessarily have an inherent "way" in which they may be conducted, we can see that the speakers' selection of certain **manner** adverbs will be a trace of their own **positional** attitudes and evaluations. For example, *wonderfully* in "She spoke wonderfully" does fulfill the ideational **circumstantial** function of **manner,** but because there is no discrete class of speaking that is "wonderful," we need to recognize the **positional** value constructed by such a choice. Other adverbs of **manner** that have a clear **positional** value include *effectively, peculiarly, beautifully, truthfully, splendidly,* and *sensibly.*

Finally, we need to recognize the attitudinal function of linking verbs that realize **relational** processes, reporting verbs used that realize **mental:verbalization** processes, and other particular verbs that realize **mental:cognitive** processes. Many of these items construct **positional** interpersonal meanings in addition to their ideational value.

In **relational:attributive** processes (see "Process Types and Participant Roles," above), such as "Mary is proud of her accomplishments," the process is realized by *is.* There are a number of other linking verbs that are used to realize attributive processes, among them *appear, feel, look, prove, seem,* and *sound.* Each of these indicates a **positional** value because all are tied to subjective evaluations of whoever makes the attribution. This seems especially evident when we can assign the attribution to a first-person speaking subject. We can see this interpersonal dimension at work when we compare "Mary is proud of her accomplishments" ("unmarked" attitudinally) with "Mary seems proud of her accomplishments (to me)" ("marked" attitudinally). Such uses are similar to certain uses of modal verbs; "Mary seems proud of her accomplishments" is close in meaning to "Mary might be proud of her accomplishments."

A wide range of reporting verbs, which realize **mental:verbalization** processes ideationally, are also significant from the point of view of the interpersonal function. They construct **positional** value because they attribute purposes and reasons for speaking. Such reporting verbs include *admit, allege, assure, boast, deny, dispute, grumble, object, plead, promise, refuse,* and *swear.* When used with first-person singular subjects, these verbs identify the speaker's assessment of the reason or purpose for speaking. When assigned to second- or third-person subjects (e.g., "You boasted you got an A+," "He denied he was at the bar"), these verbs indicate the addresser's opinion about the other's reason or purpose for speaking and therefore have a **positional** value, but in these cases they also construct specific relations by implicitly assigning a speaking role/purpose for the addressee (i.e., roughly corresponding to "You are a boaster," "He is a denier").

Finally, a number of verbs on the surface would seem to be similar to **mental:cognitive** processes, but they behave quite differently grammatically and semantically. These include *think, believe, wonder,* and *suppose.* Generally, they perform a function similar to modal verbs concerned with a speaker's assessment of probability, possibility, desirability, and so on. For example, "I think it's raining" and "I believe it's time for me to go" are roughly equivalent to "It may be raining" and "I should go." We get a clearer idea of their positional value when we recognize that they don't accept tags in the way the non-interpersonal uses of these verbs would. We would not say "I think it's raining, don't I?" The "thinking" is not at risk propositionally: It encodes the speaker's assessment of possibility. Similarly, we would tag "I believe it's time for me to go" with "isn't it?" rather than "don't I?" In this sense, these verbs signal a **positional** value. They also can have **relational** value in that they are often used for "politeness." "I wonder" and "I suppose" are often used for polite requests (e.g., "I wonder if you might give me a hand?") just as "I think" often is (e.g., "I think you should stop talking"). In these cases, we may see the construction as realizing the grammatical mood **indicative:declarative,** but the semantic speech function **command.**

SENTENCE ADJUNCTS

A number of units do not operate directly in the structure of main clauses but do attach to them to perform additional ideational, interpersonal, and textual functions. Generally, the scope of such units is the whole sentence. The four basic types of sentence adjuncts are **links, topics, attitudinals,** and **vocatives. Links** perform a textual function by signaling forms of cohesion between sentences. These include *furthermore, in addition, moreover, therefore,* and so on. **Topics** perform an ideational function by indicating a field of reference. They include adverbs formed from classifying adjectives (e.g., *technically, statistically,* *logically, geographically,* and so on) and phrases such as *speaking of X, as for X,* and *in terms of X.* The remaining two types of sentence adjuncts, **attitudinals** and **vocatives,** however, perform a specifically interpersonal function.

Attitudinals are sentence rank adjuncts that perform a number of **positional** interpersonal functions. All of them indicate the speaker's assessment of the sentence's content. Adjuncts like *unfortunately, surprisingly, curiously, admittedly,* and so on indicate an opinion or a reaction on the part of the speaker. Others can indicate the speaker's distancing or qualifying what is being spoken about. These include *in a way, in effect, so to speak, up to a point,* and so on. Some sentence rank adjuncts function in ways that correspond quite closely to model verbs indicating possibility, certainty, and probability. These include *perhaps, possibly, probably, certainly, actually, maybe,* and so on.

Vocatives are sentence rank adjuncts that assign an addressee for the sentence. They can be names (e.g., "Here's your ticket, John"), titles (e.g., "Here is your ticket, madam/Ms. Jones"), or other words that identify individuals or groups (e.g., "Have a nice day, darling / kids / folks"). Because they hail a particular addressee, they play a **relational** role in the interpersonal function; however, they can indicate **positional** value as well depending on what vocative is chosen. The level of formality, for example, can indicate the speaker's opinion of or regard for the addressee (e.g., compare being hailed as "sir" or "madam" with being hailed "Hey").

The last category included in sentence adjuncts, the **question tag,** is not really an adjunct, but because it attaches to sentences that are statements, it is included here. A tag such as *doesn't she?* in "She works in Toronto, doesn't she?" makes a statement into a question by querying about the subject of the main clause. Interpersonally, they perform a **relational** function in that they indicate question speech function, but also because they are used to check statements with addressees, see if the listener is listening or understands, and so on. They also can be interpreted as performing a **positional** function in that a tag may be used because the speaker is unsure about the content of the statement or is "hedging." Occasionally, tags are used with commands to make them sound less forceful (e.g., "Make sure you call, won't you?"). In such uses, they again indicate both a **relation** (they change addressee speech role by making the command a question) and a **position** (they may indicate "politeness").

An Illustration of Interpersonal Analysis

The linguistic resources I have outlined in the previous section focus on how language shapes interaction—how it constructs positional and relational meanings between addressers and addressees. These are certainly not all the linguistic resources that function interpersonally, but they are ones that identify the major dimensions through which interpersonal meanings are brought into existence. Interpersonal meaning is tied to acts of discourse, to social subjects speaking in social contexts. It is not conceptual meaning—seemingly transcendent of social relations—but meaning that emerges from user and use, from social role and social context. Nature has no "maybe" or "ought to" or "unfortunately." An analysis of the interpersonal function foregrounds the personal, active, and *inter*-active nature of language resources. It foregrounds the ubiquitous attitudinal component in language use. Language is not simply a series of concepts and names: It has an attitudinal and interactive component. The resources of the interpersonal function respond to motivated and interested acts between people in social circumstances.

To illustrate some of the interpersonal resources discussed here at work in a text, I will examine a transcript[3] of a largely spontaneous, face-to-face dialogue (interview). The text for analysis comes from a film documentary made in England in 1985 about the British-born painter Francis Bacon (1909-1992). The film largely consists of a discontinuous spoken, face-to-face interview between Melvin Bragg (the interviewer and a close friend of Bacon) and Bacon. The five main episodes in the film correspond with five different spatial settings: a room in the Tate Gallery, Bacon's studio, a wine bar restaurant, a pub, and a small casino. In each of these settings, the speaking participants remain the same—the interviewer and Bacon. The five main segments are interspersed with shots of Bacon's paintings, photographs, street scenes showing Bacon walking, and other illustrations of Bacon's life and work. These scenes have a narrator voice-over concerning biographical information about Bacon.

The section chosen for analysis is my transcription of the talk between the interviewer and Bacon from the restaurant segment. It is a complete transcript of their dialogue in one scene from this segment. In this whole segment, Bacon and the interviewer are seated at a restaurant table drinking wine. The camera establishes the segment with an exterior shot of the front of the wine bar and then adheres to simple head-and-shoulder shots of Bacon during his speaking turns and uses a medium-range shot of both the interviewer and Bacon during turns taken by the interviewer. Bragg, the interviewer, clearly has a sheaf of notes in front of him on the table, to which we see him occasionally glance. Bacon has no notes. The extent to which this episode unfolds in continuous space and time is obviously not fully determinable because there clearly has been some editing of the interview in terms of cutting away to pictures of Bacon's paintings and to other shots. No cutaways were made in the scene given in the transcript, so we can assume that Text 2.3 is a relatively self-contained, complete text.

We have here a partially spontaneous[4] dialogue in a face-to-face setting. The hesitations, false starts, shared completion of sentences, overlapping, interruption, repetition, and so on suggest that the discourse unfolded in a fairly spontaneous way. It is not so spontaneous, however, that it does not structure itself as an interview—the interviewer clearly initiates several of the exchanges either based on topics arising in previous discourse or, as we see in this text, based on what seems to be a prepared topic (e.g., *the history of painting of flesh*). Interactionally, Bragg and Bacon seem to engage with each other with solidarity: They use each other's first names, they are not hesitant to interrupt each other, they laugh together, and there are no prosodies of anger, hostility, or agitation in either of their voices. Of course, there is a certain amount of deference on the part of Bragg toward Bacon: After all, the documentary is about Bacon and his art, his impulses, his influences—not about Bragg. There is evidence, however, that Bragg is not gratuitous with Bacon, not overly polite to him: At a few points, he contradicts Bacon, he occasionally interrupts him, and they seem to be intimate enough that it is appropriate for Bragg to indicate ideational content to complete Bacon's often incomplete sentences.

Speech function has a predominantly **relational** value: It constructs speech roles (questioner, commenter, answerer, etc.) for participants in the dialogue. With an interview, such as Text 2.3, we might expect there to be a series of **question** and answer (**statement**) pairs, where the interviewer initiates and the interviewee responds. In fact, the choices in speech function are a large part of what constitutes the forms of interaction we recognize as interview. In Text 2.3, the interviewer does indeed initiate interaction in this way at the beginning of the text. He uses **questions** in 1, 3, 5, 7, and 9. After this, he begins to use **statements** to initiate dialogue (11, 13) and from 15 onward uses **statements** almost

TEXT 2.3
Documentary interview.

(1) I: Will you tell me about the history of painting of flesh, Francis.

(2) B: Well, perhaps the, one of the greatest painters of, of female flesh was, uh, Ingres. I think he made the most marvellous images of them and I think they are probably some of the greatest, um, in a curious way, the most sexual bodies that have been made of, um, in, in painting. No man probably who didn't love women's flesh would've been able to have painted something as beautiful as a /bændyuk/.

(3) I: And do you find the same when you paint.

(4) B: I have, I have different attitudes to life than to you and, uh, of course, but, um, my attitudes are different.

(5) I: Do you want to talk about that or do you not want to talk about that.

(6) B: Well, I can talk about it.

(7) I: Well, let's talk about it. What attitudes do you have.

(8) B: I like men. Of course males, male flesh is, is very interesting. It always attracts me, but, um, that's a, that's a different thing all together.

(9) I: And what attracts you about men.

(10) B: I just like men. I like their brain. I like the quality of their flesh.

(11) I: You obviously love Michelangelo's men.

(12) B: I, I think the greatest things he ever did were the drawings because I think they're the most, they're the greatest drawings that exist.

(13) I: You've said . . . I've read that you have said . . . that he gave the most, uh, expansive—you used better words—you said the most—

(14) B: I'll tell you what he, I said, I think he gave the greatest male voluptuousness . . .

(15) I: Voluptuous, voluptuousness, that's it. That's the word.

(16) B: Yes.

(17) I: Voluptuousness.

(18) B: . . . to the male body . . .

(19) I: That's right, that's right, that's the word

(20) B: . . . than any other man has ever done.

(21) I: Don't you think it's a bit kind of—

(22) B: And /vólupte/ is all we want. Voluptuousness.

(23) I: Yes, I know. It's a wonderful [sic], isn't it.

(24) B: Isn't it a lovely word.

(25) I: Absolutely amazing. And actually that—we want to live in a state of voluptuousness.

(26) B: How right you are. Whatever, whatever it is.

(27) I: And everything else is a falling away.

(28) B: Whatever it is.

(29) I: Ha, ha.

(30) B: Everything else . . .

(31) I: . . . is a falling away.

(32) B: . . . is a falling away.

(33) I: That's right.

SOURCE: From *Francis Bacon,* produced and directed by Hinton, ©copyright 1985 by Home Vision. Reprinted with permission.

exclusively—not so much to initiate, but to continue the dialogue by commenting on Bacon's responses, and in several cases providing additional material to "complete" Bacon's responses. By the end of the text, Bacon himself is commenting on the interviewer's responses—almost a reversal in the interviewer/interviewee role. This pattern indicates that speech function is a multivalent structure that, particularly in dialogic texts (as opposed to monologic texts), gets its **relational** value (what it does to construct interaction) as much from its place in the dialogue as from its particular structure as **statement, question, command,** or **exclamation.** That the interviewer uses **statements** rather than **questions** and that Bacon himself comments on responses and even asks a question himself (24) indicates the close social distance between him and Bacon:

Topic initiation and turn assignment are not controlled by the more formally structured question-answer pair common to interviews.

The text contains very few modal verbs. The instances of **modality** that are present deal with Bacon's assessment of his ability to speak about a particular topic (*Well, I* can *talk about it* [6]) and his intentions to speak (*I'll tell you what* [14]). These examples of modality index Bacon's high affinity for what he can and will speak about. In other cases, we need to recognize that he does not modalize his statements. For example, when answering the interviewer's question about men, Bacon responds, (10) *I just like men. I like their brain. I like the quality of their flesh.* In response to this topic, Bacon's turns are marked by other structures that signal high modality and certainty. For example, the **attitudinal** sentence adjunct *Of course,* in *Of course males, male flesh is, is very interesting,* signals his high affinity, his level of conviction, concerning the topic. This sort of response differs markedly with his other turns, which are marked by much less convicted **positional** interpersonal meanings.

Many of Bacon's turns are marked with **attitudinal lexis** that indexes a lower affinity, or perhaps a bit of hedging, with regard to the content of his responses. His first response (2) is an example:

> Well, perhaps the, one of the greatest painters of, of female flesh was, uh, Ingres. I think he made the most marvellous images of them and I think they are probably some of the greatest, um, in a curious way, the most sexual bodies that have been made of, um, in, in painting. No man probably who didn't love women's flesh would've been able to have painted something as beautiful as a /bændyuk/.

Here we have *I think* being used positionally to indicate he is expressing a possibility. *In a curious way* is a **manner adverb** that indicates his position in relation to his proposition. *Probably* and *perhaps* are sentence adjuncts marking his attitude by assessing the proposition in terms of probability rather than certainty. Bacon's position is also indicated by his generous use of the **superlative** (*the most marvellous* images, *the greatest, the most sexual bodies*) and the **comparative** (*as beautiful as*). He is indicating his position with regard to gradable phenomena. Turns like this one and others (e.g., [4] and [8]) are also marked by hesitation markers and fillers (*um, uh*), perhaps indicating if not a lower affinity, at least an effort to contemplate at what level of conviction he will speak.

These interpersonal meanings construct a particular style of inter-action in the text. Initially, the interviewer asks **questions**. This, it seems, sets up a rather conventional expectation on Bacon's part: He is to provide a response. In his initial responses, he stays with the ideational content queried in the questions (e.g., *the history of painting of flesh, attitudes,* etc.), but his responses are marked by interpersonal structures that indicate his uncertainty, his slightly lower affinity for what he is responding with. Later, the interviewer uses **statements** rather than **questions** to initiate conversation. These seem to hold Bacon less rigidly to a particular responding role, and his turns begin to be marked for higher affinity (e.g., in [10], [22], and [26]). By the end of the text, interviewer and interviewee are "sharing" the discourse by commenting on responses and in several cases interrupting and completing responses for the other. Modality, attitudinal lexis, and sentence adjuncts drop away. The interaction at this point consists largely of indicating agree-ment about the **polarity** of the turns (i.e., something *is* or *is not* the case). Some might call this a bad interview because we "get" less and less detail and opinion from the interviewee. Others might see it as a successful interview because we see a fusion of the two voices—an arriving at consensus—that is an indication of solidarity between the interviewer and interviewee. The interview seems to be as much about negotiating a shareable orientational space as it is about getting "hard facts" and experiential details about Bacon's life and art.

Textual Resources

The textual function concerns language's resources for organizing mes-sages. Language as representation (the ideational function) and language as interaction (the interpersonal function) need, of course, to be orga-nized in linguistic messages. As a serial and temporal medium, language presents different possibilities for organizing messages in sequence and in time, for drawing attention to one part rather than another, and for relating parts of messages to each other. Halliday, noting that "language can effectively express ideational and interpersonal meanings only be-cause it can create text," calls the textual function the "enabling" func-tion (1978, p. 130). The resources of the textual function are used to structure the flow of information, link different parts of the text with one another, and link the text with its context.

Two principal language resources are drawn on in creating texture in linguistic messages: thematic structure and cohesive devices. Thematic structure concerns the organization of message within the sentence, whereas cohesive devices structure interpretive relations between sentences. Both of these dimensions contribute to the "texture" of text, its structuring of information and its overall cohesion. Because there is a certain amount of choice in terms of how text is organized as message, the textual function is as much concerned with "meaning" as the ideational and interpersonal functions. The contrast between active and passive voice, for example, is a property of the textual function: "Six hundred workers were laid off (by GM) today" contrasts quite meaningfully with the active "GM laid off six hundred workers today." The former passive variant enables the **agent** (in the ideational structure of the event) to be specified (in the *by* phrase) or not, whereas the active variant necessitates mentioning the **agent.** This contrast concerns the **thematic** structure of the two variants. The first thematizes the "done to," whereas the second thematizes the "doer." In "John was out until three a.m. last night. Therefore, I don't think he'll make the meeting today," both "Therefore" and "he" are **cohesive** elements that create an explicit link between the second and first sentences. "Therefore" sets up a conjunctive relation between the two sentences (it signals that the first sentence is to be interpreted as a cause or condition for the second) and "he," as **reference,** creates cohesion between the two sentences because its referent ("John") occurs in the first sentence.

I will discuss the resources of the textual function under the categories of **theme** and **cohesion.**

THEME

In English, thematic information in messages is structured in terms of the ordering and position of elements in a sentence. The **theme** of a sentence—what the sentence is concerned with, what it is "about"—is marked as thematic in English by occurring in initial position. Halliday (1994) uses the gloss "I'll tell you about . . ." to characterize the function of the **theme:**

> There is a difference in meaning between *a halfpenny is the smallest English coin,* where *halfpenny* is Theme ("I'll tell you about a halfpenny"), and *the smallest English coin is a halfpenny,* where *the smallest English coin* is

Theme ("I'll tell you about the smallest English coin"). The difference may be characterized as "thematic"; the two clauses differ in their choice of theme. (p. 38)

We need to consider the contributions of the ideational and interpersonal functions when looking at theme. If theme is the point of departure for a message, what it is "about," then the mood of the clause (an aspect of its interpersonal meaning) is important, especially with the interrogative and imperative mood. When we use the interrogative mood (e.g., to ask questions), our messages query either for information (i.e., in wh-questions) or for affirmation or negation (i.e., in yes/no questions). Hence, the theme will be the wh- word in information questions (e.g., *Who* in "Who wants dinner?") or the auxiliary or operator verb in yes/no questions (e.g., *Can* in "Can he stay for dinner?" or *Did* in "Did he stay for dinner"). When we use the imperative mood (e.g., to give commands), we assign actions that we want our hearers to carry out; the sentence is about doing something. Hence, the theme will be the main verb of the imperative sentence (e.g., *Eat* in "Eat your dinner!" or *Try* in "Try some of this lasagna"). When we use the declarative mood (e.g., to make statements), we are, more often than not, giving information about the element that fills the role of grammatical subject in the sentence (e.g., *John* in "John came to dinner" or *What I did* in "What I did was go to dinner"). In each of these cases, the theme is **unmarked**.

Occasionally, other sentence elements can occur in first position and therefore become thematic. The theme is **marked** in the declarative mood when some element other than the grammatical subject occurs in initial position and **marked** in the interrogative when some element other than the wh- word or verb operator occurs in the initial position (e.g., "After the movie" in both "After the movie, I need to go home" and "After the movie, can we go home?"). Themes also can be **marked** by a predication of the form *It* + *be* + (other sentence element)—as in "It was on Thursday that John came for dinner," in which "It was on Thursday" is **marked** theme. Any element that fulfills a role in the ideational structure of the clause may be made prominent in **marked** predicated themes (e.g., "It was John who came for dinner on Thursday," "It was for dinner that John came on Thursday").

Finally, there are cases in which more than one sentence element is thematized. In Halliday's account, this phenomenon is called "multiple theme" (1994, p. 52). Multiple themes occur when one or more **sentence**

rank adjuncts (see the "Sentence Adjuncts" section above) occur initially. Four types of sentence adjuncts can occur alone or in combination in theme position: **links** (e.g., "however," "but," "nevertheless"), **vocatives** (e.g., "Madam," "Sir," "John," "Mary," "Your Lordship"), **attitudinals** (e.g., "unfortunately," "happily," "admittedly"), and **topics** (e.g., "technically," "speaking of X," "as for X"). Halliday treats these elements as thematic when they occur singly or in combination. Each of these varieties is related to a particular function. **Links** signal relationships between sentences, so therefore function textually. **Vocatives** assign addressees, and attitudinals signal speakers' opinions, assessments, and so on, about the sentence's content: They function interpersonally. **Topics** identify a field of reference or matter for speaking and therefore function ideationally. When one or more of these sentence adjuncts appears initially, the theme extends to include the first element that plays a role in the ideational structure (i.e., a participant, circumstance, or process) of the sentence.

When analyzing a text for theme, we are not interested in what the theme of a particular sentence is in isolation; we are concerned with the progression of themes throughout a text or section of text. The thematic development in a text is a major means through which a writer or speaker structures the text's flow of information. We will need to consider actual texts to see thematic development in action, but we may, for now, keep general questions in mind, such as What gets to be theme? Are there marked themes? Are there multiple themes? and Do themes remain similar, or are they differentiated? Answers to these questions will make it possible to discuss the effects and consequences of the structuring of information in a text.

COHESION

The second major resource of the textual function used to create texture is **cohesion:** the devices that are used to relate parts of one sentence to parts of another across spans of text. Halliday and Hasan (1976) say that:

> Cohesion occurs where the *interpretation* of some element in the discourse is dependent on that of another. The one *presupposes* the other, in the sense that it cannot be effectively decoded except by recourse to it. When this happens, a relation of cohesion is set up, and the two elements, the

Table 2.7   **Textual Resources and Functions**

Resource	Theme	Cohesion
Structures	• theme • marked theme • multiple theme	• reference • ellipsis • conjunction • lexical cohesion
Organizational functions	• structures thematic development and information flow	• creates texture • relates text to context

presupposing and the presupposed, are thereby at least potentially integrated into a text. (p. 4)

Cohesion gives text unity, enabling it to be interpreted as a whole, rather than as an unorganized collection of words. It operates as a part of the overall process of text: Like the act of making, exchanging, and interpreting text, the construction of textual cohesion (on the part of writers/ speakers and readers/listeners) is a part of the ongoing process of meaning-making. An analysis of **cohesion** in a text points to the interpretative ties that are made possible by the text. I will briefly discuss four main types of cohesion: **reference, ellipsis, conjunction,** and **lexical cohesion.**

Cohesive **reference** occurs in text when some participant or circumstance introduced at one point in a text is taken as the reference point for interpreting some third-person pronoun (e.g., he/him, she/her, it, they/them, his, hers, its, theirs, their), demonstrative (e.g., the, it, this/ these, that/those, here/now, there/then), or comparative word that assumes a standard of reference from previous text (e.g., same, similar, other, more, fewer, such). **Reference** may be made to referents that occur previously in the text (anaphoric reference), occur "later" in the text (cataphoric reference), or are "outside" the text in the context (exophoric reference). The first few sentences of Text 2.4 contain an example of each of personal, demonstrative, and comparative reference. The type and "direction" of each referring item is noted in square brackets.

Cohesion through **ellipsis** occurs when a piece of wording (a part of a clause, nominal group, or verbal group) is presupposed at a subsequent place in a text. The omitted wording is recoverable in previous text.

TEXT 2.4
Introduction

In June 1977, I thought I had *the beginnings* [*demonstrative:exophoric*] of two books. One I called *The Evolutionary Idea* and *the other* [*comparative:anaphoric*] *Every Schoolboy Knows*. *The first* [*comparative:anaphoric*] was to be an attempt to reexamine *the theories of biological evolution* [*demonstrative:exophoric*] in *the light of cybernetics and information theory* [*demonstrative:exophoric*]. But as I began to write *that book* [*demonstrative:anaphoric*], I found *it* [*personal:exophoric*] difficult to write with a real audience in mind who, I could hope, would understand *the formal and therefore simple presuppositions* [*demonstrative:exophoric*] of what I was saying.

SOURCE: From *Mind and Nature: A Necessary Unity* (pp. 89-90), Bateson, ©copyright 1979 by Dutton. Reprinted with permission.

Occasionally, a **substitution** element (e.g., "do" for verbal groups, "one" for nominal groups) replaces the ellipted wording. The following turns in an imaginary dialogue illustrate varieties of **ellipsis** and **substitution**:

A: Can you tell me a joke?
B: Yes. Here's a good one.

B's *Yes* response contains clausal ellipsis (i.e., "I can tell you a joke"), and *one* is a substitution for *joke*. Both *Yes* and *one* are interpretable only in terms of previous text.

Cohesion through **conjunction** occurs when one sentence is marked as having a particular "logical" relation to previous text. The presence of a conjunction makes the sentence interpretable in light of previous text. The four basic types of conjunctive relations are **additive** (e.g., "and," "furthermore," "in addition," "for instance," "likewise"), **adversative** (e.g., "yet," "but," "however," "instead," "at any rate"), **causal** (e.g., "so," "therefore," "because," "for this reason"), and **temporal** (e.g., "finally," "first," "meanwhile," "secondly," "in short"). Although most conjunctive relations are made explicit by the presence of one of these words, occasionally we may interpret an implicit conjunction between sentences. Between the two sentences "Jill broke her leg skiing" and "She won't be in to work today" we may recognize a **causal** relationship (we may make an implicature) that could be made explicit with the use of "therefore" or "as a result" or some similar conjunction in the second sentence. An interesting case for discourse analysis occurs when there is potential ambiguity about certain conjunctive relations. For example, "and" is the most basic conjunction and normally is used additively. In certain uses, however, it may disguise (or make only implicit) another type of conjunctive relation. An advertisement for an upscale travel magazine had the headline "Read this and you may want to leave town." Clearly, the advertisers would be thrilled to have readers entertain different interpretations of the conjunctive relation. Some possibilities include **adversative** ("Read this, *but* [we're warning you] you may want to leave town"), **causal** ("Read this, *then/as a result* you may want to leave town"), and **temporal** ("Read this, *then afterwards* you may want to leave town").

Lexical choice can create cohesion in texts when words are repeated; when choices are related to previous words through synonymy, hyponymy, meronymy; and when pairs of words have a more than ordinary tendency to co-occur. **Repetition** may involve the same word being repeated, or a word with different morphology (e.g., "work," "working," "worked," and so on). **Synonymy** involves a lexical item being similar in meaning, sense, or denotation to a previously occurring item (e.g., "work," "strive," "toil"). **Hyponymy** involves a specific-general relationship between lexical items (e.g., "table," "chair," "desk," in relation to "furniture"), and **meronymy** involves part-whole relationships between lexical items (e.g., "hard drive," "CPU," "sound card," in relation to "computer"). Instances of pairs of words having a more than ordinary tendency to co-occur, like all aspects of cohesion, depend on the **register** (see the section on "Register" below) being instantiated by the text. This type of lexical cohesion is called **collocation**. It does not depend on a general semantic relationship between items in the way synonymy, hyponymy, and meronymy do, but rather involves a "co-occurrence tendency" (Halliday, 1994, p. 333). Collocation involves setting expectations: The presence of a particular item creates a greater than random chance that a related item will occur. In the play-by-play commentary for a hockey game, for example, cohesion is provided by collocation of such items as "shoot," "pass," "stop," "send," and "puck."

Lexical cohesion is closely related to the topic of **concept taxonomies** that I discussed previously as a resource of the ideational function. From the point of view of the textual function, we are concerned with lexical sets as one of the means by which text is made cohesive. Concept taxonomies often are constructed out of the same items, but when interpreted in terms of the ideational function, these items are a part of how text represents experience. The particular selection of sets, what items do and do not get included, and what hierarchical arrangements may hold between items and sets are all issues that are related to how concepts represent experience (see analysis of speech pathology text, Chapter 5).

Context

So far in this chapter, I have focused on a variety of functional resources that can be drawn upon in the construction of text. These are inventories for describing the different, but complementary, functions of linguistic structures. I have focused on these structures as **resources**—as the things that can be done with language to construct ideational, interpersonal, and textual meaning potentials. This, of course, is only a part of the picture because text always occurs in a context that enables it to function ideationally, interpersonally, and textually. The functional meaning potentials of linguistic resources become relevant only in relation to contexts of their use.

The term *context* has been used to refer to both the accompanying text of a particular stretch of language under consideration (sometimes called "co-text" or the "verbal context") and the situational, nonlinguistic, context of which a text is a part. I will use the term *context* in the latter sense.

FIELD, TENOR, AND MODE

Halliday (1989) comments on the symbiotic relationship between text and context:

> The text . . . is an instance of the process and product of social meaning in a particular context of situation. Now the context of situation, the context in which the text unfolds, is encapsulated in the text, not in a kind of

piecemeal fashion, nor at the other extreme in any mechanical way, but through a systematic relationship between the social environment on the one hand, and the functional organisation of language on the other. If we treat both text and context as semiotic phenomena, as "modes of meaning," so to speak, we can get from one to the other in a revealing way. (pp. 11-12)

We have seen that a functional discourse analysis understands the patterns of linguistic structures in texts in terms of their contribution to the realization of ideational, interpersonal, and textual meaning. These meaning types respond to the structure of the situational context of the text. Halliday (1978) identifies three general characteristics to describe situations:

(i) The social action: that which is "going on," and has recognizable meaning in the social system; typically a complex of acts in some ordered configuration, and in which the text is playing some part, and including "subject-matter" as one special aspect;

(ii) The role structure: the cluster of socially meaningful participant relationships, both permanent attributes of the participants and role relationships that are specific to the situation, including the speech roles, those that come into being through the exchange of verbal meanings;

(iii) The symbolic organization: the particular status that is assigned to the text within the situation; its function in relation to the social action and the role structure, including the channel or medium. (pp. 142-143)

Respectively, these situational features are labeled **field, tenor,** and **mode.** The type of social activity involved (field) activates the resources of the ideational function, the role relationships involved (tenor) activate the resources of the interpersonal function, and the mode activates the resources of the textual function. The **field** of Text 1.1 (the student note), for example, involves seeking permission to submit late work in a university course. It is one constitutive activity of the larger field activity of attending (in terms of the student's participation) and conducting (in terms of the professor's participation) a university course. The **tenor** characteristics of the context of Text 1.1 involve the relationship between a student and a professor, which is asymmetrical in terms of authority and power as far as the granting of permission is concerned. The **mode** characteristics of Text 1.1 involve the expectations that both parties have for written communication in relation to the field and tenor characteristics of the situation. In this context, a short, handwritten note

Table 2.8   Situational Resources in Relation to Text Resources

Resource	Situation (Context)		Text
Structures	Field of discourse— social activities	realized by	Ideational meanings
	Tenor of discourse— social relationships	realized by	Interpersonal meanings
	Mode of discourse— role of language	realized by	Textual meanings
Functions	Situation type— organizes recurring, recognizable social situation types	corresponds with	Register—recurring configurations of ideational, interpersonal, and textual choices

delivered with the paper is construed as an appropriate transaction with which to "perform" the request for permission.

REGISTER

Field, tenor, and **mode** are used to refer to recurring situational features: They characterize recurring situation *types*. The terms are also meant to identify aspects of the situation that affect what functional resources are typically drawn upon in making, exchanging, and understanding text in context. Situations can be described in many different ways, but this particular set of criteria is meant to draw out the relationship between the structure of situations and the functional potential of the linguistic resources of the language system. The functional resources that are typically drawn upon in response to recurring situation types are called **registers**. A register is a "particular configuration of meanings that are typically associated with a particular situational configuration of field, mode, and tenor" (Halliday, 1989, pp. 38-39). Registers are thus varieties of language use—described in terms of the typical patterns of realization of ideational, interpersonal, and textual meaning—that are deployed in response to typical, recurring situation types. We may think of registers as "sublanguages" that are "characteristic of particular activities in which language is used, defined by systematic differences in the probabilities of various grammatical and semantic features" (Lemke, 1995, p. 26). Buying a jug of milk at a local convenience store, for example, calls upon very specific functional meaning potentials of the language system because the whole range of ideational, interpersonal, and textual resources of the language are not at risk in this type of situation. A president's televised state of the union address, although a less restricted register, still calls upon specific and predictable meaning-making resources of the language.

Beyond raising questions concerning what ideational, interpersonal, and textual meanings are typically deployed in relation to recurring situation types, an analysis of register draws attention to two particularly significant issues concerning the social functions of discourse and discourse types. First, the possible configurations of ideational, interpersonal, and textual meanings in texts (i.e., registers) are not open ended. There are some combinations that do not occur. Martin (1985) gives an example:

> Some fields do not combine with particular tenor and mode values because of taboo. Sex for example does not readily combine with power (tenor) and spontaneous dialogue (mode). It is not always "polite" in our culture to talk about sex to our inferiors; if one does so, it may be construed as a rather threatening, often sexist, demand for sexual favours. Similarly, there is a general constraint against talking about sex while doing it, regardless of the tenor involved. (p. 251)

Lemke (1985) comments that "missing registers" are both "a powerful stabilizing mechanism for a community's social order" ("we don't talk about that that way") and "a system of critical points of potential change should these meanings come to be made and recognized in a community where they formerly were not" (p. 277).

Second, the characteristics of registers (what linguistic features correspond with what situational characteristics) are objects of social analysis because they are a significant feature of the symbolic power that certain social agents have over others. Control over registers—the ability to make and understand texts in particular situation types—is a significant prerequisite to having one's authority recognized as legitimate. Lemke (1995) gives an example concerning authority and scientific registers:

A discourse, a way of speaking, is considered less scientific, or even rendered "unscientific" exactly to the extent that it includes elements either of the language of feeling or the language of action and values. Use the linguistic and stylistic resources of the poet or artist for scientific communication, and you will not have standing as being scientific. (p. 178)

I return to the relationship between registers and symbolic power in Chapter 4.

Summary of Resources and Functions

This chapter has worked toward providing a vocabulary with which to identify and analyze the social and functional characteristics of text in context. The categories used to describe patterns in the language of texts are functional categories: They focus on how language structures function in representing experience (the ideational function), constructing role relationships (the interpersonal function), and organizing messages (the textual function). The categories used to describe contextual variables—**field, tenor,** and **mode**—interpret context in terms of how recurring social activities, social roles, and recognized modes of communication systematically correlate with the functional patterns of texts.

Tables 2.1 and 2.6-2.8, presented earlier, summarize these vocabularies in terms of structures and functions. Tables 2.1, 2.6, and 2.7 identify "structures" as the resources of the language system that are typically drawn upon in realizing the social "functions" of text in context. Table 2.8 displays the relationship between **field, tenor,** and **mode** as situational variables and the functional resources of the language system.

Notes

1. Representative works in these three related areas include, for systemic-functional linguistics, Halliday (1978, 1989, 1994); for communication linguistics, Gregory (1985, 1988, 1995); and for social semiotics, Hodge and Kress (1988), Lemke (1995), and Thibault (1991).

2. Fairclough (1989, 1992) makes a similar distinction.

3. The transcription was prepared from an audio recording of a documentary film. Long dashes ("—") are used to indicate when a speaker is interrupted. Ellipsis points (". . .") are used to indicate points where the speaker hesitated. I have transcribed the interview into a written form that recognizes major independent

and dependent clauses. Coughing, clearing of the throat, and other such speech elements have not been included in the transcription, although it can be noted that these generally occurred at points of hesitation within a single turn. In the transcript, "I" indicates the interviewer and "B" indicates Bacon, the interviewee. For ease of identification, I have numbered each new turn in the text. Unclear material is transcribed phonetically within slashes (/. . . /).

4. We can assume the interviewer prepared somewhat for the interview. Bacon may have been alerted to the content or type of questions to be asked. Indeed, he may have suggested some.

3 The Resources of Rhetorical Theory

This chapter outlines the second of the three perspectives taken here on the rhetoric of discourse as social practice. From the work of Kenneth Burke, I derive a framework for the rhetorical analysis of language as symbolic action that both complements and extends the social and functional discourse analysis presented in the previous chapter. The framework complements discourse analysis by offering a perspective that is, once again, systemic, functional, and social. Burke, like Halliday and others interested in the social functions of discourse, interprets the structures of discourse in a functional vein: He is concerned with understanding how, in drawing upon the meaning-making resources of symbolic systems, instances of discourse constitute socially motivated, oriented, and consequential acts, and he is concerned with understanding how the nature of systems of symbolic resources not only enables symbolic acts to be recognizably meaningful but also powerfully constrains symbol users by circumscribing the conditions and consequences of their acts.

We saw in Chapter 2 a framework for identifying text structures and interpreting their functions with reference to context. Discourse analysis focuses on the language of text as both constrained by and constitutive of the social conditions of its use. Burke's rhetorical perspective extends discourse analysis, however, by introducing different vocabularies to understand how and why symbolic action occurs. Burke's rhetoric shares an object of analysis with discourse analysis—real instances of text in context—but because it draws on drama, philosophy, and theology, a different, but complementary, perspective is enabled. To discuss the grammatical resources (systems and structures) of symbolic action, Burke draws on an understanding of human relations and activities as drama: The language of text arranges acts, agents, agency, scenes, and purposes in different structures (which Burke calls "ratios"), each constructing different motives, reasons, and orientations for human actions. To discuss the overriding functions of symbolic action, Burke offers "identification" and "consubstantiation" as key terms: Rhetorical acts initiate congregation and segregation in social orders based on the symbolic acts' positing of the terms through which participants may share or not share "substance." To discuss both the social conditions and the social consequences of symbolic action, Burke offers "logology": a study of how symbol systems themselves constrain human perspectives (our practices of vision and division) and also structure the social consequences—for example, guilt, imperfection, hierarchical psychosis—of living in terms of symbolic systems.

Before dealing with the key terms of Burke's rhetoric, I will return to Text 1.1 to introduce some of the considerations of a rhetorical analysis.

A Rhetorical View of Text 1.1: Changing Exigencies

Text 1.1 occurs in what is very much a *rhetorical* situation. The student's paper is overdue, and an explanation is forthcoming if it is to be accepted. The student's success in the course hangs in the balance.

Extrinsically, in terms of meeting exigencies presented by the situation, the text performs a number of key rhetorical functions. Put simply, the note is meant to persuade me to accept the late paper—that is, to grade it and record the mark. This is not all there is to the note rhetorically. Burke describes the principal function of rhetoric as rooted in the function of language as "a symbolic means of inducing cooperation in beings that by nature respond to symbols" (1950/1969b, p. 43). This function—to induce cooperation—is evident enough in the student's act of giving me the note: The student does so to create the means through which we can "see" the situation in complementary terms and thereby "resolve" a pressing exigency that currently divides us. Cooperation and being united by a (new) shared vision of the situation do not necessarily imply a complete consensus between participants; they imply the sharing of the means with which to characterize and understand the situation. The meaning potentials of the text provide the terms through which a shared vision of our roles, responsibilities, and different but related authority is negotiated. They are the substance we have to shape cooperation.

The rhetorical act's function to induce cooperation is conditioned by its nature as an addressed act. We have interactants assessing each other as audience, predicting reactions, scoping out appropriate initiations and responses, and so on. The rhetorical act hails its audience. The meaning-making resources instantiated in the rhetorical act not only create the "I" that addresses but also the "you" being addressed, thus enabling (and constraining) meaning-making potentials for what the "you" can see and how the "you" can respond. The student's note creates a multifaceted addressee. I am hailed by my role (*Professor Stillar*); I am shown deference of a sort (*Thank you . . . , I'm sorry . . .*); but I am also given a rather strong (though implicit) injunction to accept the terms of the explanation—to comply with the request. In other words, I am also constructed as a compliant addressee. This is most salient in the student's characterization of the *difficulty getting back into semiotics mode*. Recalling that this was a semiotics course, we see that, to resist this appeal (which asks me to see the student in terms I would presumably use to characterize myself), I would be calling into question a "mode" that I, as a semiotics professor, helped create. Also, ending with *Have a good summer* (which points to a span of time in which I would have no contact with the student) clearly indicates that I need not "take a turn" now—the matter is closed. On one hand, then, I am addressed as someone who would quite naturally accept the grounds of the explanation (having been, as a semiotics professor, presumably subject to the difficulties of "semiotics mode"), and on the other, I am addressed simply as a "reader" who, through textual clues like the foreclosing *Have a good summer,* should recognize that my next "turn" consists only of complying by grading the paper.

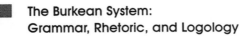

The Burkean System: Grammar, Rhetoric, and Logology

Rhetorical analysis, in a Burkean perspective, focuses on our dual relation to symbolic action and symbolic systems. That is to say, symbol systems enable us to construct a world of experience and orientation. Through symbols, we actively shape and interpret worlds and orient ourselves to those represented worlds and the other agents in them. They constitute our ways of knowing and acting in the world. At the same time, the symbol systems and symbol-using patterns of our cultures define us as social agents. They constitute our ways of being in the world. Burke (1945/1969a) comments:

> Dialectically considered (that is, "dramatistically" considered) men [sic] are not only *in nature*. The cultural accretions made possible by the language motive become "second nature" with them. . . . [S]ymbolic communication is not a merely external instrument, but also intrinsic to men as agents. Its motivational properties characterize both "the human situation" and what men are "in themselves." (p. 33)

Most of Burke's works revolve around the simple, but very consequential, fact that life is lived *in terms of*—that is, it is lived through a variety of "terministic screens." He says:

> We *must* use terministic screens, since we can't say anything without the use of terms; whatever terms we use, they necessarily constitute a corresponding kind of screen; and any such screen necessarily directs the attention to one field rather than another. Within that field there can be different screens, each with its way of directing the attention and shaping the range of observations implicit in the given terminology. (1966, p. 50)

The terministic screen (whether it is as "grand" as the discourses of capitalism or as "mundane" as our occasional chat with the proprietors at our local convenience store) conditions and constrains the scope and effect of our symbolic action, but such screens also always produce consequences because they "direct the attention" and are by nature not simply neutral, but orientational and attitudinal. Burke prioritizes the orientational and attitudinal aspects of symbolic action over the representational. We are not simply overdetermined subjects blindly operating with particular terministic screens: We are social agents with attitudes and motives. Our words negotiate relations of power, legitimacy, and authority. Orientation is concomitant to every representation. In a dialogue between Satan and The Lord (concerning the "symbol-using" animal-humans) at the end of *The Rhetoric of Religion*, Burke has The

Lord tell us of the ubiquity of attitude in language and its embodiment in language users:

> **TL (The Lord):** The nature of language as petition, exhortation, persuasion and dissuasion implies that, first of all, their words will be modes of posture, act, attitude, gesture. If one of their creatures strikes an attitude, such as kneeling in obeisance, that's real enough—and the same kind of reality can be carried into any words that go with it. . . .
>
> **S (Satan):** Their task in ranging linguistically, then, will be to round out their sheer attitudinalizings as thoroughly as possible?
>
> **TL:** Yes, and some quite grandiosely architectonic enterprises will emerge in the process. . . .
>
> **S:** Their most comprehensive symbol-systems, then, will be but a constant striking of attitudes?
>
> **TL:** Yes, . . . (1961/1970, pp. 288-289)

We will see, in working out the key terms in Burke's work, that in answering the basic question for rhetorical analysis—"What is said by whom in terms of what?"—we are compelled to focus on how attitude and motive are omnipresent in all language use (indeed, in all semiotic practice). Both have active consequences: Attitude for Burke borders on action "since attitude contains an implicit program of action" (1941/1973, p. 143) and is "the *preparation* for an act" (1945/1969a, p. 20).

This chapter deals with Burke's theory (using terms he provides) in three sections: **grammar, rhetoric,** and **logology.** Each section focuses on the constitutive elements and functions of symbolic action. **Grammar** deals with analysis of the vocabularies and structures of texts used in the construction of motives. Burke's grammar is a "dramatistic" one because it focuses on language as motive and as "act." **Rhetoric** deals with language's role in identification and division among social agents; it focuses on the exchange of discourse as a central mode through which social orders are constructed and transformed through addressed symbolic action. **Logology**—words about words—deals with the conditions and consequences of symbol systems in relation to "symbol-using animals": It focuses on the implications of symbolic action as conditioned by the negative and by the attendant forms of transgression that are invited by the implicit "perfection" of various semiotic orders.

▓▓▓ Grammar

Burke's grammar is not a grammar in a traditional linguistic sense, although it is a grammar that focuses on language in its own terms, seeks to make explicit and replicable statements about the function of combinations of language units, and operates with a coherent and consistent set of terms with which to generate a descriptive analysis. The grammar focuses on how patterns in discourse (from actual texts to whole philosophical schools) index, construct, and embody motives. He calls his method of analysis "Dramatism"—a "method of analysis and corresponding critique of terminology designed to show that the most direct route to the study of human relations and human motives is via a methodological inquiry into cycles or clusters of terms and their functions" (1968b, p. 445). The dramatistic orientation focuses on language as "primarily a species of action, or expression of attitudes, rather than an instrument of definition" (1968b, p. 447).

The key concepts that figure in Burke's dramatistic analysis are the **pentad, ratios,** and **substance.**

THE PENTAD AND RATIOS

As with Halliday and others who practice functional discourse analysis, for Burke form and function in discourse are not antithetical. An analysis of text processes focuses on patterns of selection and combinations of various semiotic resources available for making meaning. Burke's pentadic model consists of five terms (**act, agent, scene, agency,** and **purpose**) used to identify the structures (what goes with what) and functions (indexing, constructing, and shaping attitudes) of elements of symbolic action:

> In a rounded statement about motives, you must have some word that names the *act* (names what took place, in thought or deed), and another that names the *scene* (the background of the act, the situation in which it occurred); also, you must indicate what person or kind of person (*agent*) performed the act, what means or instruments he used (*agency*), and the *purpose.* (1945/1969a, p. xv)

The object of a pentadic analysis is the language of the text itself. By identifying how a text construes each element, we begin to get a picture of how it constructs a representation of "reality"; more important, the representation is attitudinal and motivated because every representation is the situated social practice of real social agents who necessarily construct "reality" with reference to their practices and the terminologies that are a part of them. Burke (1966) comments: "Even if a given terminology is a *reflection* of reality, by its very nature as a terminology it must be a *selection* of reality; and to this extent it must function also as a *deflection* of reality" (p. 45). A particular pentadic pattern in a text is both a "selection" and a "deflection": A text deploys selected pentadic resources and the elements can combine in different ways, each leading to a different construction of motive. These particular combinations Burke calls **ratios.** Ratios are principles of "determination" and "selectivity" (1945/1969a, pp. 15, 18). For example, a **scene:act** ratio imputes motive by constructing the act as appropriate to or determined by the scene; a **purpose:act** ratio would characterize the act as made necessary by some purpose. The particular ratio being foregrounded in a text or part of a text is an indication of how symbolic action frames and shapes experience and orientation. A pentadic analysis would be a mere cataloging of the ideational structure (**process, participants,** and **circumstances**) of a text if it did not recognize the structuring capability of ratios. Different ratios construct different motives, different orientational and attitudinal dispositions. In Text 2.1, the instantiation of the circumstantial element **role** (e.g., *As a teacher of composition, linguistics, and literature for twenty years, as a director of a large writing program for eight years, As a teacher of linguistics, as a teacher of literature and composition*) as the apparent condition for **mental:reactive** actions (e.g., being *appalled* and *distressed*) constructs an **agent:act** ratio: One can develop such strong reactions (the act) because of one's qualities as a particular type of agent (holding particular authorizing roles such as "teacher" and "director"). In Text 2.2, which introduces a similar type of book, motive is couched in a **scene:act** ratio (particularly in the second paragraph): The authors *wrote The Scribner Handbook for Writers* (act) because of what they *found* in a particular scene—that is, other writing textbooks that, in the authors' estimation, were flawed. Here, then, the act is conditioned by the scene, whereas in the previous example it was conditioned by the qualities of the agent. Both these texts are explicitly about *why* the authors wrote their books and implicitly why we should read them. An analysis and comparison of the dominant ratios constructed by the forms of the two texts (in their "own terms") distinguishes two different motives. In the first case, we are implicitly invited to read on with the assurance that what the author writes (the act) comes from authority and experience, and in the second case because the act is positively influenced by a "negative" scene that it promises to transcend.

A text is not framed in terms of one ratio because making, exchanging, and understanding text is a dynamic process that instantiates various and shifting textual, contextual, and linguistic resources. As this heterogeneity develops, ratios are transformed. The resources of the pentad are deployed in patterns that evolve in text exchange processes. This becomes very salient when we support a pentadic analysis with the tools of discourse analysis in a functional perspective. From one point of view, act, agent, scene, agency, and purpose are analogous to the **ideational** functions **participant, process,** and **circumstance** (see Chapter 2).[1] Shifts in patterns of realization of process type will likely affect the type of ratio being foregrounded. A text does not rely on one type of ideational structure throughout. A text's **textual** pattern contributes to transformations in ratios as well; for example, a concentration of theme-marked (see Chapter 2) circumstances of **time** and **place** may indicate that scene will figure in the ratio. The instantiation of **interpersonal** resources is not monotonous in text either. Patterns of realization of **positional** and **relational** interpersonal meaning will affect ratios because **positional** resources are a major resource for the construction of attitude in text—something that can affect any element of the pentad. **Relational** resources (such as the choice of speech function) largely concern the nature of language as act (giving information, demanding, commanding, etc.), thus minimally falling under a consideration of the act element of the pentad.

These sorts of considerations need to be placed in the context of analysis of an actual text. The point here is simply that the functional heterogeneity of text indicates that there will necessarily be heterogeneity in terms of what ratios are being foregrounded. We will pay close attention to those cases where there seems to be a transformation from one ratio to another because these points indicate shifts in how symbolic action both constrains and enables (by directing the attention with particular ratios) interpretation by transforming *what* is being said in terms of *what*. The pattern of realization of the ideational, interpersonal, and textual functions is just one resource for determining pentadic ratios.

As we go on, we will consider the effect of other meaning-making resources such as register and situation type (i.e., field, tenor, and mode).

SUBSTANCE

Ratios are the means through which the elements of the pentad can frame and construct motive and attitude. To establish a **scene:act** ratio, for example, is to invite interpretation of acts in terms of scene: The whisky priest in Graham Greene's *The Power and the Glory* attempts to evade his pursuers and hide his identity as a priest because he lives in a "godless State"—Mexico during its anticlerical purges of the 1920s. We are led to understand and identify with his actions through the perspective of this ratio. So, the elements of the pentad, instantiated in various ratios in texts, direct the attention; to be directed to see *in terms of* is to adopt an attitude, to be predisposed to act *according to* the ratio. Burke's grammar, therefore, is concerned with how symbols act, how they are substantive in several senses. Ratios of the pentad form attitudes having practical consequences that make them substantial, but the very framing action of the ratios and the elements of the pentad presuppose a whole series of substantives—things that *are*. A text's construction of ratios from elements of the pentad presupposes identities, classes, and attributes for those elements. At the same time, the symbolic action of the ratio produces and reproduces identities, classes, and attributes; it constructs substances. Burke gets at this dual relation to substance in the following:

> The transformations which we here study as a Grammar are not "illusions," but citable realities. The structural relations involved are observable realities. Nothing is more imperiously there for observation and study than the tactics people employ when they would injure or gratify one another—and one can readily demonstrate the role of substantiation in such tactics. To call a man a friend or brother is to proclaim him consubstantial with oneself, one's values or purposes. To call a man a bastard is to attack him by attacking his whole line, his "authorship," his "principle" or "motive" (as expressed in terms of the familial). An epithet assigns substance doubly, for in stating the character of the object it at the same time contains an implicit program of action with regard to the object, thus serving as motive. (1945/1969a, p. 57)

Burke maintains that the whole issue of "substance" resides in paradox: Normally in saying what something or someone *is* (that is, characterizing its substance), we must say what it *is not* (1945/1969a, pp. 21-58). We see this very clearly in the grammar of **relational** processes (see Table 2.4). **Identification, attribution, classification, possession,** and **location**—each concerning something "substantial" about the central participant—all paradoxically characterize participants *in terms of* what they are not. For example, to say of an acquaintance, "Mary is my friend," is to assign substance to *Mary* via a social relation, not through some intrinsic or inherent quality *Mary* possesses. To say "Mary is a teacher," analogously, is to assign substance to *Mary* through the properties of members of a class rather than a property of *Mary*.

Our purpose here is not to plunge headlong into the philosophical quagmire of identity. Rather, it is to recognize, following Burke's lead, that motive and attitude, constructed *in terms of* ratios, are dependent upon the assignation of substance. Because we can never really say what "it" *is* directly, but can do so only *in terms of,* the ambiguities of substance play a significant role in the shaping of attitude and the construction of ratios with the pentad: Assigning substance to an entity is not *the* way of its being, but *a* way of its being. Assigning substance is hence a selection and a deflection, just as a particular ratio (**scene:act,** for example) constitutes a selection (one of many) of the ways in which motives may be attributed or understood, and it is a deflection because it impels us to see in *its* terms, not in *others:*

> What we are here considering formally, as a paradox of substance, can be illustrated quickly enough by example. A soldier may be *nationally* motivated to kill the enemies of his country, whereas *individually* he is motivated by a horror of killing his own enemies. Or conversely, as a patriot he may act by the motive of sacrifice in behalf of his country, but as an individual he may want to profit. Or a man's business code may differ so greatly from his private code that we can even think of him as a "split personality" (that is, a man of "two substances," or "divided substance"). (Burke, 1945/1969a, p. 37)

The functioning of ratios is conditioned by the "type" of substance presupposed by their elements. The different types of substance (presuppositions of "what *is*") affect the meaning potentials of the ratios. A dramatistic grammatical analysis must consider both ratio and substance because they are different resources, each allowing different selection and combination of grammatical elements.

The different types of substance presuppose different alibis for "being." As a "taken-for-granted," seemingly inalienable resource, substance functions as ground or foundation for motive. Substance enables a type of defining, a way of delimiting and marking boundaries—first for what *is* and *can be,* and by extension for what is therefore legitimate. Burke identifies three main types of substance: **geometric, familial,** and **directional** (1945/1969a, pp. 29-33). Geometric substance concerns definition in terms of temporal and spatial context. The character of geometric substance derives from "participation in a context":

> Contextual definition might also be called "positional," or "geometric," or "definition by location." . . . Historicists who deal with art in terms of its background are continually suffering from the paradox of contextual definition, as their opponents accuse them of slighting the work of art in its esthetic aspects; and on the other hand, critics who would center their attention upon the work "in itself" must wince when it is made apparent that their inquiries, in ignoring contextual reference, frustrate our desire to see the products of artistic action treated in terms of the scene-act, scene-agent, and agent-act ratios. (Burke, 1945/1969a, p. 26)

When Canadians are called "our northern neighbors" by American politicians, they are being defined in terms of contextual substance.

Familial substance concerns definition in terms of descent, lineage, and membership. The character of familial substance derives from shared ancestry:

> In its purity, this concept stresses common ancestry in the strictly biological sense, as literal descent from maternal or paternal sources. But the concept of family is usually "spiritualized," so that it includes merely social groups, comprising persons of the same nationality or beliefs. Most often, in such cases, there is the notion of some founder shared in common, or some covenant or constitution or historical act from which the consubstantiality of the group is derived. (Burke, 1945/1969a, p. 29)

An interesting subclass of familial substance is the case of "nutritive substance" (1945/1969a, p. 30). Burke (1945/1969a) characterizes definition by **nutritive** substance as a combination of contextual and familial definition:

Since the taking of nourishment involves a *transubstantiation* of external elements into elements within, we might treat nutritive substance as a combination of the contextual and familial. . . . (p. 30)

Discourses of dieting, weight training, and the wonders of high-tech pharmaceuticals, for example, rely on definition by ("magical") nutritive substance. Definition in terms of nutritive substance can be the essential element in familial definition:

Totemic rites and the sacrament of the Eucharist are instances where the nutritive emphasis becomes submerged in the notion of familial consubstantiality. "Tell me what you eat, and I'll tell you what you are." (Burke, 1945/1969a, p. 31)

Directional substance concerns definition in terms of trajectory, path, and motion. Being and motive are constructed as products of tendency, of conformity to general trend:

The directional has encouraged much sociological speculation in terms of "tendencies" or "trends." With such terms, the substantial paradox is not far in the offing. If a man did *not* make a certain decision, for instance, we might nonetheless choose to say that he had a "tendency towards" the decision. (Burke, 1945/1969a, p. 32)

Directional substance posits motive in dispositions—habit, will, and inclination—that have their alibis in historical, cultural, even statistical trends. Demographic explanation of individual social action might be considered a paradigm case where motive is constructed in terms of directional substance. Cliché attributions that so-and-so is "up-and-coming," "going straight to the top," or "a social climber" also betray a definition of being in terms of directional substance.

Burke's assiduous treatment of the paradox of substance is not aimed at claiming that all substantiation collapses into nonsense. Rather, it is a reminder that although substance—as the "taken-for-granted" of being—would seem to be inalienable and natural; it is as much a social construction, as much a selection and deflection, as any other speaking *in terms of.* Precisely because substance is taken for granted (presupposed as essential and foundational and therefore not contestable), Burke (1945/1969a) seizes upon its ambiguities:

[T]here is cause to believe that, in banishing the *term* [substance], far from banishing its *functions* one merely conceals them. Hence, from the dramatistic point of view, we are admonished to dwell upon the word, considering its embarrassments and its potentialities of transformation, so that we may detect its covert influence even in cases where it is overtly absent. (p. 21)

AN ILLUSTRATION OF GRAMMATICAL ANALYSIS

Text 3.1 consists of the running text appearing on the front and side panels of a box of President's Choice "Too Good to Be True" Ancient Grains™ breakfast cereal. Here is a very common sort of text we encounter in unremarkable situations: We may read such texts in grocery stores, we may read them while we sit eating. The symbolic action involved in such texts, however, is as complex and consequential as other types of discourse (advertising being one relevant intertext), as indexical of our culture and social practices. Flakes of cereal would seem to be a fairly mundane thing, but differentiating one brand of flakes from another, persuading consumers to eat particular flakes, summoning the appropriate symbolic distinctions with which to identify and capture market share—these are the stuff of grammar, rhetoric, and logology.

"Too Good to Be True" is the name for a whole line of low-calorie and low-fat foods available in the President's Choice product line. The President's Choice line itself consists of a whole variety of products offered as in-house, "generic" alternatives to national brand-name items.

The side panel consists of two sections of running text. The first talks about the importance of eating these grains, and the second lists the four grains and gives descriptions. The first section (*By supporting the use of these rare and ancient varieties of grains, you're encouraging the continued cultivation of these treasures from the past, which might otherwise be lost forever*) sets up a **purpose:act** ratio that advocates eating the cereal (the act) as something that should be done to help preserve the grains' continued cultivation (the purpose). Motive here would seem to apply in a scope much greater than simply eating because one is hungry or because one likes the taste of the cereal. The preservation of these "ancient" treasures is a "cause" to be championed.

A transformation takes place across the two sections on the side panel: We move from a **purpose:act** ratio in the first section (where the addressee is the implied agent) to a **scene:agent** ratio in the second section, where the grains are described. In the second section, the grains

TEXT 3.1
Ancient Grains cereal box.

Front panel:
Made with organically grown ancient grains
"TOO GOOD TO BE TRUE"™
PC™
President's Choice™
ANCIENT GRAINS cereal

- Only 115 calories per serving
- Contains organically-grown ancient grains Spelt, Millet, Kamut and Quinoa
- 13.5 grams dietary fibre per serving
- No refined sugar added—sweetened with honey
- Only 2% calories from fat
- No preservatives added
- No artificial flavors or colors

Side panel:
By supporting the use of these rare and ancient varieties of grains, you're encouraging the continued cultivation of these treasures from the past, which might otherwise be lost forever . . .
Spelt
dates back to biblical times and grows well without fertilizers, pesticides and insecticides. It's a versatile grain, perfect for baking, pastas and cereals.
Millet
is a hardy, small grained annual cereal grass believed to have originated thousands of years ago in central Asia. It has a pleasant nutty flavor.
Kamut
pronounced "Ka-moot"—commonly known as "King Tut's Wheat"—originated in the Near East and is believed to be an ancient relative of modern durum wheat. It has a rich, buttery flavor.
Quinoa
pronounced "Keen-wa"—was a staple of the Inca Empire and is appreciated for its delicious taste and fluffy texture.

become agents characterized as having particular attributes that result from their temporal and geographical origins. This ratio relies on definition in terms of **nutritive substance** (quite literally). The taste (*a pleasant nutty flavor; a rich, buttery flavor; delicious taste and fluffy texture*), characteristics (*versatile, perfect, hardy*), and source (*dates back to biblical times, originated thousands of years ago in central Asia, originated in the Near East, a staple of the Inca Empire*) all characterize the grains in terms of nutritive substance. We are even given glosses of two of the grains' phonetic substance (*pronounced Ka-moot, pronounced "Keen-wa"*). The **scene:agent** ratio constructs the grains as particularly magical and powerful because of their characteristics and origins.

I pointed out earlier that Burke conceives of definition in terms of nutritive substance as a combination of contextual and familial definition (1945/1969a, pp. 30-31). **Contextual** definition is realized in terms of both a temporal (*ancient, thousands of years ago*) and geographical (*central Asia, the Near East, the Inca Empire*) context. **Familial** definition presupposes the recognition and renown of a special class, the members of which share "ideal" features. The text presupposes a long-standing recognition of a class of *Ancient Grains:* This is realized quite clearly in the use of **mental:cognitive** processes in *believed to have originated thousands of years ago, commonly known as, is believed to be an ancient relative, is appreciated for its delicious taste.* Because these processes have no **processors,** we are being invited to think that "anyone" would "believe," "know," and "appreciate": The reputation and characteristics of the grains are constructed as "true," in the generic sense, as "true" in principle.

Motive is constructed through what we might call a doctrine of nutritive substance in this case. Because they are old (*ancient*), are geographically exotic (*central Asia, the Near East, the Inca Empire*), and belong to a recognizable class (*commonly known, believed,* etc.), they are "good." Because they are "good," we are (should be) motivated to eat them.

Burke's dramatistic grammar provides two related vocabularies for understanding how motive is constructed in discourse. The **ratios** highlight the relationships between the terms of a text as the means for giving reasons, thereby constructing motives, thereby striking attitudes and shaping incipient actions. The elements of the ratios rely on definition in terms of particular types of **substance** that furnish them with ostensibly inalienable kinds of "being." Investigating the paradox of substance allows us to understand the text's implicit and usually unspoken "this *is*" as "this is *in terms of,*" thereby disclosing that substantiation is itself an act (i.e., tied to agents, their interests, their motives, their attitudes) because to define *in terms of* is to select and valorize one kind of substance, one kind of "being," over others.

▓▓▓▓ Rhetoric

Two phrases from Burke's definition of the "symbol-using" animal specifically bear upon his characterization of the features and functions of rhetoric: "separated from [our] natural condition by instruments of [our] own making" and "goaded by the spirit of hierarchy (or moved by the sense of order)" (1966, p. 16). The first identifies what Burke sees as our condition as biological and social beings: We are divided in interest, ability, access to resources, attitude, and so on. To this end, the function of rhetoric is to overcome division through **identification** and consubstantiality. To identify with someone or something is to construct "the real" in the same terms as another, to construct it as united by similar **substance.** Burke (1950/1969b) says:

> A is not identical with his colleague, B. But insofar as their interests are joined, A is *identified* with B. Or he may *identify himself* with B even when their interests are not joined, if he assumes that they are, or is persuaded to believe so.
>
> Here are ambiguities of substance. In being identified with B, A is "substantially one" with a person other than himself. Yet at the same time he remains unique, an individual locus of motives. Thus he is both joined and separate, at once a distinct substance and consubstantial with another. (p. 21)

The second clause ("goaded by the spirit of hierarchy [or moved by the sense of order]") recognizes that any identification is always contextualized by some type of social **order** or hierarchy that sets the conditions for what kind of identification is possible and what sorts of substance "count" as "legitimate" terms for consubstantiality. Identification becomes possible when the rhetorical act draws on grammatical resources that function in terms of substances appropriate to a particular hierarchy. This is particularly clear when we consider the forms of hailing that are required in any rhetorical act. Rhetoric is always **addressed:** A primary requirement to identification is addressing one's audience in appropriate terms and constructing one's own subjectivity in terms that make congregation possible. The rhetorical act is also a transaction that seeks to bring about a change in the exigencies inherent to the particular social order in which it takes place. To initiate identification (to overcome a division) is to initiate a **transformation** in the hierarchy, to change the way *what* is seen *in terms of what*.

I will explore Burke's key rhetorical terms—**identification, transformation, addressivity,** and **order**—with reference to Text 3.1.

IDENTIFICATION AND TRANSFORMATION

The grammatical analysis of Text 3.1 went as far as identifying two ratios: A **purpose:act** ratio that assigned motive to the reader along the lines of "by eating this cereal, you are preserving important grains," and a **scene:agent** ratio that characterized the grains as particularly enticing because of their scenic (temporal and geographical) origins. Both these ratios rely on definition in terms of nutritive substance—a combination of contextual and familial definition where time and place origins and belonging to a class of "renowned" things are the alibis of substance and being.[2] These are the grammatical resources that form the basis for what is a rhetorical act: They are patterns (particular ratios and substances) that function in addressed rhetorical action. They are aimed, we can presume, at initiating a basic transformation—getting readers to "see" the cereal in the same terms (that is, identify) such that they would be likely to consume the product. Identification here relies on sharing substance—consubstantiality—in both the literal and symbolic senses. To eat the cereal is to become literally a part of a congregation of Ancient Grains cereal-eaters; to identify with the substantiality of the ratios (to accept their "slant") is to become symbolically a part of a congregation that identifies with preserving the heritage of "ancient" grains and eating "healthy" foods. The rhetorical act seeks to unite the audience in substance by having them (pardon the pun) "swallow" its terms.

Identification and consubstantiality presuppose division. Burke (1950/1969b) says:

> Identification is affirmed with earnestness precisely because there is division. Identification is compensatory to division. If men were not apart from one another, there would be no need for the rhetorician to proclaim their

unity. If men were wholly and truly of one substance, absolute communication would be of man's very essence. It would not be an ideal, as it now is, partly embodied in material conditions and partly frustrated by these same conditions; rather, it would be as natural, spontaneous, and total as with those ideal prototypes of communication, the theologian's angels, or "messengers." (p. 22)

In the Ancient Grains case, there are a number of ways in which the parties to the rhetorical act are divided. The most obvious division is between those who have eaten the cereal and those who have not. This is the division that the producers, the Ancient Grains people, would like to overcome. A more interesting and complex division—and one that creates the exigency for constructing motive in the ways it is constructed in this text—concerns the difference between those who would accept this particular doctrine of nutritive substance and those who would not. The reader is invited to share in a social purpose (help "save" the grains), to believe in the renown of their taste (e.g., *a pleasant nutty flavor*) and healthy potency (e.g., *3.5 grams dietary fibre*). These two broad divisions—one literal, the other symbolic—are the principal obstacles to be transcended and transformed by the rhetorical act.

ORDER AND ADDRESSIVITY

The particular ratios and appeals to seeing in terms of nutritive substance that constitute the grammatical patterns of the text both presuppose and reproduce various social practices and the systems and structures that enable and constrain them. Social orders are marked by hierarchy (those who have and those who have not, those who are up and those who are down, those who are on the inside and those on the outside, and so on), and rhetoric negotiates potential movement and understanding between levels of hierarchy. Burke (1950/1969b) understands hierarchy as a product of symbolic action:

> [I]n any order, there will be mysteries of hierarchy, since such a principle is grounded in the very nature of language, and reinforced by the resultant diversity of occupational classes. That claim is the important thing, as regards the ultimate reaches of rhetoric. The intensities, morbidities, or particularities of mystery come from institutional sources, but the *aptitude* comes from the nature of man, generically, as a *symbol-using animal*. (p. 279)

To be invited to become consubstantial with, to identify with, a doctrine of nutritive substance instantiates tensions inherent in several discourses of our culture's social orders. The rhetorical act attempts to build a congregation of addressees who would share interest and have a stake in these social orders. It hails addressees who would fancy themselves as "connected" with the past, environmentally conscientious, and health conscious.

One such order is built around the mysteries of past civilizations and the need to "transcend" time and cultural difference to become consubstantial with "ancient" practices. Such an order contains an implicit hierarchy: What is constructed as "ancient" in time and "exotic" in place and culture is presupposed to be good and superior to what is contemporary and commonplace. The Ancient Grains text invites readers to participate in a communion with the past and with exotic cultures, to transcend their mysteries.

Another social discourse/order that the text appeals to is constructed quite clearly in the **purpose:act** ratio, in which the reader is motivated to eat the cereal because it will help preserve *continued cultivation of these treasures from the past, which might otherwise be lost forever* (side panel). This general appeal to "doing the right thing" echoes what we might call the discourse of environmentalism and conservation. A basic hierarchy constructed by such a discourse includes those who would make things worse and those who would make things better. We are enabled by the text to join the latter because it provides a symbolic motive for the simple act of consuming the product. By doing so, we support the use of a grain that *grows well without fertilizers, pesticides, and insecticides.*

Finally, there is the implicit hierarchy endemic to the discourse of health and diet. Definition in terms of nutritive substance obviously plays a role in inviting readers into this hierarchy: Not only is the cereal "good" because it is made with *ancient* grains, they are *organically-grown* and have all the characteristics (listed on the front panel) of a healthy food—low in calories, high in fiber, low in fat, and so on. The **scene:agent** ratio motivates us (gives us the reason and the means) to encompass the benefits of two temporal worlds: the "exotic" past with its legendary grains and the "practical" present with its dietary emphasis—a healthy anachronism.

The Ancient Grains text sets up ratios that invite participation in *and* a way to the "top" of each of these hierarchies. It provides the rhetorical means to fulfill its eponymic promise *Too Good to Be True*. This name itself stands as a very good example of what is at risk whenever we would, as it were, forget the paradoxes of substance. Substance can be asserted only in terms of what it is not: A flake of cereal does not have *intrinsic* symbolic qualities, only constructed ones (e.g., being a *staple of the Inca Empire* constructs it as "good" by presuming that whatever the Incas ate was good). Constructing the substance in terms of history, renown, healthy characteristics, and so on is an attempt to stabilize the paradox, to make identification and consubstantiation possible through persuasion and consensus—ultimately through literal "communion." The interesting consequence of this, for readers, is that the very possibility of transcending this paradox (or temporarily stabilizing it)—and the resources we have at our disposal to do so—are constructed and constrained by the rhetorical act itself. That is, to sidestep the paradox that Ancient Grains are "Too Good to Be True," we must accept the transcending vision offered to us in the ratios and substance of the text. This makes the text very rich in terms of symbolic capital because it largely controls the means to satisfy a paradox it both relies on (speaks *in terms of*) and re-creates. This last point takes us into the realm of **logology**.

Logology

In the second half of *A Rhetoric of Motives* (1950/1969b), Burke analyzes how rhetorical and symbolic action create and reproduce different social orders that are inscribed with different types of hierarchies. Hierarchies calibrate the social order by charging it with rankings and evaluations of things, words, people, acts, and so on. These values are determined with reference to social practices, relations, institutions, and social norms and expectations, as well as the forms of symbolic action (the "terministic screens") that articulate, reproduce, and legitimate them. Burke's grammatical and rhetorical analysis focuses on the resources drawn upon in symbolic acts and characterizes these as instances of ratios, substance, identification, addressivity, and transformation. They focus on symbolic acts as dynamic processes. His **logology** extends this analysis to the symbol systems themselves. Logology—words about words—seeks to understand the conditions and consequences of motives that are inherent in symbol systems. It inquires into how systems of symbolic resources themselves—with their completeness, their perfection, their "systematicity"—compel the subject that would make use of their resources. It is concerned, very simply, with what transpires when we would live through—live in terms of—symbol systems. Borrowing a term from Hodge and Kress's (1988) *Social Semiotics,* we can say that logology focuses on the social functions of "logonomic systems." Hodge and Kress give the following gloss:

> [F]rom the Greek *logos,* which means a thought or system of thought, and also the words or discourse through which the thought is presented, and *nomos,* a control or ordering mechanism. A logonomic system is a set of rules prescribing the conditions for production and reception of meanings; which specify who can claim to initiate (produce, communicate) or know (receive, understand) meanings about what topics under what circumstances and with what modalities (how, when, why). (p. 4)

Logonomic systems would therefore include the language system, registers, expectations about the structure of situation types (field, tenor, and mode), discourses (in the sense of "the discourse of . . . discussed in Chapter 1), systems of intertextuality (a community's typical practices of relating texts to each other), and other meaning-making systems. An instance of text (including the discoursal practices involved in its exchange) not only draws on logonomic systems but also in itself forms a more or less stable instantial logonomic system that circumscribes its meaning potential. The analyses in Chapter 5 deal with several instances of how texts set up (and often contradict) their own logonomic "rules."

We interact with and through logonomic systems in all symbolic action. In attempting to characterize logonomic systems, however, our recourse to their features comes from an analysis of the records (texts) of instances of interaction. In his outlines of logology, Burke draws on records of symbolic action, in the form of texts, to provide the evidence with which to construct the terms, features, and functions of elements of logonomic systems. After introducing the concept of logology in practice (though not in name) in *A Rhetoric of Motives,* he later turned to theology and theological texts in *The Rhetoric of Religion* (1961/1970) as a source for understanding the nature of language as motivational system—that is, as a logonomic system, one whose words and discourses "ordered" and "controlled" its subjects:

Insofar as man is the "typically symbol-using animal," it should not be surprising that men's thoughts on the nature of the Divine embody the principles of verbalization. And insofar as "God" is a *formal* principle, any thorough statements about "God" should be expected to reveal the formality underlying their genius as statements. . . . [I]nsofar as religious doctrine is verbal, it will necessarily exemplify its nature as verbalization; and insofar as religious doctrine is thorough, its way of exemplifying verbal principles should be correspondingly thorough.

   Thus it is our "logological" thesis that, since the theological use of language is thorough, the close study of theology and its forms will provide us with good insight into the nature of language itself as motive. Such an approach also involves the tentative belief that, even when men use language trivially, the motives inherent in its possible thorough use are acting somewhat as goads, however vague. (pp. 1, vi)

Logology, then, is concerned with "language itself as motive," with word/*logos* and "order"/*nomos*. It is concerned with both the conditions and consequences that logonomic systems bestow upon the social agents who are subjected to them. Although our characterization of logonomic systems is an abstraction, they are themselves inherently social phenomena arising out of situated, historical, and mediated symbolic practice. Burke remarks, for example, that "vocabularies" [of a particular logonomic system] "are not words alone but the social textures, the local psychoses, the institutional structures, the purposes and practices that lie behind the words" (1935/1984b, p. 182). A focus on the social conditions and consequences of logonomic systems keeps logology from being a mere spinning out of the possibilities of the system in a purely internal way. In typically dramatic and portentous terms, Burke links the logonomic system ("Order") with the decidedly social practice of "victimage" (1961/1970, pp. 4-5):

Here are the steps
In the Iron Law of History
That welds Order and Sacrifice:

Order leads to Guilt
(for who can keep commandments!)
Guilt needs Redemption
(for who would not be cleansed!)

Redemption needs a Redeemer
(which is to say, a Victim!).

Order
Through Guilt
To Victimage
(hence: Cult of the Kill) . . . .

Logology does not replace grammatical (dramatistic) and rhetorical analysis: It complements them with meditation on the ontological conditions and epistemological consequences for us as "bodies that learn language."

BODIES THAT LEARN LANGUAGE

Near the end of his career, Burke made some final modifications to his "definition of man" (later, "human beings"), which he had first introduced in *The Rhetoric of Religion* (1961). This definition, which he eventually came to call a "Poem," contains in very condensed form the essences of his grammar, rhetoric, and logology. It is, as it were, a kind of logonomic system for Burke's language. With it we could "generate" the implications of his work:

BEING BODIES THAT LEARN LANGUAGE

THEREBY BECOMING WORDLINGS

HUMANS ARE THE

SYMBOL-MAKING, SYMBOL-USING, SYMBOL-MISUSING ANIMAL

INVENTOR OF THE NEGATIVE

SEPARATED FROM OUR NATURAL CONDITION

BY INSTRUMENTS OF OUR OWN MAKING

GOADED BY THE SPIRIT OF HIERARCHY

ACQUIRING FOREKNOWLEDGE OF DEATH

AND ROTTEN WITH PERFECTION (Burke, 1989, p. 263)

I will use this "Poem" to explore issues related to what I have called the conditions and consequences of living through logonomic systems.

Wordlings

In the first two lines ("Being bodies that learn language/Thereby be-coming wordlings") we are alerted to Burke's recognition of the comple-mentarity between action ("language") and motion ("bodies"): Humans are biological entities, and our social practices bear relations to physical constraints. We are, however, also "wordlings" that act with symbols. Burke was critical of terminologies (logonomic systems) that described social practices *as if* they could be reduced to the terms of motion. Burke recognized that any contemplation of motion (the physical, biological, etc.) involves action (in the form of symbolic action, directing of atten-tion with particular terministic screens and so on). This recognition cuts two ways for logology. First, logology cannot focus on words/action alone without a recognition that they operate within "physical" con-straints and have practical, material consequences. Second, logology must recognize that any human engagement with the physical world is framed by social practices that are themselves products of symbolic action. The complementarity between action and motion that Burke's definition thematizes resonates with a social semiotic conception of the complementarity of action/semiosis and motion/materiality:

> A "social practice" is a semiotic cultural abstraction, but every particular, actual instance of that social practice is enacted by some material processes in a complex physical, chemical, biological, ecological system. Every action thus enters into two systems of relations, for which our culture has two different sorts of descriptive discourses. As an instance of a social practice, it enters into relations of meaning with other social practices. These are semiotic relations. As a physical event, it enters into relations of energy, matter and information exchange with other events. These are material relations. Every instance of a social practice is simultaneously also an instance of some material process. Every system of social practices, linked in semiotic formations according to their meaning relations, is also a system of material processes linked by physical, chemical, and ecological relations. (Lemke, 1995, p. 106)

To be a "symbol-making, symbol-using, symbol-misusing animal" means that logonomic systems will be both a link to and a screening of the "reality" of the physical world of motion. Words, registers, discourses, and terministic screens condense "reality" by picking out certain parts of it for our engagement and attention. We become "symbol-misusing animals" in Burke's eyes when we would forget the deflecting action of terministic screens, when we would, in Alfred Korzybski's terms, mistake the map for the territory and initiate all sorts of confusions, inequities, and errors. Logological analysis alerts us to the consequences of the selective and deflective nature of terminologies by reminding us that the efficacy of the symbol is to be found in its relationship to other terms in the terminology, not in its inherent accuracy in "summing up" the symbolized.

Inventor of the Negative

The next clause, "inventor of the negative," is crucial to Burke's logology. Burke made much of the recognition that there are no negatives in nature: "To look for negatives in nature," he says, "would be as absurd as though you were to go out hunting for the square root of minus-one. The negative is a function peculiar to symbol systems, quite as the square root of minus-one is an implication of a certain mathematical symbol system" (1966, p. 9). Burke characterizes the function of the negative in symbol systems as more than a simple assertion of *is* or *is not*. Because the negative always functions with reference to particular logonomic systems—including its contexts and participants—it is hortatory, admonitory:

> Dramatistically, the stress should be upon the hortatory negative, "Thou *shalt* not." The negative begins not as a resource of definition or information, but as a command, as "Don't." (1966, p. 10)

Every logonomic system has its resources for marking the negative and hence constraining symbolic action in terms of the "rules" of the system. The negative, whether marked very explicitly as in the Decalogue, or implicitly, as for example, in the Ancient Grains text, compels participants in the particular logonomic system to act accordingly because transgressing the negative courts guilt. Our recognition of the source of this guilt may be obscured, however, making the possibility of understanding or even transcending the negative difficult. "The negative principle," Burke comments, "is often hidden behind a realm of quasi-positives" (1966, p. 11). It may not be a serious case of moral judgment, but the Ancient Grains product-line name "Too Good to Be True" is a good example of an implicit and complex negative injunction. It invites us, paradoxically, to yoke the negative and the positive: To be "Too Good" implies a kind of *negative* (in the sense that it is "excessive") and to be "True," a kind of *positive* (in the sense that the "true" equates with the good). We need to at least entertain the negative reading to "believe" (with whatever type of conviction—this is cereal, after all!) the positive reading. Lighthearted or not, the phrase invites us to oscillate between the positive and negative "readings." This indeterminacy is exactly what makes the implicit negative of logonomic systems effective: An explicit connection between instances of the negative and the wide-scale implications of the negatives of the logonomic system would be too self-evident, too easily challenged. In the seemingly trivial case of the "Too Good to Be True" implicit negative, there is ultimately a connection between it and a negative on a greater cultural scale that says, in effect, "Don't be fat or unhealthy; overweight and sick people are inferior." The negative implies choice on the part of those subjected to it. The "paradox" or ultimately the "poison" of the negative, however, is made clear when we recognize that the negative itself is created by the logonomic system— something beyond "individual" choice. Being "moralized by the negative" (as Burke had at one time modified his definition) means to accept the shifting of burden, as it were, from the system to the agent. We may reinterpret Burke's clause "inventor of the negative," then, along lines he suggests:

> I am not wholly happy with the word, "inventor." For we could not properly say that man "invented" the negative unless we can also say man is the "inventor" of language itself. So far as sheerly empirical development is concerned, it might be more accurate to say that language and the negative "invented" man. (1966, p. 9)

Separated by Instruments of Our Own Making

This clause emphasizes the ubiquity of the framing—and alienating— effect of logonomic systems in our social practices. The "rules" of logonomic systems, such as the classificatory function of registers, for example, do not exist in a vacuum: They are established, recognized, and practiced by social groups in real contexts. They are "instruments" of our own making. An "instrument" in the sense of a property of a logonomic system is not a mere "tool": It is a semiotic practice. It "separates" us from our "natural condition" (our place in physical, chemical, biological, and ecological systems) in several ways. First, signs are not the "things" signified: the word "hunger" is not the sensation of hunger. Second, as we've seen at other points in this chapter, symbolic action (naming, for example) selects and deflects; it directs attention to particular aspects of the symbolized *in terms of* the terministic screen being used. It therefore "separates" us from other aspects through deflection (e.g., what other terministic screens emphasize). Third, and perhaps most significant, logonomic systems reflect, construct, and reproduce divisions and inequities in social systems. For example, not every person has access to and "control" of the particular registers that help construct the social fields in which they participate.

The "alienating" or "separating" function of logonomic systems is amplified by the reflexive dimension that consists of the recognition of the propriety of the system's rules and forms. The reflexivity (e.g., discourses about the efficacy or propriety of a particular logonomic system) can be alienating because the subject and scope of such reflexivity is the system itself—its rules and forms—not the social practices to which it "applies." The following comment from Bourdieu—which anticipates material that I will explore in Chapter 4—resonates with Burke's emphasis on this alienating power of the instruments of logonomic systems:

> There is a properly symbolic effectiveness of form. Symbolic violence, of which the realization *par excellence* is probably law, is a violence exercised, so to speak, in formal terms, and paying due respect to forms. Paying due respect to forms means giving an action or a discourse the form which is recognized as suitable, legitimate, approved, that is a form of a kind that allows the open production, in public view, of a wish or a practice that, if presented in any other way, would be unacceptable. . . . The force of the form . . . is that properly symbolic force which allows force to be fully exercised while disguising its true nature as force and gaining recognition, approval and acceptance by dint of the fact that it can present itself under the appearances of universality—that of reason and morality. (1990a, p. 85)

This reflexivity (here couched in terms of proper "respect" and recognition of form) is more alienating when we consider that in most social fields only certain people are endowed with the authority to remark on the propriety and appropriateness of rules.

Goaded by the Spirit of Hierarchy

Logonomic systems create and reproduce hierarchies of many different varieties. On one hand, logonomic systems are based in rules for the production and exchange of discourse that are intended to function in particular social fields. Hierarchy results because access to and control of the resources of logonomic systems is unequal: Division and difference structure a field of "haves" and "have nots" or participants whose "competence" is more positively valued than others. On the other hand, the "perfection" of a logonomic system itself—the entelechy of its rules and resources—constructs a kind of graded hierarchy in which sanctioned and proper combinations of its resources, by virtue of their formal "elegance," are valorized.

Burke links social hierarchy with the "mystery" inherent in differential access and control of the resources of logonomic systems. "King and peasant are 'mysteries' to each other," he says. "Those 'Up' are guilty of not being 'Down,' those 'Down' are certainly guilty of not being 'up' " (1966, p. 15). Other examples abound. For instance, handbooks aimed at teaching the "communication" practices of business or technical writing trade on "debunking" such forms of mystery by providing student readers with explicit systems and methods for "writing like professionals." The hierarchical incentive can be fulfilled by following the system. Here is one example from a business communication text's preface:

> The 3 × 3 process, a practical and helpful approach to written and oral communication, is developed fully and applied consistently. With the book's strong graphics you'll understand and remember this multi-stage process of *analyzing-anticipating-adapting, researching-organizing-composing,* and *revising-proofreading-evaluating.* . . . By consistent repetition and application of the process, you will learn and retain an invaluable problem-solving strategy you can take with you and use every day in your future career. (Guffey, Rhodes, & Rogin, 1996, p. xxii)

The emphasis here on *repetition and application of the process* (that is, following the logonomic system) and the projection of a certain state likely to follow from practice (*your future career*) illustrate well the relationship between the logonomic system itself as motive (that is, the *source* of motive) and transcending mystery (in this case, transforming from student to practitioner). The features of the system itself posit the mystery (the *process* implies that a change needs to take place) and constrain the means with which to transcend it (*By consistent repetition and application of the process, you will learn . . .*). The lurking irony of all such "expert" systems of advice (see Chapter 5) is that in seeking to help readers transcend the mystery, they must reproduce it; otherwise, they would have nothing to offer. If there is no mystery, no hierarchy to be transcended, there is no need for expert advice. Mystery, Burke notes, is very persuasive:

> Rhetorically considered, Mystery is a major resource of persuasion. Endow a person, an institution, a thing with the glow or resonance of the Mystical, and you have set up a motivational appeal to which people spontaneously ("instinctively," "intuitively") respond. In this respect, an ounce of "Mystery" is worth a ton of "argument." Indeed, where Mystery is, we can be assured that the arguments will profusely follow. (1952, p. 108)

Most business and technical communication textbooks now include profiles of professionals in the fields to which they would have their readers aspire. These are the models at the top of the hierarchy—exemplary communicators to learn from and admire:

> Each chapter begins with an interview of a front-line employee from a leading company. These interviews provide insights, tips, and, in many instances, role models for readers. (Guffey et al., 1996, p. xvii)

Mystery helps preserve hierarchy by foregrounding those differences that would motivate participants in the hierarchy to "change," rather than those differences that would provide the grounds for contesting the apparent stability of the hierarchy. We do not expect a business communication textbook to explore methods for a systematic critique of, say, social inequities that may be reproduced by "accepted" business communication practices. In fact, logonomic systems often neutralize potentially destabilizing differences either by ruling them "out-of-court" (not "our" concern) or by actively precluding them (i.e., the system does not contain the resources for making those types of meaning). Material concerning "ethical" and "cross-cultural" issues in business and technical communication textbooks, for example, often sidesteps a concern for critical, social analysis by offering instead a series of checklists and questions designed to "stimulate discussion" or "draw attention to issues."

To be "goaded by the spirit of hierarchy," Burke notes, may be "too weighted" an expression. He offers "Moved by a sense of order" to compensate (1966, p. 15). In either case, we are asked to recognize that logonomic systems create hierarchy "externally" (project organization onto a social practice) and "internally" (mark "good" and "bad" application of its resources/forms), and in doing so, move or "goad" people to participate in the hierarchy accordingly. Hierarchy becomes corrosive when the means with which to understand its terms and the motives it constructs are obscured, suppressed, or trivialized.

Rotten With Perfection

This final clause sums up an overall condition and consequence of logology. We are in the condition of living through symbol systems that are "perfect" in the sense that the rules and resources combine in a logic proper to the system itself. We face the consequences of transgressing that logic when we would be moralized by its negatives and goaded by its spirit of hierarchy. Burke points out:

> By the very fact of setting up an order, you make men potentially transgressors. For you give order only to the kind of being who might possibly disobey them. Thus, order makes man *in principle* subject to temptation. (1972, p. 44)

Burke says that the lure of the formal completeness of logonomic systems is a motivation for participants who would use it. Forgetting that they are ultimately social constructs, born of practice, history, and power, we engage with and through logonomic systems *as if* they had their own entelechy, their own internal motivational principles aimed at attaining perfection proper to their kind (the "perfect" sonnet, the "perfect" report, the "appropriate" response, the "obvious" answer, etc.): "A given terminology contains various *implications*, and there is a corresponding "perfectionist" tendency for men to attempt carrying out those implications" (Burke, 1966, p. 19).

The "perfectionist tendency" of logonomic systems functions, in many cases, regardless of the "ends" that some or all participants in a situation consider relevant. Stories and jokes about dealing with bureaucracies in which hapless clients and civil servants are led through a comic dance of form-filling and frustration are merely funny or ironic, but cases such as a wrongful conviction resulting from "strict adherence" to "proper investigative practice" have resulted in disaster for the accused. In Chapter 5, I explore entelechy and perfection as they relate to the register of a diagnostic speech pathology progress report. I will make a case that the text provides evidence of implied "requirements" of the register the "rules" applicable to the writing of the report—that are a significant factor in blocking the clinicians from exploring alternative diagnosis and interpretation of their subject's speech characteristics. The "perfection" of a terministic screen enables a construction of its objects—it allows a "picking out" of relevant features, it makes situations "manageable" by naming them—but it also constrains our ability to entertain other views. "Every way of seeing is also a way of not seeing," Burke says (1935/1984b, p. 49).

The Scope of Grammar, Rhetoric, and Logology

Burke's grammar, rhetoric, and logology, outlined here in separate sections, all share in the substance of symbolic acts. They comprise three complementary and complex vocabularies with which to link text structures with social functions, addressers with addressees in transformative acts, and instances of text and symbol-users with the logonomic systems that direct and inculcate them. The different perspectives enable us to identify and interpret significant, salient features and functions of discursive practice: Grammar focuses on discourse as drama by targeting the text's construction of ratios of act, agent, agency, scene, and purpose and sorting out the antinomies of substance that every symbolic act betrays; rhetoric focuses on discourse as the means through which social subjects build identification and overcome division through addressed symbolic acts; and logology focuses on the conditions and consequences attendant to all symbolic acts, the significant—often deleterious—effect of the limited and limiting potentials of the various systems of meaning-making resources we live through. The key terms of Burke's grammar, rhetoric, and logology together constitute a theory of language as symbolic action enabling us to identify its features, structures, relationships, and functions. They construct objects of analysis by picking out elements of discourse for our attention.

We can also use Burke's grammatical, rhetorical, and logological theory to interpret some of the recurrent, "overall" functions of discourse. The grammar proposes that an overall function of discourse is to project attitudes into acts, that speaking/writing *in terms of* functions to represent, select, and deflect attention. The rhetoric proposes that an overall function of discourse is to consummate transcendence, to consubstantiate what, under some description, was formerly divided. The logology proposes that an overall function of discourse is to embody the dramatic, comedic, and all too often tragic consequences of the symbol systems at risk in discourse.

Notes

1. Lining up the two vocabularies, we could arrive at: act/**process**; agent/**participant**; scene/**circumstance:place** or **time**; agency/**circumstance:manner**; purpose/**circumstance:purpose**. I would, however, resist reducing the pentad to these terms. The two vocabularies, ideational structure and the pentad, have different scopes and purposes in analysis.

2. Note that these ratios could have been made to function in terms of a different type of substance, leading to a different assignation of motives. Imagine that the side panel told a story about how popular the cereal was becoming, about how more and more people were eating it, about how the "rage" for the cereal was catching on. We might then be working with definition in terms of directional substance; the text would be trading on the persuasive aspects of trend, tendency, and inclination ("Everyone's eating it, now!").

4 The Resources of Social Theory

The previous two chapters developed theories—discoursal and rhetorical—of language acts that include a social dimension as part of their foundations. Both perspectives, for example, view the systemic and functional nature of language use as intimately connected both to the social conditions out of which texts arise and to the social consequences that follow from them. This chapter seeks to investigate social theory to provide a means for systematically and explicitly exploring the social meanings of language acts in terms that complement and extend the discoursal and rhetorical theories. The social theory explored here complements these theories by relating **systems** of social resources to the typical social **functions** they enable in symbolic action. It extends the other two theories by providing a specialized vocabulary with which to identify and interpret the properties of social systems and social functions and by emphasizing the dialectical relationship between social and symbolic practices.

Bracketing social theory in its own chapter perhaps artificially separates it from discourse and rhetorical theory, but there is greater unity than a separate chapter implies. First, I will demonstrate this unity among these perspectives by summarizing some of the principal features of discourse analysis and rhetorical theory that are inherently concerned with social structures, meanings, and functions. Then, in the remainder of the chapter, I introduce the particular aspects of the social theories of both Anthony Giddens and Pierre Bourdieu that will form the third theoretical component for our perspective on the rhetoric of discourse as social practice.

Social Aspects of Discourse and Rhetoric

Both discourse analysis and rhetorical theory understand symbolic acts as social phenomena in terms of what occasions them, how they are to be theorized, and what their effects are. In the first case, both discourse analysis and rhetoric see social organization and practice as giving rise to meaning-making acts. In the second case, the terms of the theories and their relationships are organized with reference to their social functions. In the third case, both theories aim to shed light on the social effects and outcomes of symbolic acts; that is, analysis is aimed at investigating and understanding how discoursal and rhetorical acts shape and reflect the social practices of groups in particular contexts, rather than theorizing the nature of linguistic knowledge as a cognitive property of individual minds or brains, or investigating rhetorical acts as mere exemplars of more or less "effective persuasion." In the following two sections, I will show that the fundamental principles of the versions of discourse analysis and rhetorical theory presented here are both derived from and directed toward understanding symbolic acts as social acts.

SOCIAL DISCOURSE ANALYSIS

The framework presented in Chapter 2 focuses on understanding the meaning potentials of instantiated linguistic structures (texts) with reference to social contexts. It does not focus on linguistic structures as meaningful in their own right; rather, it conceptualizes meaning as function in context. The description is organized around three general functions exhibited by text in relation to context: the ideational, interpersonal, and textual functions. Discourse analysis, in this perspective, aims to investigate the solidary relations among the structures and functional meaning potentials of texts and the characteristics of the situations in which text plays a role. The very recognition of the three general functions is based upon the assumption that *in social contexts* language is called upon to represent social activities (i.e., perform an ideational function), construct role relationships and interactive practices (i.e., perform an interpersonal function), and, when language is a part of the situation, organize messages and construct coherence with the contexts of its use (i.e., perform a textual function). In other words, language is characterized and analyzed in terms of its role in social practice as a major means through which we represent the world for ourselves and others, orient ourselves and others to that world and our representations, and organize and articulate both representation and orientation. What Firth (1937/1964) said in the 1930s regarding meaning as function in context holds as much today:

> Most people, I suppose, regard the meaning of a word as something at the back of their minds which they can express and communicate. But the force and cogency of most language behaviour derives from the firm grip it has on the ever-recurrent typical situations in the life of social groups, and the normal social behaviour of the human animals living together in those groups. Speech is the telephone network, the nervous system of our society much more than the vehicle of lyrical outbursts of the individual soul. It is a network of bonds and obligations. (p. 113)

SOCIAL RHETORICAL ANALYSIS

Burkean rhetorical theory understands that rhetorical acts index, construct, and potentially bring about transformation in social relationships and practices. Pentadic analysis focuses on how language shapes attitudes—predispositions to act in the social world in particular ways. It characterizes the ratios and substances of text as the means by which social "realities" are not merely reflected but instead constructed through the selection of particular terministic screens and the consequent deflection of other visions. For example, a news report that characterizes the unemployed in a **scene:agent** ratio where the attributes of the unemployed (e.g., their inability to find work) are understood as a reasonable consequence of the scene they are in (e.g., a recession) constructs a particular version of the social and predisposes us to act accordingly. By contrast, another report (say, of the opinions of a conservative politician) may characterize the unemployed in an **agent:act** ratio that attributes their inability to find work (the act) to their characteristics as particular types of agents (e.g., unmotivated, lazy, waiting for "handouts," and so on). Symbolic acts are not neutral and passive because they actively construct the social and orient us to act in particular ways.

The emphasis on identification and transformation in Burke's rhetoric recognizes the fundamental divisions and differences that mark social agents and orders of their practices. Burke posits identification and consubstantiation as the fundamental functions of rhetoric because the struggles between social agents—implied by the division and segregation of their interests, motives, resources, and power—are both the grounds for and outcome of addressed symbolic action.

Logology focuses on understanding the social implications of living *in terms of* particular logonomic systems. A logonomic system lays out the rules prescribing the conditions for production and reception of meanings. Every logonomic system has ways of marking the "negative," not simply as a resource for definition but as a command "Thou shalt not." Every logonomic system has its own principles of perfection that, in practice, cannot be embodied exhaustively by its users; hence, in living with and through symbolic systems, we experience imperfection and the consequential guilt it invites. Every logonomic system reflects and constructs value-laden hierarchies that mark the social order: They project hierarchy onto the social order (e.g., those who use the system well versus those who do not) and reflect existing social hierarchies when they are understood as the product of "natural" divisions in the social order (e.g., prestige dialects, privileged ways of speaking, and so on, which correspond to dominant social groups).

The Duality of Structure

To complement and extend an investigation of the social conditions and consequences of discoursal and rhetorical acts, a social theory must illuminate two crucial kinds of relationships. The first concerns the relationship between situated, instantial social action and the wider social systems and structures that constrain and enable it. I will use the term "resource" to identify the characteristics of social systems and subsystems in general, and the term "practice" to identify what is typically done with these resources. Both are implicated in "instances" of social action of any kind. The relationship between resource and practice is analogous to the relationship between a structured system (as potential) and functions (as typically realized potential). A general example: A capitalist economy (resource, structure) both enables and constrains consumption practices.

The second crucial relationship that social theory needs to illuminate in the context of discoursal and rhetorical analysis is the relationship between symbolic acts and social action. Whether at the "level" of resource or that of practice, we will want to understand discursive and rhetorical action as both a type of social action and a constituent of social action. This understanding involves interpreting the findings of a rhetorical or discoursal analysis in social terms and necessitates an explicit and systematic vocabulary for associating rhetorical and discoursal functions with social functions.

Both these relationships (between social structure and social practice, and between social action and discoursal/rhetorical action) can be understood in the light of Giddens's principle of the "duality of structure." According to this principle, "Structure [is] the medium and outcome of the conduct it recursively organizes; the structural properties of social systems do not exist outside of action but are chronically implicated in its production and reproduction" (1984, p. 374). In our terms, resources (structures) are both the medium (meaning the modality or means) and the outcome (what is produced and reproduced) of practices (action). As systems and structures of what can be done socially, resources both constrain and enable practices. As what typically gets done in a community, practices produce and reproduce resources. For example, if I were to write a new course description for a university calendar, I would draw on registerial expectations (i.e., the typical configurations of ideational, interpersonal, and textual meanings that correspond to the situation) for course descriptions. At the same time, I am reproducing these resources by instantiating them. The registerial expectations for such a text are not so rigid that novelty and improvisation are ruled out. To a greater or lesser extent, any particular variations I introduce in my descriptions slightly reshape the resources. The structure (resource) of course descriptions is thus both a medium for my description and the outcome of it. Bourdieu often uses the phrase "structured and structuring" to indicate that all forms of social practice bear a dual relation to structure (resource): For example, he writes "instruments of domination . . . are structuring because they are structured . . ." and "discourse is a structured and structuring medium" (1991, pp. 168, 169); "the habitus is not only a structuring structure . . . but also a structured structure" (1984, p. 170). The dialectical relation between social structures and social practices is reflected in this kind of conjunctive phrasing.

▨ Social Resources and Social Practices

This section outlines the principal social resources and practices that a theory of discoursal and rhetorical action needs to address. Bourdieu's work emphasizes that any adequate investigation of the social must recognize that a given social order is dialectically related to language, discourse, rhetoric, and other symbolic systems and practices. The social and the symbolic are themselves dialectically related. Bourdieu (1990b) says:

> The established order, and the distribution of capital which is its basis, contribute to their own perpetuation through their very existence, through the symbolic effect that they exert as soon as they are publicly and officially declared and are thereby misrecognized and recognized. It follows from this that social science cannot "treat social realities as things," in accordance with Durkheim's famous precept, without neglecting all that these realities owe to the fact that they are objects of cognition (albeit a misrecognition) within the very objectivity of social existence. (p. 135)

In such a conception, the objects of social analysis (i.e., social resources and social practices) include the discoursal and rhetorical practices that both shape and are shaped by social orders. I organize my discussion of social resources and social practices around this duality, first in terms of the relations among *habitus,* distinction, and fields, which are general social resources and practices, and then in terms of the relations among linguistic *habitus,* symbolic power, and recognition, which are specifically symbolic resources and practices.

HABITUS

The key concept in Bourdieu's social theory is *habitus.* Habitus describes a set of embodied cultural dispositions that social agents bring to bear in social practice. It is an inclination to carry ourselves in particular ways: to eat certain foods, to take on certain jobs, to seek out certain types of entertainment, to speak and write in particular ways, and to feel, hope, and desire with particular inclinations. We are imbued with the preferences, dispositions, and tastes of the cultures into which we are socialized. We acquire habitus in our day-to-day lives through our

interaction with our environments and the other social agents who move
in them: at home with parents and siblings; at school with teachers and
students; in the workplace with coworkers, superiors, and employers; in
shops and restaurants with clerks and customers; and in the street with
neighbors. A culture consists of a variety of different types of habitus that
reflect the heterogeneity of its different social groups and their practices.
We may think of habitus as a very specific concept that describes the
dispositions of specific groups (e.g., opera singers) or more generally as
a concept that describes the dispositions marking differences between
different genders, classes, and age groups.

As a technical term in Bourdieu's overall theory of practice, habitus is
a multifaceted concept with a number of important features that distinguish it from a mere label for social agents' habits. On one occasion,
Bourdieu provides this gloss, which demonstrates the density of concepts
indexed by the term *habitus:*

> The conditionings associated with a particular class of conditions of exis-
> tence produce *habitus,* systems of durable, transposable dispositions, struc-
> tured structures predisposed to function as structuring structures, that is,
> as principles which generate and organize practices and representations that
> can be objectively adapted to their outcomes without presupposing a
> conscious aiming at ends or an express mastery of the operation necessary
> in order to attain them. (1990b, p. 53).

I will illustrate the key points of this definition with reference to Text
1.1 (the student note). Text 1.1 provides traces of a number of interrelated social practices, most saliently action sequences (e.g., "handing in
a paper"), social roles and circumstances (e.g., student and professor; a
late paper, course requirements, university rules and regulations), and
text practices (e.g., a note of explanation). It forms a key element of these
practices and serves to reproduce the potentials associated with these
practices. The practice of handing in a late paper with a particular type
of explanation, at a particular time, and so on, is a typical one in the
context of the university. This kind of doing is interpretable and meaningful because it bears relations to the larger systems and structures of
the university community and related practices in a particular culture
(e.g., communicating with "superiors"). Keeping in mind the duality of
structure, a social analysis seeks to link the instantiation of a particular
social act with the resources—the social system—that enabled it. For the

act to have relevance, or meaning potential, its forms and functions must be homologously related to the larger systems and structures for doing in the community. No sharp division separates the act as an instance of a particular kind of action from larger social systems and structures. As an instance of social practice, the text and the practices involved in its exchange rely on, as well as reproduce, tendencies and dispositions to act in similarly premised ways. The act reinforces these propensities as well as the social structures and systems "surrounding" it.

The habitus is embodied by social agents. It is learned, inculcated, and exercised in the particular primary socializing environments in which agents live and participate. Schooling (from primary through to postsecondary) provides a set of conditions, for example, that will affect the habitus of those who participate in the institution (e.g., students, professors, administrators). These conditions produce dispositions that are "structured structures." The student who hands in the note with the late paper has embodied, as it were, the regulation that explanation should be forthcoming for late work and that the explanation should take one of a number of sanctioned forms. Hence, this aspect of the student's habitus is "structured" (in the passive sense of being affected by the regulation), and this results in a form or structure (the sanctioned forms for seeking permission for late work—notes, phone calls, medical certificates, verbal agreement, etc.).

Habitus is also "predisposed to function as structuring structures." The student's disposition to act by way of the note in the face of the exigency of having the paper refused reproduces the sanctioned forms of seeking permission in this context. In simple terms, the attached note helps shore up the practice of handing in late work with partial or even presumed impunity ("It's o.k. because I told you what was happening."). The habitus is also a structuring structure: Similar situations will be structured by the student's perception of the situation and his or her expectations for how to respond.

That habitus is embodied as "principles which generate and organize practices and representations" is evident in this situation: The student's being inculcated in a practice that includes the injunction that work not be handed in late without explanation "generates" the practice itself (of which the text is both a constituent and a record). It organizes the practice and representations to the extent that embodying the "rule" about late work and explanation ("excuses," "reasons") also contains within it directives as to the appropriate ways to seek permission: the right modes (to write or to speak, and how), the right ways to carry oneself (the student's bodily gestures in a face-to-face request or the stealth and timing of slipping the paper and note under the professor's door after hours), the right kinds of timing (when to ask—before it's late using rational prediction or after it's late using a *mea culpa* appeal?), and so on.

The practices of the habitus, Bourdieu adds, are "objectively adapted to their outcomes without presupposing a conscious aiming at ends or an express mastery of the operations necessary in order to attain them" (1990b, p. 53). The institutional *role* of student creates the injunction that the student must embody the "rule" concerning late work. When faced with the possibility of having late work refused (and hence suffering in grades), the student has no choice, as it were, but to provide explanation or seek permission in some form. The student will *act* and does have some measure of choice within that act (e.g., concerning which route to take for explanation or permission), but just going on in the situation is already objectively adapted by the habitus. The act is constrained by the habitus (to continue, the student must provide explanation or seek permission) but also enabled by it (the habitus also "decrees" what is an appropriate form of response to the situation).

At the same time as it generates typical social activities, habitus generates classificatory schemes, ways of perceiving, and systems of classification through which it structures our representations of, our orientation toward, and our judgment of the social world:

> The habitus is both the generative principle of objectively classifiable judgements and the system of classification (*principium divisionis*) of these practices. It is in the relationship between the two capacities which define the habitus, the capacity to produce classifiable practices and products (taste), that the represented social world, i.e., the space of life-styles, is constituted. (Bourdieu, 1984, p. 170)

The student's habitus enables the production of the text (by guiding what types of meaning choices can be made): It is a capacity. The forms of classification that result from it (e.g., the representations of the student, the professor, good "reasons" for late work) are a product of the habitus as well. The student's particular experience of the university has led to a recognition that there is some measure of negotiability in such cases. For example, the construction of the social relationship between the student and professor moves between a recognition of asymmetrical (the student shows deference) and solidary (the student pleasantly forecloses against objection) power relations.

Taste and Distinction

As a resource, habitus generates not just ways of acting but also the specific kinds of acting that are enabled by systems of classification (naming, labeling, assessing, distinguishing). Habitus produces and guides the practices of what Bourdieu (1984) calls "taste":

> Taste is a practical mastery of distributions which makes it possible to sense or intuit what is likely (or unlikely) to befall—and therefore to befit—an individual occupying a given position in social space. It functions as a sort of social orientation, a "sense of one's place," guiding the occupants of a given place in social space towards the social positions adjusted to their properties [habitus], and towards the practices or goods which befit the occupants of that position. (p. 466)

Taste (and distinction—the ability to grade alternatives) transforms the necessities of habitus (e.g., a late paper *requires* explanation) into matters of choice and strategy by allowing material distributions (actual *doings*) to be read as distributions of symbolic distinctions as well. The student's "necessary" act (he or she must provide explanation to have the paper graded) becomes a "stylized" act bearing the traces of his or her assessment of distinguishing, distinctive symbols most likely to match the professor's sense of "taste" and distinction. The student speaks of having *a great difficulty getting back into semiotics mode*. In the context of a semiotics course, this way of naming the situation betrays the student's sense of a system of distinguishing *mode*[s] of practice: In his or her assessment, *semiotics mode* falls, we may suppose, somewhere between a nondistinctive "great deal of difficulty getting back into the paper" and a highly distinctive (for this context) "great deal of difficulty getting back into Saussure's notion of *valeur*," for example.

Field and Capital

The practices enabled and constrained by a particular habitus always operate in relation to a particular social context just as the resources of a language system become "meaningful" or "functional" only in reference to some context of use (i.e., with reference to particular field, tenor, and mode variables). John Thompson explains in his introduction to Bourdieu (1991):

> [W]hen individuals act, they always do so in specific social contexts or settings. Hence particular practices or perceptions should be seen, not as the product of the habitus as such, but as the product of the *relation between* the habitus, on the one hand, and the specific social contexts or "fields" within which individuals act, on the other. . . . A field or market may be seen as a structured space of positions in which the positions and their interrelations are determined by the distribution of different kinds of resources or "capital." (p. 14)

Field, in Bourdieu's sense of the term, is also structured by and structuring of social practices: It is not merely a "setting" or unstructured context for practice. If we think of habitus as a "feel for the game" (a metaphor Bourdieu often uses), then the field is the "game." Games are both structured (i.e., they include rules, positions, players, sequences, etc.) and structuring (i.e., their structures are capable of generating sequences of actions, outcomes, and so on). The structure of a particular field does not determine the function of habitus; it constrains it and makes certain of its aspects relevant or not.

A field is structured in terms of the distribution of agents and capital. The kinds of capital that agents can have in relation to particular fields take the form of economic capital, cultural capital, and symbolic capital (Bourdieu, 1991, p. 230). Capital is a resource (economic, cultural, or symbolic) that has value in relation to a particular field. Economic capital takes the form of material resources (money, credit, allocative resources); cultural capital is a resource of the habitus—the particular schemes of perception, taste, and distinction that compose the habitus; and symbolic capital is the "form assumed by these different forms of capital when they are perceived and recognized as legitimate" in reference to a particular field (Bourdieu, 1991, p. 230).

LINGUISTIC HABITUS

Our principal concern in relating discourse analysis and rhetorical theory to social theory is with understanding the social conditions and consequences of discursive acts. Bourdieu's concept of habitus bears upon this concern in two ways. First, the concept of distinction—a constituent and product of habitus—reminds us that social practices not only involve what social agents typically *do* in relation to particular fields but also involve the typical representations, perceptions, and classifications of those practices and their outcomes. The latter involve linguistic practices that are one of the means through which the products of habitus (practices, dispositions, preferences, and so on) are evaluated, distinguished, and judged. Habitus and distinction are fused when "[s]ocial divisions become principles of division, organizing the image of the social world" (Bourdieu, 1984, p. 471). Our engaging in social practices is mediated by symbolic representations and evaluations of those practices. This leads us to the second way in which Bourdieu's concept of habitus bears upon our understanding of the relationship between discourse, rhetoric, and social practice: A significant part of social agents' habitus is their particular linguistic habitus. Linguistic habitus governs not only our meaning-making practices in terms of the kinds of discourse we can control but also the evaluative dispositions we take toward discourse. Thompson glosses linguistic habitus as such:

> The linguistic habitus is a sub-set of the dispositions which comprise the habitus: it is that sub-set of dispositions acquired in the course of learning to speak in particular contexts (the family, the peer group, the school, etc.). These dispositions govern both the subsequent linguistic practices of an agent and the anticipation of the value that linguistic products will receive in other fields or markets. (Bourdieu, 1991, p. 17)

On one hand, discourse and rhetorical analysis provide the means with which to characterize different kinds of linguistic habitus: Texts are records of these practices, and a characterization of the discoursal and rhetorical resources drawn upon in instances of text constitutes a statement about the nature of a particular linguistic habitus. On the other hand, texts also provide traces of their producers' evaluations of the products of linguistic habitus. The student's use of a written note, the representation of the situation as one involving **mental processes** (to signal *difficulty*), and the interpersonal markers of deference, for example, imply that the student considers these symbolic features appropriate for the situation and the acts and actors involved.

Symbolic Power

Depending on the field, some types of linguistic habitus endow speakers/writers with more symbolic capital than other speakers/writers. In a field that is structured in part by linguistic resources (Bourdieu also calls it a "market"), power is based on unequal distributions of linguistic capital (1991, p. 57). Put simply, linguistic capital denotes the availability, value, and circulation of specific linguistic meaning-making resources—the distribution of what is said, how it is said, by whom, on what occasions, with what effects. The field/market of Text 1.1—the academic institution, in general—is characterized in part by differentiated distribution of linguistic capital. The student exercises a linguistic habitus different from the professor's. Our different institutional roles, for example, set the conditions for the practical efficacy or value of our utterances in this field. Bourdieu (1991) says,

> The value of an utterance depends on the relation of power that is concretely established between the speakers' linguistic competences, understood both as their capacity for production and as their capacity for appropriation and appreciation; it depends, in other words, on the capacity of the various agents involved in the exchange to impose the criteria of appreciation most favourable to their own products. (p. 67)

Text 1.1 is an excellent example of the complexities of power exercised through the "capacity for appropriation and appreciation." It would be simplistic to focus solely on the "fact" that, as the student's professor, my utterances are more valuable and have more currency in the field because I can accept or reject the request, call for more explanation, and so on. I do not want to deny that this possibility exists, but I would like to focus instead on the significant overlap of the student's and my linguistic capital as evidenced in this text. In my rhetorical view of the text I focused on identification, addressivity, and transformation—how I thought the text functioned rhetorically to create common ground (consubstantiation), to exploit the social meanings of addressivity (it exhibits deference of a sort but also constructs and constrains its addressee), and to effect a transformation or transcendence in the situation (a "division" between interests concerning rejection or acceptance on my part is at least potentially transcended). These effects, I think, would not be possible without the tension created by the meeting of different, but obviously related, forms of linguistic capital in this particular exchange in the academic field. The student, faced with the possibility of losing a significant portion of the final grade of the course, I have argued, maximizes the potential of his or her linguistic capital by having it directly address what he or she habitually and objectively (embodying "student-ness") sees as my particular linguistic *habitus,* hence the explanatory, but also foreclosing, aspect of admitting a *great deal of difficulty getting back into semiotics mode.* The student assesses, we can imagine: How can he, as a semiotics professor, not recognize the value, power, or currency of such a naming of the situation?

The exercising and success of the linguistic habitus depend on "anticipation of profits," an unconscious, embodied disposition to assess the market and possible future states of capital resulting from linguistic interaction. An analogy: Our linguistic *habitus,* in relation to particular markets, acts like a governor in a steam engine or like a control mechanism in a homeostatic system. It "takes information" from a state of the market, "adjusts" the information, and "feeds" new information back to the system, thereby changing the state of the market. This reflexive, cybernetic vision of the linguistic habitus is apparent in Bourdieu's emphasis on production and reception as inseparable and on the lack of "conscious calculation" in the anticipating practices of the linguistic *habitus:*

> In reality, the conditions of reception envisaged are part of the conditions of production, and anticipation of the sanctions of the market helps to determine the production of discourse. This anticipation, which bears no resemblance to a conscious calculation, is an aspect of the linguistic habitus which, being the product of a prolonged and primordial relation to the laws of a certain market, tends to function as a practical sense of the acceptability and the probable value of one's own linguistic productions and those of others on different markets. (1991, p. 77)

The student's "prolonged and primordial relation to the laws of a certain market" (e.g., in this case, the student's involvement in educational institutions, particularly the university) has been tempered, of course, by the recent and specific instantiations of market tensions in the course taken with me. What has "worked" in the past (in terms of requests for extensions in other courses, etc.) conditions what may work now. What seems to be the current state of the market (as practiced in

my course) becomes a factor affecting how the student shapes the text
and anticipates his or her chances of success.

Recognition

Symbolic power and the value of linguistic capital presuppose recognition on the part of those party to them. Bourdieu insists that what
makes symbolic capital (including linguistic capital) powerful is that it is
recognized as arbitrary; that is, it is recognized as *not* being the product
of social agents' habitus in relation to a particular field. He says,

> Symbolic power—as a power of constituting the given through utterances,
> of making people see and believe, of confirming or transforming the vision
> of the world and, thereby, action on the world and thus the world itself, an
> almost magical power which enables one to obtain the equivalent of what
> is obtained through force (whether physical or economic), by virtue of the
> specific effect of mobilization—is a power that can be exercised only if it is
> *recognized,* that is, misrecognized as arbitrary. (1991, p. 170)

The relationship between particular forms of symbolic power and the
distributions of capital in a particular social field are not arbitrary. The
efficacy and authority of a medical doctor's diagnosis, for example, does
not derive from some special power of the language he or she uses to
communicate it. The language is efficacious and authoritative because it
is redounds with the significant authoritative and allocative resources
medical doctors command in their field.

Misrecognition does not render symbolic capital "false," impotent, or
ineffective. In fact, it does exactly the opposite. By acknowledging
symbolic power as arbitrary (that is, not motivated by habitus, field, and
social divisions), distributions of capital, economic power, and material
divisions in the social order are converted to purely symbolic divisions—
different ways of characterizing the social world, different discourse
types, registers, schemes of perception, classification, and distinction—
all of which have the alibi of being "mere" representations. Bourdieu
(1990b) comments,

> In an economy which is defined by the refusal to recognize the "objective"
> truth of "economic" practices, that is, the law of "naked self-interest" and
> egoistic calculation, even "economic" capital cannot act unless it succeeds

in being recognized through a conversion that can render unrecognizable the true principle of its efficacy. Symbolic capital is this denied capital, recognized as legitimate, that is, misrecognized as capital. (p. 118)

The relationship between a form of symbolic capital and the social orders it is produced by and productive of is constantly and vigorously maintained by social agents who have advantage in particular fields:

> The relationship between distributions [of a social field] and representations [of forms of symbolic capital] is both the product and the stake of a permanent struggle between those who, because of a position they occupy within the distributions, have an interest in subverting them by modifying the classifications in which they are expressed and legitimated, and those who have an interest in perpetuating misrecognition, an alienated cognition that looks at the world through categories the world imposes, and apprehends the social world as a natural world. (Bourdieu, 1990b, pp. 140-141)

Symbolic power is a power, therefore, that must continually be guarded and policed. Texts are both the site for this struggle and the stake of this struggle. They are the site in the sense that as symbolic acts they presuppose (mis)recognition. They are the stake in that "legitimate" texts are the ones that characterize the social world, that reflect, select, and deflect "reality."

Recognition (or misrecognition) binds the social with the symbolic. It allows representations of a social order to stand as legitimate realities of divisions in the social order, rather than as products of the divisions. Representations of the social are a product of habitus and the organization and distribution of resources in the social. Just as we turn the necessities of habitus into matters of choice, preference, taste, and distinction—that is, treat the products of habitus as if they were products of choice—we treat representations of the social (i.e., our linguistic habitus and symbolic capital) *as if* they were matters of choice and preference rather than products of the divisions and distribution of capital that characterize the social world. To understand symbolic power *as if* it were preference (i.e., not largely determined by our habitus and relation to fields) is to misrecognize it as "arbitrary." Paradoxically, to misrecognize the constructedness of representation (symbolic capital, linguistic habitus) is to recognize representation as unmotivated, not self-interested, but "natural." Representation, in Bourdieu's scheme, is both a product of and a site of reproduction of the divisions in the social world.

Misrecognition is analogous to the "paradox of substance" that Burke sees lurking in every symbolic act (see Chapter 3). We misrecognize the constructed nature of symbolic acts when we interpret their terms *as if* they were "natural," substantial, and inalienable representations rather than as representations that are always *in terms of,* that is, as terms that have meaning-potential only with reference to particular systems of classification, identification, attribution, and so on. In Bourdieu's theory, these particular systems of classification, identification, and attribution are products of habitus and a relation to a particular social field: They are distinctions made *in terms of* the habitus and field. A seemingly natural and substantial attribution such as "James is a wonderful ball-room dancer" defines (classifies) "James" *in terms of* a kind of gradable ("wonderful" versus "awful") social activity ("ballroom dancing"). The substance of the definition—the power of its *is*—relies on its relation to a social field where these sorts of classification are recognized (or not) as legitimate, not in the words themselves. In Burke's terms, we misrecognize when we would not see that the classification is made *in terms of* a particular type of substance that is itself not some inalienable category of "being" but a category that has meaning-potential only in relation to other types of definition and to the social fields it seeks to represent and out of which it arises. Both the concepts—misrecognition and the paradox of substance—remind us that the "meanings" of text and its constituents are determinable only with reference to the systems they instantiate (e.g., language systems, registers, discourse types, systems of intertextual relations, and so on) and with reference to the social contexts of their use (e.g., the field, tenor, and mode characteristics of the situation, the particular social market at risk, and so on).

Discourse analysis emphasizes that the meaning-potential of text is a relational phenomenon; rhetorical theory emphasizes that all representations are both selections and deflections of "reality"; and social theory emphasizes that treating representations of the social as "natural" involves misrecognition. Each thus creates a powerful impetus for critical analysis by providing the means with which to systematically investigate a text as a social act involving choice, paradox, and misrecognition. The next chapter delves into all these issues in the context of an extended analysis of three instances of text.

5 Text Instances and Critical Practices

In the last three chapters, I outlined and exemplified three vocabularies for investigating text as a simultaneously discoursal, rhetorical, and social practice. Each of these vocabularies has its own way of identifying and interpreting patterns of textual practice in terms of its systemic, functional, and social features.

Discourse analysis understands texts as instances of meaning-making systems: When we make and understand linguistic meanings in situations of language use, we draw on the resources of the language system, the resources of the particular register or registers that are relevant to the situation, as well as our experiences and expectations of similar situation types in terms of what sort of language resources are appropriate for the field, tenor, and mode characteristics of the situation. Discourse analysis organizes its description of linguistic resources and their meaning potentials around the concept of function. Linguistic structures—as the "output" of linguistic systems—are interpreted as the realization of three general functions simultaneously: the ideational function (for representing experience), the interpersonal function (for representing social relations), and the textual function (for organizing cohesive and coherent messages). Discourse analysis conceptualizes both the resources for linguistic meaning-making and the functions they perform in actual texts as social in their origins, contexts, and effects.

The Burkean framework for rhetorical analysis investigates texts in terms of their systemic, functional, and social aspects as well. Rhetorical acts are instances that are realized in terms of logonomic systems. They are functional in that they instigate both congregation and separation among participants in the rhetorical act. Every rhetorical act bears relations both to hierarchies in the social order and to the symbol systems that are a major means through which social orders are structured and coordinated. Instances of rhetorical acts therefore have social consequences because they contribute to the production and reproduction of social orders. For example, rhetorical acts help transcend or reconstitute difference and "mystery." At the same time they are acts that bear out the social consequences of the terms and implications of the logonomic systems that enable them. For example, rhetorical acts are subject to the hortatory negatives of logonomic systems: Every rhetorical act is a potential transgression of some symbolic order.

The social theory presented in Chapter 4 organizes its understanding of textual practice in terms of its systemic, functional, and social characteristics as well. First and foremost, it recognizes that all textual practices have social consequences. Symbolic action is not something that is appended to social life but instead is one of its primary constituents. The theory of the duality of structure posits that textual practices (symbolic action) bear a dual relation to social structures and systems of resources: The functions of textual practices are seen as one of the principal products of social systems (e.g., habitus and field shape the social agents' access to and control of symbolic capital) and textual practices are a constituent of social systems and structures (e.g., the exercise of symbolic power in particular fields reproduces, justifies, and legitimates existing social orders).

These vocabularies are presented as resources for understanding text as discoursal, rhetorical, and social action. The vocabularies can be called upon to identify and interpret—explicitly and systematically—the social, functional, and systemic nature of textual practice from three different points of view. In this chapter, I demonstrate how the three perspectives complement one another in the analysis of actual instances of text. Previously, we have seen the parts of each perspective exemplified in the context of illustrating individual points of the theories. My emphasis now is on how particular patterns in instances of text can be interpreted in terms of discoursal, rhetorical, and social theory. Not all the resources of these three theories are brought into play in these analyses, but a significant number are relevant. More important, the analyses will demonstrate the three theories at work and provide exemplars of their complementarity in producing textured and critical close readings.

Case 1: Saturn Automobile Advertisement

The Saturn advertisement reproduced as Text 5.1 is a full-color, two-page spread that appeared in the January 1995 issue of *Harper's* magazine. Advertising texts for products like automobiles, it seems simple enough to say, are aimed at persuading readers (of verbal and visual texts) to buy. The *way* this is done and the host of other social meanings that are drawn upon and constructed in the process, however, present us with the traces of a variety of social, discursive, and rhetorical practices whose scope and consequences require more than a discussion of the text as more or less "effective" persuasion.

Saturn's slogan is "A Different Kind of Company, A Different Kind of Car." For "difference" to be discernible, a set of contrastive and distinctive features needs to be constructed in the semiosis of the verbal and visual texts. These enable something to be "different" from something else. In this particular advertisement, Saturn creates "distinction," *diacrisis, discretio* . . . difference out of the undifferentiated" (Bourdieu, 1984, p. 479) by instantiating a series of oppositions, expressed implicitly as binaries, and by valorizing the traditionally depreciated terms of these social oppositions.

The following analysis explores the rhetorical, discoursal, and social construction of this series of oppositions. The binary oppositions reductively sum up a representation of some aspect of social life. Some of these binaries include mind/body, rational/emotional, action/inertia, serious/ironic, and additional pairs that index sociocultural classifications of gender (male/female), race (white/black), economic class (wealthy/poor), and physical ability (abled/disabled). Presented as such, these binaries are abstract categories for ideational representations of participants, processes, events, and relations in contemporary social life. Lurking in every binary construction, however, is a real discursive history marked by contest, struggle, power, and ideology. The terms of such binaries are not simply neutral opposites: They are *partial* representations in the sense that they reduce dynamism to a false stasis (the terms are "fixed" representations abstracted from social practice) and in the sense that they

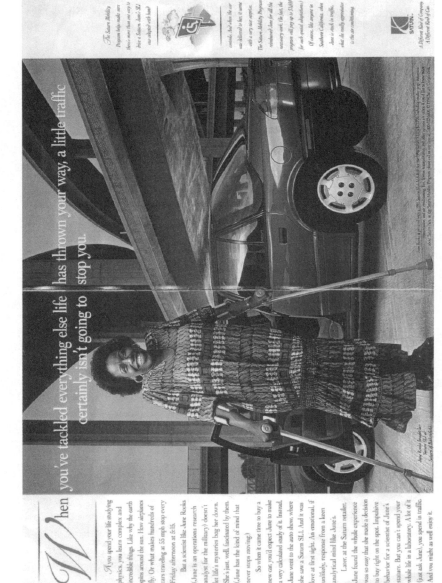

Text 5.1. Saturn Advertisement

reflect particular social orientations, attitudes, and interests. When contextualized in actual discourse, the terms become weighted: They are marked interpersonally and orientationally. One term dominates and is more positively valorized. This suppresses the other term, makes it pejorative, and silences its representational and orientational functions. Wilden (1987) has said of such pairs:

> Only in the imaginary can these categories be seen as symmetrical opposites rather than as relations between levels. The second term of each pair (e.g., emotion) is in fact the environment that the first term (e.g., reason) depends on for subsistence and survival. (Similarly labor is the source and sustenance of capital.) But by turning each hierarchy upside down like the inverted image of a camera obscura, the first term (e.g., culture) either appears to dominate the second (e.g., nature), or does in fact dominate it (e.g., white and non-white). [The first term in each pair] is an open system apparently free to exploit whatever it defines as its environment; and any open system that exploits its environment in the short range inevitably exploits itself in the long range. (p. 82)

We are constrained by the symbolic action of the binary in three significant ways. First, representation in the form of binaries artificially constrains the inherent complexity and dynamism of that which would be represented: It is a strong "deflection" of "reality" in Burke's terms. Second, binaries trade on a kind of logico-semantic purity: Something is either this or that, is or is not, and so on. They reflect a pursuit for what Burke calls the "semantic ideal" that seeks to function *as if* "accuracy" of representation were the only issue (1941/1973, pp. 138-167). Orientational, interpersonal, and rhetorical meaning potentials are ruled out-of-court. Third, even if we attempt to "recoup" the orientational value of the terms of the binary pair, by virtue of their discursive history—the past semiotic practice involving the terms—the ability to "speak" certain suppressed terms is so constrained (by convention, propriety, "good sense," etc.) that critique or "recovery" seems impossible. The binaries I explore here are constructed as opposites engaged in a zero-sum game of social classification. The bind that binary oppositions create for those subject to them could be summed up: We are forced to construct representations through binaries. The binaries are ill-equipped, but we must use them nevertheless. We are invited to engage with the binaries as "mere" representations, not value-charged in any way. Even if we transcend this fiction and engage with them as the orientational and rhetorical classifications that they are, we may not—without severe reproach that is made possible by the binaries in the first place—"speak" or express the suppressed, depreciated, "second" term. We cannot re-*orient* something that is not assumed to be oriented in the first place.

Let me try to concretize this process by discussing the advertisement's photograph before getting into the details of the analysis. This is not going to be very pleasant because I have to make explicit a series of oppositions and differences that the advertisement implicitly forces the reader/viewer to draw upon. I have to make explicit what *is not* there to speak about the meaning potentials of what *is* there. Before doing so, I have to say that I in no way support the corrosive and inequitable effect of such oppositions, but they are nevertheless a part of my analysis because I will argue that the advertisement forces readers/viewers to acknowledge them.

The photograph depicts a woman standing beside her Saturn car. She uses crutches. Her skin color and hair are indices of African American descent. She is, by some cultural standards, heavyset. None of these characteristics needs to be construed as a term from a binary pair. In conjunction with the text of the advertisement, however—and the oppositions it construes—the visual features of the depicted participant become signs, I will argue, of "second," suppressed terms to be recuperated, championed, by Saturn ownership. The photograph implicitly trades on the following oppositions: male/female, white/black, able-bodied/disabled, and trim/heavyset.

THE DISCURSIVE CONSTRUCTION
OF BINARY OPPOSITIONS

We live in more or less "ad literate" cultures where advertising, in its myriad forms, is ubiquitous. When we engage with advertising texts, we draw on linguistic, visual, social, and cultural meaning-making resources. All factor in the reading practices we would bring to a text in a particular instance. Our reading practices are also structured by, and structuring of, the logonomic systems of contemporary advertising: who produces it, what resources are used, where it appears, how it is organized, and how it should be read. The rules and resources for how advertising is read allow for considerable variability: Our readings may be compliant (we "accept" the social roles assigned to us by the text), resistant, or even "deviant." (Cook [1992] discusses the "ways of hearing" advertising.) In each case, however, our reading is constrained by the semiotic patterns of the text. The kind of reading I will develop here seeks to understand the Saturn text as an indicator of how stereotypic representations—implicitly constructed as binary oppositions—are both constructed and exploited in advertising discourse. I do not believe that in attempting to analyze the processes through which this occurs we are looking for "hidden" meanings. The text is a record of a series of social acts, the premises of which are contained in the terms of its own semiosis. My analysis of linguistic semiosis in the text focuses on the headline and main body of copy appearing in the left margin of the advertisement.

In Chapter 2, I discussed two main dimensions of meaning for language's interpersonal function: **relational** value, which concerns language's resources for constructing interaction between speakers/writers and hearers/readers, and **positional** value, which concerns language's resources for signaling addressers' attitude, orientation, and assessment both of addressees and of the ideational content of their discourse. The particular characteristics of both these dimensions of interpersonal meaning are clearly influenced by who is being addressed in text. Typical of advertising registers, the Saturn advertisement addresses *you,* but it is not the same *you* that normally simply designates the addressee (as in the "I/you" of casual conversation): here, *you* refers to both *June* and the reader of the text. This *you* thus functions as a kind of fantasy address: Readers are invited to put themselves in June's role. Readers are told about June's world via second-person pronominal address (*So when it came time to buy a new car, you'd expect June to make a very calculated study of it*), but at other points are vicariously conflated with June (*But you can't spend your whole life in a laboratory*). This form of address allows the reader to both "be June" and "not be June." This kind of "conflation" fantasy would not be possible if the constructed "I" of the text was June's voice (e.g., "I am an operations analyst for the military" . . . "So when it came time to buy a car, you'd expect me to make a very calculated study of it."): It is constructed by implicitly multivalent addresser/addressee relations in the text. On one hand we have:

First person (implicitly): Saturn voice
Second person: *you* (the reader, e.g., *you'd expect June* . . .)
Third person: *June* (e.g., *June is an* . . .)

On the other hand, we also have:

First person (implicitly): Saturn voice

Second person: *you* (*June*/the reader, e.g., *If you spend your life studying physics, you learn . . .*)

The duplicity of second-person address is very clear in the last few lines of copy, where we are addressed first as You/June and then simply as *you: But you can't spend your whole life in a laboratory. A lot of it (just ask June), you spend in traffic. And you might as well enjoy it.* Considered rhetorically, this shifting second-person address is one of the means by which the text attempts to construct identification: To be the "You/June" combination is to be consubstantial with June, to see life (the ironies of traffic, for example) from her point of view.

The text constructs a particular representation of experience by instantiating the resources of the ideational function. This is a text dominated by **mental** processes (with *June/You* as **processor**) and **relations** that identify and locate June. It is not a text about June (or you) doing much (by way of actions), but rather one that characterizes June/You by describing **mental reactions** (*doesn't let life's mysteries bog her down;* [i]s . . . *fascinated; enjoy*[s]) and **cognitions** (*studying, learn, expect, study, found*) and **circumstantially** situating her in time and space (*when it came time to buy a new car, at the Saturn retailer, right on the spot, in the laboratory, in traffic*). **Relational** processes characterize June and her mental life rather than tell what she does/can do: *a scientist like June Rooks; June is an operations research analyst; June has the kind of mind that never stops moving; An emotional, if unlikely response; a keen analytical mind like June's; Impulsive behavior for a scientist of June's stature.*

These ideational structures create an opposition between dynamism and stasis. Characterized as a **processor** (rather than an **agent**) and as positioned in **time** and **place** (the **circumstances** *Later, at the Saturn retailer,* etc.), June represents stasis—so much so that we are even told parenthetically that it is her *mind* that *never stops moving.* Also, her only overt **actions** (in ideational terms) either are very nonspecific (*June went to the auto show*) or are metaphors of action that actually encode **mental** processes (*June . . . doesn't let life's mysteries bog her down; June . . . ma[d]e a very calculated study of it*). By characterizing June/You in terms of stasis and inertia, we are implicitly directed to identify with this sort of opposition. Western culture, in general, valorizes dynamism and action: We admire "movers and shakers," wildly successful Nike advertisements tells us to "Just Do It," the Marlboro man works the ranch, and so on. This Saturn advertisement, however, implicitly has us experience dynamism's opposite via June. It valorizes the traditionally negative, less-valued term of the action/dynamism opposition and in doing so not only summons our knowledge of such an opposition but also invites us, as it were, to not admit of valorizing dynamism and action because that would not only contradict our identification with June (in the visual text we can see that her actions are "restricted," but cannot "say" so) but also show that we, unfairly, prejudicially, construct the world through an unbalanced and inequitable opposition in the first place. The opposition courts guilt, in Burke's terms, but it is a guilt that is a consequence of the logonomic systems instantiated by the text itself. We are, in this particular ideational construction of experience (who can do what, etc.) asked to operate with a false binary opposition and then, being constructed as representative of the dominated term of the binary, we are compelled to not admit (for fear of paradox or some kind of cruel irony that now applies to *us* as June, for example) to subscribing to that view of things in the first place. The text operates on a kind of characterizing *in terms of* which we must then "forget" so as to not experience the guilt of reproducing an inequitable and ultimately false opposition.

The text constructs other related binary oppositions that, I suggest, function in a similar way. One such opposition concerns what we could label rational/emotional behavior. Many of the lexical items of the text cluster in two conceptual sets that could bear these labels:

Rational: *physics, studying, learn, complex, scientist, operations research analyst, mind, calculated study, analytical mind, laboratory*

Emotional: *love at first sight, emotional, on the spot, unlikely, easy, impulsive*

Again, the first of these terms ("rational") tends to be more highly valued in Western culture, whereas the second ("emotional") is less valued. Often, "emotional" or "impulsive" behavior is tolerated or positively valued only because we construe it as a temporary or playful digression from reason and rationality (hence we "*return* to our senses" or "*lose* all sense," as if rationality and sensibility were the norm, the default case). Carnival is meaningful because it temporarily "inverts" its overall scenic context of structured, civil society. The rational/emotional pair construes a similar dynamic in the Saturn advertisement. The first two paragraphs of the copy introduce June as rational: This is the context for the ironic surprise to come. Later, June's behavior is characterized as *emotional,* *[i]mpulsive,* and *unlikely.* The text presupposes the rational as the dominant term setting the context for the (ironic) emotional behavior, so the two sets of collocations outlined above are not logically parallel, but skewed. We are even told: *you'd expect June to make a very calculated study of it. Instead . . . it was love at first sight.* By the logic of this text, one cannot, without inviting the ironies of paradox, be both an *operations research analyst* and *impulsive* and *emotional.*

The **thematic development** (see Chapter 2) of the last two paragraphs reinforces this progression *toward* the emotional, irrational, and the impulsive. We have **marked themes** that foreground conjunction and temporal connections (*So when it came time to buy; Instead . . . ; And . . . ; Later, at the Saturn retailer; But . . . ; And . . .*). These **marked themes** explicitly construct a narrative sequence (they identify time and place settings and link events) but implicitly (because they set up the "emotional" behavior events) mark what appears to be a natural, logical sequence. That is, the thematic progression corresponds to what the text presupposes is the logical relationship between rationality and emotion. The assumed logical priority of "rationality" to "emotion" is couched in a seemingly "natural" narrative. Burke describes this phenomenon in *A Grammar of Motives* (1945/1969a) under the title "The Temporizing of Essence." He notes that "[b]ecause of the pun whereby the logically prior can be expressed in terms of the temporally prior, and *v.v.,* the ways of transcendence, in aiming at the discovery of *essential* motives, may often take the historicist form of symbolic *regression*" (p. 430)—a process that is clearly at work in the Saturn text. The narrative pattern makes a presupposed logical relation look like a consequence of time and cause-and-effect events. It is a natural alibi. Again we are invited to identify with the less valued term of the opposition; that is, if the text constructs us as as likely as June to be "emotional" or "impulsive," it is advocating this behavior (on the assumption that it does not seek to alienate addressees intentionally). Finding ourselves constructed by the traditionally dominated and depreciated representation, we are again implicated in a kind of apologetics for another false dichotomy.

SOCIAL CLASSIFICATION AND DISTINCTION

I have not yet emphasized that the kinds of classificatory practices that binary oppositions enable are a part of systems of intertextuality in our culture. The binaries I identify in the Saturn text function in relation to other texts, other discursive practices, which give them meaning potential. The rational/emotional binary, for example, is at risk in other discourses of our communities. Other discourses that involve this opposition are accessed when we would write, speak, read, and hear texts such as the Saturn advertisement. What other texts are relevant depends on the reading practices of the particular social group involved. Our interest is not so much in *that* texts are made and read against the backdrop of other texts, but in *how* they are read—what resources are drawn upon and what social consequences can follow. Classification, as one constituent of a particular form of discursive practice, is structured by and structuring of the different social relationships and positions that characterize the social field; the construction of social representations and orientations through binary oppositions is intimately related to other resources and practices that mark difference (in power, access to resources, etc.) in social hierarchies. In this section, I explore some of the social meanings and functions involved in classification through binary oppositions as they are evidenced in the Saturn advertisement.

The Saturn text, as an instance of advertising, is a part of the social meanings and practices of consumption. Consumption is not a strictly material practice involving the exchange of capital for goods and services: It is a meaning-making practice involving classification and distinction. *What* is to be consumed, by *whom,* and with *what* meanings is a consequence of how classification and distinction are negotiated in discursive practices. What Bourdieu (1984) says in relation to the "reading" of works of art applies equally well to adverting discourse:

> Consumption is . . . a stage in a process of communication, that is, an act of deciphering, decoding, which presupposes practical or explicit mastery of a cipher or code. In a sense, one can say that the capacity to see (*voir*) is a function of the knowledge (*savoir*), or concepts, that is, the words, that are available to name visible things, and which are, as it were, programmes for perception. (p. 2)

The Saturn advertisement presupposes a practical knowledge of the binary oppositions it instantiates, including the knowledge that one of the terms usually dominates the other (e.g., being rational is more highly valued than being emotional; to be white, male, and able-bodied is to be among the dominant). It operates with oppositions deeply ingrained in the social order and strategically brings them into play by indexing both terms of the opposition and constructing a discursive site where readers can experience a championing of the traditionally dominated term. The binary oppositions called upon are a "programme for perception."

Classification and distinction involve an exercise of "taste": It calls upon and constructs the classificatory means with which we would discriminate, choose, and evaluate the agents and objects of consumption. Advertising discourse is emblematic of how we would/should fancy ourselves and our ability to exercise taste. Whereas habitus and position in social fields would determine our access to goods and services, taste—partially constructed by advertising discourse—turns necessity (our "real" access to goods and services) into preference (our "perceptions" of what we like and want). Classification practices do not simply apply externally to persons and objects; they construct the agents of classification as well:

> Taste classifies, and it classifies the classifier. Social subjects, classified by their classifications, distinguish themselves by the distinctions they make, between the beautiful and the ugly, the distinguished and the vulgar, in which their position in the objective classifications is expressed or betrayed. (Bourdieu, 1984, p. 6)

The Saturn advertisement, by offering a generative system of binary opposition, explicitly engages and invites the reader to make distinctions: It supplies a practice with which to classify oneself (e.g., us as June). Saturn is as much in the business of selling distinction (and *ways* to make distinctions) as it is in the business of selling cars. More than selling a "lifestyle" (which has been attributed to advertising), it is selling distinction and classificatory practices. The advertisement does not address the June Rookses of its audience: It addresses anyone who can identify what kind of person June "is" and can engage in the practice of recognizing the terms and meaning potentials of a whole series of binary oppositions (based in gender, class, physical ability, race, and so on). By "playing the game," readers will have classified themselves: Compliant readers, or Saturn's ideal readers, learn to make these distinctions and thereby classify themselves as consubstantial with a group who would construe the social order in these terms.

Making distinctions in this way is not a mere playing out of the potentials inherent in a particular code because the oppositions instantiated here are embodied in the social order that the advertisement both indexes and reproduces:

> All the agents in a given social formation share a set of basic perceptual schemes, which receive the beginnings of objectification in the pairs of antagonistic adjectives commonly used to classify and qualify persons or objects in the most varied areas of practice. The network of oppositions between high (sublime, elevated, pure) and low (vulgar, low, modest), spiritual and material, fine (refined, elegant) and coarse (heavy, fat, crude, brutal), light (subtle, lively, sharp, adroit) and heavy (slow, thick, blunt, laborious, clumsy), free and forced, broad and narrow, or, in another dimension, between unique (rare, different, distinguished, exclusive, exceptional, singular, novel) and common (ordinary, banal, commonplace, trivial, routine), brilliant (intelligent) and dull (obscure, grey, mediocre), is the matrix of all the commonplaces which find such ready acceptance because behind them lies the whole social order. (Bourdieu, 1984, p. 468)

The oppositions Bourdieu speaks of here are an abstraction from the oppositions that are realized in actual discursive practice. Saturn's instantiation of similar oppositions presupposes "ready acceptance" of them but goes a step further by having readers identify with the traditionally dominated, depreciated term of the opposition. This strategically precludes a critique of the opposition: First, we must call upon our knowledge of such oppositions to make a reading of the advertisement; second, we are invited to identify, to be consubstantial with, the traditionally dominated, depreciated term that effectively "silences" critique because it would then presuppose that the dominated term *really* does exist, really does need championing. The advertisement creates real potential for guilt. Who would want to admit the oppositions are real? To do so seemingly supports the inequitable classifications. Bourdieu (1984) says that,

> The seemingly most formal oppositions . . . always derive their ideological strength from the fact that they refer back, more or less discretely, to the most fundamental oppositions within the social order: the opposition between the dominant and the dominated. (p. 469)

As a social act that both reflects and reproduces the opposition between the dominant and the dominated, the Saturn advertisement seemingly provides the means to overcome this inequity—"June is doing all right"—

but the very practice through which it constructs this possibility relies on reproducing the inequity. Rather than provide the means with which to champion the traditionally dominated, it reproduces the inequity through what Bourdieu (1984) calls "the logic of stigma":

> The logic of stigma reminds us that social identity is the stake in a struggle in which the stigmatized individual or group, and, more generally, any individual or group insofar as he or it is a potential object of categorization, can only retaliate against the partial perception which limits it to one of its characteristics by highlighting, in its self-definition, the best of its characteristics, and, more generally, by struggling to impose the taxonomy most favourable to its characteristics, or at least to give to the dominant taxonomy the content most flattering to what it has and what it is. (p. 476)

The dominated, depreciated terms are constructed as positive in the Saturn advertisement, but they are done so still only in terms of their relation to the dominant term. Hence, we read that June's *impulsive* and *emotional* behavior is acceptable only because she is also an *operations research analyst for the military;* we see that June's acting *right on the spot,* blinded by *love at first sight,* is construed as ironic given her *stature* as *scientist.* In other words, no "myth" ("black, female, disabled African Americans are not usually scientists") is really shattered, only recast. The championing of the dominated term is still sanctioned, tempered by, the dominant term. This is a significant function of (ideological) symbolic power: It can control the oppositions to the extent that it can proffer them as ceasing to be oppositions. The discursive practice presents a unity of opposites that masks very real division in the social orders out of which it arises:

> The dominant culture contributes to the real integration of the dominant class (by facilitating the communication between all its members and by distinguishing them from other classes); it also contributes to the fictitious integration of society as a whole, and thus to the apathy (false consciousness) of the dominated classes; and finally, it contributes to the legitimation of the established order by establishing distinctions (hierarchies) and legitimating these distinctions. The dominant culture produces this ideological effect by *concealing the function of division beneath the function of communication:* the culture which unifies (the medium of communication) is also the culture which separates (the instrument of distinction) and which legitimates distinctions by forcing all other cultures (designated as sub-

cultures) to define themselves by their distance from the dominant culture. (Bourdieu, 1991, p. 167; emphasis added)

The Saturn advertisement engages us in a double fantasy: First, we are compelled to represent the world in terms of binary oppositions and consent to the legitimacy of this seeing *in terms of;* and second, we are compelled to believe that the inequities of this form of representation can be transcended (e.g., June can be both *calculated* and *impulsive,* etc.). In Burke's terms, we are persuaded to transcend the paradox of divided substance. I turn now to examining the text in terms of rhetorical analysis.

DIVIDED SUBSTANCE AND GUILT

This section develops a grammatical, rhetorical, and logological analysis in a Burkean perspective to further substantiate and interpret the discursive and social analysis of the Saturn advertisement. Let's begin by examining the relationship between ratio and substance in the advertisement. Two ratios dominate the text: **agent:act** and **scene:agent**. In the first two paragraphs (telling us about June), an **agent:act** ratio characterizes June (and by extension *you*) as being capable of certain acts (*learn complex and incredible things, not let life's mysteries bog her down,* be *fascinated*) because of the kind of agent she/you is/are (someone who *spend[s] your life studying physics,* is *a scientist like June Rooks, an operations research analyst for the military,* and *has the kind of mind that never stops moving*). With such a ratio, motive is constructed along the lines that persons act according to their nature as particular types of agents. This ratio is transformed in the latter half of the text into a **scene:agent** ratio, in which we get a "new" type of agent—one who has particular characteristics (*impulsive, emotional*) because of the effect of context (**time** and **place** circumstances) on the agent (*when it came time to buy a new car;* at *the auto show; Later, at the Saturn retailer; on the spot; in the laboratory; in traffic*). This ratio implies that we "become" a certain type of agent given our surroundings: We do not really get details of June's acts, just details about how she (ironically) changed (or acted "out of character") in the presence of the Saturn car and dealership. Such a motive is clearly reflected in the **process type** used to convey June's response to the context: *Later, at the Saturn retailer, June found the whole experience was so easy that she made a decision to buy right on the spot.*

June's perception (*found*) of a phenomenon (*the whole experience*) in the context (*at the Saturn retailer*) motivates her. This form is analogous to a conversion story in which someone becomes a different kind of agent because of what was perceived in the context (e.g., a person becomes a fervent environmentalist after seeing pollution in a local stream; a reluctant party-goer decides to join the fun once she sees what fun everyone else is having, etc.).

The instantial functions of these ratios depend upon the kind of substance presupposed by their elements. In particular, agents are characterized *in terms of* some kind of substance that functions *as if* it were a statement of "being," rather than a motivated selection from a variety of ways of characterizing agents. The issue of substance is implicated in the implicit characterization through binary oppositions in the advertisement. First, we note that characterization of June/You as an agent is done in terms of **familial** substance. We are working with constructions of classes of agents who, by virtue of membership in a particular class, share certain characteristics (or alternatively, positing particular characteristics presupposes a substantial class of a certain type). The linguistic text (as opposed to the visual text) characterizes June in terms of a set of stereotypic qualities we would *expect* a scientist to possess (*calculated, fascinated,* studious) and a series of "counter-to-expectation" qualities we would *not* expect a scientist to have (*impulsive, emotional*). The first set of qualities deals in definition in terms of the expected "inherent" qualities of scientists. It relies on us seeing June as an exemplar of a class of "scientists" who share defining features. Later, when June acts counter to expectation for members of this class by forming an *emotional, if unlikely, response,* we are forced to either abandon the original definition or expand the class to include (paradoxically) features it would not normally contain (e.g., succumbing to *love at first sight*). To stay with definition in terms of familial substance and accept this later modifications means to accept definition in terms of divided substance: June can be both *calculated* and *impulsive.* This is the contradiction expressed in the binary opposition "rational/emotional," and others, throughout the text. By virtue of the fact that the "story" ends well (and June is smiling, etc.), we are asked to "transcend" the contradiction rather than stay mired in paradox. Putting the ratios and substance together, we get the following picture: June can do certain things (acts) because she is a particular type of agent—one defined in terms of familial substance (the qualities of scientists). June undergoes a transformation and becomes a different kind of agent defined by contradictory substance—the qualities of emotional behavior—when placed in a different scenic context. The rhetorical act of transcendence/transformation here unifies the opposites of the binary pair—surely a very persuasive strategy: Rather than settling for "either-or" (as the binary opposition implies), we are offered the means to triumph with a "both-and" (the ultimate way to fulfill desire—to have one's cake and eat it too).

In Chapter 3, I discussed Burke's key terms for rhetoric: identification, order, addressivity, and transformation. Identification is effected through consubstantiation, by sharing substance. In the Saturn advertisement, as I have noted, two addressees ("you" the reader, and "you" June Rooks) are conflated. This pattern links June and the advertisement's readers at the level of discourse. It sets up the possibility of identifying with, or being consubstantial with, the terms of the binary oppositions that are used to construct June. I have discussed how these terms tend to be the traditionally dominated, "second" terms of a set of social classifications based in binary oppositions: male/female, white/black, able-bodied/disabled, trim/heavyset, rational/emotional, and so on. To be conflated with June and to be constructed in these terms (each of which relies on definition *in terms of* particular types of substance) is to be consubstantial with June, and by extension, with the Saturn ethos in general. Any reader who literally is not June can become "different" through this process of identification and consubstantiation: To be like June is to be "different," and to be "different" ultimately is consubstantial with Saturn itself, the slogan of which is "A Different Kind of Company, A Different Kind of Car." The advertisement constructs substantial means for the readers/viewer to be a "different kind of person" as well. This possibility for change is the principal transformation that the advertisement seeks to initiate: Readers are offered the means to change their identities, to see (and, however temporarily or tentatively, *be*) *in terms of* an alternative social identity.

A fundamental irony is at stake in such a transformation, however. To engage in the transformation, readers are called upon to exercise their knowledge of a series of binary oppositions that mark the social order. Burke notes that the rhetorical act instantiates (and creates) hierarchies implicit in the social order and that it creates social cohesion by constructing identity and difference among and between different social groups. The Saturn advertisement invites readers to treat classificatory schemes in the social order *as if* they were not hierarchical: To be transformed in this context relies on an ability to reconcile the divisions in the social order encoded in the binary oppositions the advertisement clearly indexes. The easiest way to reconcile these divisions would be to treat them as if they were simple alternatives (difference equates with choice) rather than hierarchical divisions (difference equates with discrepancy in power, resources, social capital, etc.). The advertisement invites us to (mis-)recognize division as cohesion. This is the central logological consequence of the advertisement.

The Saturn advertisement would seem to be exemplary of what Burke means by being "goaded by the spirit of hierarchy" (1989, p. 263). The binary oppositions that we are asked to entertain in the process of identifying with June, I have argued, are hierarchical: They mark divisions in the social order that have traditionally favored the "first" term of the pairs (e.g., white, male, able-bodied, trim, rational, and so on). By identifying and being consubstantial with June, who represents the second terms of the binaries (black, female, disabled, heavyset, emotional, and so on), we are put in a situation where it is difficult to avoid the "guilt" that transgression of this kind of order makes possible. On one hand, if we do not identify with June, we in a sense deny that being black, female, disabled, and so on, are desirable qualities: In effect, we would be erasing these features as aspects of legitimate social identity. On the other hand, if we do identify with June, we are doubly guilty: First, we reproduce the hierarchy by "consenting" to this form of social classification (i.e., acquiesce to the "logic of stigma"); and second, being consubstantial with June, we would not (for fear of depreciating her and ourselves) overtly draw attention to (champion) this identity as "different" because that would imply the legitimacy of the dominant/dominated binary in the first place. The different possibilities for being "guilty" that the Saturn advertisement sets up rely on a reader's sense of propriety about classification, labeling, and stereotyping: It's all right to "know" these oppositions—perhaps even firmly "believe" in them—but it is not all right to acknowledge them openly, especially in the context of a "simple" automobile advertisement.

▓▓▓ Case 2: Royal Bank Financial Advice Booklets

My second analysis focuses on a selection of text from a series of financial advice booklets produced by Royal Bank of Canada. The series is called

"Your Money Matters." The booklets (each approximately 40 pages in length) are given away free of charge to customers of Royal Bank. The series has seven titles:

- *Buying a Car*
- *Renovating Your Home*
- *Taking Action When Something Goes Wrong*
- *Investments*
- *Budgeting*
- *Buying a Home*
- *Retirement*

A sample cover and a selection of inside pages appear in Figure 5.1.

I treat this series as an example of the kind of discursive practice produced by and constitutive of what Giddens (1991) calls "expert systems." Expert systems "bracket time and space through deploying modes of technical knowledge which have validity independent of the practitioners and clients who make use of them" (p. 18).

The analysis begins with a exploration of the exchange of expert systems and "gifts" (the booklets are given away to customers) as social practices. I discuss the ways in which the Royal Bank booklets are exemplary of expert systems, as Giddens defines them. I then investigate some of the conditions and consequences of gift exchange—especially the function of time, self-interest, and the binding of obligation in gift exchange. These comments regarding the social meanings associated with expert systems and gifts are then substantiated by a discoursal and rhetorical analysis of the texts.

My discourse analysis of the Royal Bank texts focuses on the role played by the language of the texts in the discursive construction of expert systems and the "gift." A gift, in general, requires an appropriate recipient, and it needs to be something the recipient will recognize as valuable. My analysis focuses primarily on the introductory letter from the Chief Executive Officer of Royal Bank that opens each booklet. I show how discursive patterns in these letters function to create a particular type of addressee who will be constituted as potential gift recipient and how the gift is promoted (made "valuable") for such a recipient.

My rhetorical analysis explores the relationship between expert systems, perfection, and guilt. Here I focus on the booklets as a kind of

Figure 5.1. Sample of "Your Money Matters" series.
SOURCE: From *Budgeting* (cover, p. 3, p. 25), ©copyright Royal Bank of Canada. Permission for use of this material has been provided with the courtesy of the **Royal Bank of Canada.**

Spending habits

There's no more accurate an observation than the saying that people are creatures of habit. It's especially apt when it comes to the way we manage the money that passes through our hands.

Most people get their first experience with money-handling at an early stage of their lives — looking after allowances, special-occasion gifts, earnings from part-time work. A great deal of this experience is based on ideas, examples and values learned at home and school and, good or bad, has a powerful effect on the formation of our money habits.

It doesn't necessarily follow that if money was a point of contention when you were growing up that it will be so with you. However, most people would agree that early experiences do influence. Of course, as people branch out in independent directions, they develop their own ideas and create their own unique spending priorities, which may differ from their earlier upbringing.

No matter how good we may consider our money planning to be, once in a while, we need to stand back and re-examine the spending habits we've slipped into.

The detailed advice that follows outlines techniques others have found beneficial in taking a fresh look at their household money management. It applies equally to the single-parent unit, the average Canadian family or the one-person enterprise. It is not intended to be a foolproof formula or to suit all cases. Rather, it lays out a series of guideposts to aid you in finding your own way.

The starting point is to have a firm idea of how and where you spend the money you already have.

Figure 5.1. (Continued)

How household assets are owned

Name of household: _____

Assets	Owned by			
	Me	Partner	Jointly	Other
Chequing account				
Savings account				
Investments				
Value of house				
Home furnishings				
Automobile				
Cash value of life insurance				
Pension holdings				
RSP				
Other				
Total				

Figure 5.1. (Continued)

logonomic system that constructs an order of rules and procedures for what we might call, for now, "financial perfection." Because expert systems have a "validity independent of the practitioners and clients who make use of them," any actual instance of their application is bound to be muddied and imperfect in light of the entelechy of the system. The consequences of "transgressing" Royal Bank's system are further complicated by the fact that its producers have two alibis potentially releasing them from culpability for such transgressions: First, the advice is construed as an "ideal," as being sound "in principle"; and second, the advice is exchanged as a "gift." In the first case, the producers are beyond reproach because they simply present "commonsense" advice not strictly bound to the interests of Royal Bank; in the second case, they absolve themselves of responsibility for any deleterious effect of transgressing the system because they simply offer the advice as a "free" gift that does not explicitly presuppose obligation on the part of the recipient.

EXPERT SYSTEMS AS GIFTS

Each title in the Royal Bank "Your Money Matters" series presents detailed information on how to profit and prosper in some activity involving finances. For example, the *Buying a Home* booklet presents a series of questions readers can use to find out if they are the right kind of people to buy homes (e.g., *Are you a saver at heart? Do you take pride in owning things?*); it defines and gives examples of key terms involved (e.g., *The mortgage; property taxes; interest; The down-payment,* etc.); it provides balance sheets and budgeting charts readers can fill out; it outlines activities involved in buying a home (*The offer; The down-payment; How to look for housing; Planning your move*); and it provides checklists and a glossary of technical *terms to help you when buying a home*. Like the rest of the booklets in the series, it is a primer of expert advice providing readers with a complete system to follow. It sets clearly defined goals (reflected in the booklets' titles), provides sequential and exhaustive steps to follow in order to fulfill those goals, and does so authoritatively.

In his discussion of "expert systems" (in which I would include a subcategory called "expert advice"), Giddens (1991) remarks:

> Such systems penetrate virtually all aspects of social life in conditions of modernity—in respect of the food we eat, the medicines we take, the

buildings we inhabit, the forms of transport we use and a multiplicity of other phenomena. Expert systems are not confined to areas of technological expertise. They extend to social relations themselves and to the intimacies of the self. The doctor, counsellor and therapist are as central to the expert systems of modernity as the scientist, technician or engineer. (p. 18)

"How-to" advice produced by banks for their customers falls squarely in the category of expert system. A number of features characterize the booklets as part of a large financial institution's expert system. First, the booklets outline procedures for engaging in financial transactions (spending, saving, investing) that are constructed as valid for any reader who has the means to engage in the transactions. The validity of the advice is not dependent upon its users; rather, it is judged with reference to internal systemization. That is, the system is not invalidated if it does not apply to a particular individual or particular case: It simply does not apply. Its own internal consistency and logic remain. For example, in the *Buying a Home* booklet we read: *The larger the down-payment you are able to make, the less your home will cost in the long run. Your mortgage will be smaller, therefore, your interest charges lower.* This is "true" no matter to whom it applies.

An expert system relies upon and constructs trust on the part of its users. Because the expert system constructs knowledge of practices not known in entirety by its users, trust "presumes a leap to commitment, a quality of 'faith' " (Giddens, 1991, p. 19). Most adults have some idea about what is involved in buying a home, for example, but most do not have the complete or systematic knowledge of all the constitutive factors that expert advice like the *Buying a Home* booklet contains in an internally consistent system. In general, there is no day-to-day need for us to make our knowledge of buying a home systematically consistent in analogous ways. Expert advice constructs trust on the part of its users— indeed, presupposes it—in fashioning itself as a *complete* guide (its rules and procedures are internally consistent) as it so often does. By doing so, it uses trust to systematize and structure the limited or nonsystematic knowledge that its users have of the information relevant to the field of the advice. The codified expertise of the financial information mediates users' interaction in the field of finance.

Expert advice sells (or occasionally "gives away") an intangible commodity—information. By providing customers with the booklets, Royal Bank is not directly selling financial "products" but offering the information as a part of its customer service. The only direct solicitation for goods and services in the booklets comes on the inside of the back cover, where toll-free phone numbers are listed *Should you have questions about bank services*. In instances involving commercial enterprises like banks, the "giving away" of expert advice is directly tied to other marketing efforts aimed at securing and preserving a customer base (financial planning, special services, longer hours, etc.). This free expert advice performs a so-called "goodwill" function, but more significant, it *shapes* its audience as potential users of financial services while masquerading as benevolence.

The social context in which expert advice is exchanged does not, of course, go unnoticed by the producers of such advice. In an award-winning speech[1] on the subject of corporate philanthropy and social responsibility, the (then) chairman and chief executive officer of Royal Bank, Allan R. Taylor, made the following remark about the relationship between bank activities and social context:

> There is no lack of discussion in the business community on the subject of corporate responsibilities, both economic and social. Milton Friedman's "profit-is-the-only-measure" philosophy has been called the "fundamental-ist" position. Contemporary thinking is now moving toward a somewhat different model, one which is based not only on buying and selling goods and services, but on what has been called an "interpenetrating systems" model. A mouthful, yes, but clearly descriptive of the recognition of two key points: First, that a corporation is in, and of, society, an integral part of it, inextricably linked with other parts of society in myriad complex ways; and second, that economic activities and responsibilities have a variety of social results and implications. (1996, p. 19)

Taylor's remark provides us with a clear example of what Giddens calls "institutional reflexivity"—the "regularised use of knowledge about circumstances of social life as a constitutive element in its organisation and transformation" (1991, p. 20). As Giddens repeatedly asserts, all social action involves a routine and reflexive monitoring of practice—and the forms of discursive knowledge this monitoring produces "re-enter" and affect social practices. This makes reflexivity a part of the object social analysis. Much reflexivity is concerned with explicitly legitimating and justifying practices, so it not only informs us about agents' conception of *what* is done but also is indicative of their orientation and attitude toward their practices—their conceptions of *why*

things are (or should be) done. Such remarks provide us with evidence
of the real, monitored, and symbiotic relationship between what are
referred to as "corporate philosophies" and the social realms in which
they hold sway.

Taylor's speech focuses on the corporation's philanthropic responsibilities. He speaks on a grander scale about "gifts" and what they can
mean to the corporation and to the gift receivers. Taylor is eager for
corporations to think about more than "profit," for them to recognize
that "giving" has other benefits. Although as CEO of a large bank he
almost certainly has other ends in mind. Taylor's remark, "a corporation
is in, and of, society, an integral part of it, inextricably linked with other
parts of society in myriad complex ways; and second, that economic
activities and responsibilities have a variety of social results and implications," squares perfectly with the approach to the social implications of
discourse explored in this book. On a smaller scale, the gifts of financial
advice in the booklets fit into his view of "interpenetrating systems."
Taylor himself signs the introductory letter to each booklet in the "Your
Money Matters" series. Although the booklets would not be characterized as "philanthropy" (in the same way that multimillion-dollar
donations to hospitals, for example, would), they are still constitutive of
the bank's systems of practices that are "inextricably linked" to society.
They are still "gifts" and, as such, have "value" and social meaning.

As expert advice, the booklets are both a product of and a constituent
of expert systems; as gifts, the booklets are situated in the exercise of
symbolic power between the giver and receiver. Gifts are a part of power
relations because they bind receivers by obliging them to give a counter-
gift (which may be realized "simply" as recognition of the initial gift) and
by creating indebtedness on the part of receivers. Among other things,
they are symbolic because it is not so much the gift itself, but the meanings
associated with giving it, that structures its consequences for agents
involved in its exchange. Giving allows "self-interest" to be concealed
and allows the binding of obligation to be recognized not as an imposi-
tion but as an act of generosity. Although giving away financial advice
booklets would not seem to oblige receivers too stringently (one could
quite easily ignore the obligation) and although the expectations for what
would constitute an appropriate counter-gift appear to be fairly innocu-
ous (one could "use" the information, become a Royal Bank customer,
ask questions in response, etc.), the act of giving a gift nevertheless
creates the opportunity for the bank to fashion "ideal" (and, hence,

compliant) customers without paying the cost of having the booklets recognized as a "blatant" attempt to capture customers. Free gifts of advice vindicate against possible charges of self-interest. "Gift exchange," Bourdieu remarks, "is one of the social games that cannot be played unless the players refuse to acknowledge the objective truth of the game" (1990b, p. 104).

The **tenor** (social relationship) and **field** (social activity) characteristics (see Chapter 2) implied in situations of gift exchange are not rigid, static structures. Despite the fact that gift exchange as a general social practice has defining features (such as those discussed in the previous paragraphs), any particular instance of gift exchange is made dynamic and unique by the effects of timing and improvisation on the part of participants. Bourdieu (1990b) cautions against an overly mechanistic vision of gift exchange that is implied by identifying a giver-gift/receiver-counter-gift structure:

> "Cycles of reciprocity," mechanical interlockings of obligatory practices [e.g., gift and counter-gift], exist only for the absolute gaze of the omniscient, omnipresent spectator, who, thanks to his knowledge of the social mechanics, is able to be present at the different stages of the "cycle." In reality, the gift may remain unreciprocated, when one obliges an ungrateful person; it may be rejected as an insult, inasmuch as it asserts or demands the possibility of reciprocity, and therefore of recognition. (p. 98)

There must be an interval between the giving of the gift (obligation created) and the giving of the expected counter-gift (obligation fulfilled). This is not "empty" time, but "marked" time, meaning that participants are aware of the meaning of the amount of time between gift and counter-gift. It allows for actions that seem improvised, that allow the practice to be recognized as bounded, but not determined. Because the exact nature of what would constitute an appropriate counter-gift to Royal Bank's gift of expert advice is not explicitly specified in the material itself (or even in the practice of giving it away: nowhere are readers advised to reply or respond by such and such a time), the booklets initiate an indefinite temporal interval between giving gifts and a time when a counter-gift would be expected. Time is still "marked," however: The appropriate timing of the counter-gift is implied to be "if and/or whenever it applies to you." The gift of the booklets gets the best of both eventualities: Even if recipients never "respond" with a counter-gift, the booklets nevertheless remain a gift given (recipients are "forever indebted"); if one does "respond," then one repays with the counter-gift of engaging with the expert system offered (by seeking the bank's services, etc.). The indefinite interval projected between gift and counter-gift allows the booklets to stand as an inexhaustible gesture—surely the ultimate goal for "goodwill," image-building discourse.

The "gift" is a symbolic act that presupposes an appropriately constructed recipient and a gift of significant "value." I turn now to exploring how the language of the booklets, particularly the introductory letters signed by Royal Bank CEO Allan Taylor, functions discursively to both interpellate their ideal addressee/recipients and promote the booklets' content as a desirable and valuable gift.

INCLUSION AND PROMOTION

A discourse analysis of the linguistic text of the Royal Bank booklets reveals functional patterns that contribute to their meaning potentials as expert advice and as "gift." I have noted that expert advice (being both a product and constituent of expert systems) aims at having validity independent of the practitioners and clients who make use of it: It is designed to apply to as wide a scope of situations as possible within its field. The *Buying a Car* booklet in the series, for example, contains information and procedures that apply no matter what kind of car is being purchased, where it is purchased, or who is purchasing it. A second feature of expert advice is that it aims to present authoritative, comprehensive, and exhaustive field knowledge (hence, "expert" advice). For the expert advice to be successful as "gift," two exigencies must be met. First, the social roles of the giver and the receiver must be appropriately complementary: *Who* gives the gift to *whom* determines the social meanings of the relationship initiated by gift exchange. Second, the gift must be mutually recognizable by both parties as a gift of appropriate value—something worth giving and something worth receiving. A giver's evaluation of the gift may differ, of course, from the recipient's, but in the exchange some kind of intersubjective criteria of evaluation are necessary for the gift to be recognized as a gift. My analysis of the introductory letters of the booklets aligns these features of expert advice and gift with linguistic patterns in the text that both construct and respond to the social exigencies of expert advice and gift. I identify these patterns with two labels meant to sum up their discursive functions: Inclusion and Promotion.

Inclusion concerns the ways in which the linguistic text functions to interpellate both as wide and as "ideal" (from the Bank's point of view) an audience as possible for the expert advice offered in the booklets. For expert advice to have validity and applicability in as wide a scope as possible, it must be addressed to a wide audience: Ideally, it must address "everyone" who would ever be involved in the activities on which it gives advice. For the giver to maximize the social credit of the gift, the recipient must be construed as an "ideal" recipient. While discussing structures of Inclusion in the texts, I note how the addressee of the letter is construed as ideally suited to participating in the methods and procedures offered in the expert advice of the booklets.

The second pattern, Promotion, concerns the ways in which the linguistic text functions to construct (and claim) the value, expertise, and authority of the advice being offered and the ways in which it makes the gift of advice an appropriate and desirable gift for its interpellated recipients. For expert advice to be recognizably "expert," both the source of the advice and the advice itself need to be appropriately promoted and valorized: It needs to be constructed in terms that allow its audience to recognize expertise and value. Similarly, in gift exchange the giver and the gift must be endowed with recognizable symbolic capital to count as "suitable."

Each of the letters (signed by Allan Taylor, Chairman and Chief Executive Officer of Royal Bank) introduces the topic of the booklet, describes its usefulness, and closes by thanking the contributors. The last paragraph and signed closing, the same for each letter, is included in the first letter of Text 5.2 and marked by ellipsis points in the subsequent letters.

My analysis of Inclusion and Promotion ranges over all seven of these introductory letters. Each letter individually exhibits these general functions, but looking at all seven together demonstrates the pervasiveness of the patterns in general. I will deal first with the linguistic patterns that realize Inclusion and follow with the patterns that realize Promotion.

Inclusion

Readers of the letters are addressed as *you,* and although the letter is signed by Allan Taylor, CEO of Royal Bank, the addresser is *we* (*We thank them and hope that this effort will prove useful to Canadians*). In each letter, however, there is a seamless transition from third-person referents (e.g., *they/individuals, most people, a good many Canadians*) in the

TEXT 5.2
Introductory letters from "Your Money Matters" series.

In recent years there has been increased interest and concern about a relatively new phenomenon—retirement. Will those years be a time of joy? Will they be fruitful and healthful? Will they be financially secure?

Your Money Matters—Retirement is designed to prompt you to consider and investigate these key points so that this important stage of life is indeed satisfying and invigorating.

Many people, including members of our staff, contributed their experience, expertise and insight to the development of this booklet and others in Royal Bank's *Your Money Matters* series. We thank them and hope this effort will prove useful to Canadians.

[signature]
Allan R. Taylor
Chairman and Chief Executive Officer

The house you always dreamed of could be the one you have. Maybe you're thinking of an extra room or bathroom or a home that is more efficient. If so, turning your dream into reality may simply be a matter of renovating your present home.

Bringing ideas to life requires imagination and careful planning whether the job is large or small. *Your Money Matters—Renovating Your Home* includes key points you should consider before undertaking home improvements including tips for organizing your finances to pay for the work.

. . .

Even though the costs of buying and maintaining a car have risen considerably in recent years, most people still prefer to own their own "wheels" whether they choose a standard sedan, a station wagon or a camper.

With so significant a portion of a household's dollar involved in buying a vehicle, it's important that the purchase be well planned. *Your Money Matters—Buying a Car* covers key points to evaluate your financial and vehicle requirements and includes shopping tips to help you meet your transportation needs at a price you can afford.

. . .

Whatever type of housing you choose, a sizable sum will go to pay for the roof over your head. And, if you're like a good many Canadians, you'll prefer to own that roof.

Buying a home can be the beginning of an exciting adventure. To ensure that it is, it's important to end up with a home that both meets your needs and is a good fit with your financial situation.

Your Money Matters—Buying a Home takes you through the home buying process and includes detailed information about financing your new home, too.

. . .

The investments individuals make play a vital role in the development of the country in which they live. The benefits go to the individual and also to the nation in the form of improved growth, efficiency and profitability. However, because the world of investment can be complex and the range of opportunities diverse, it's important to gain an understanding of the options available so that the investments you make are right for your personal short- and long-term goals.

Your Money Matters—Investments provides basic investment information designed to encourage you to search out the advice and counsel needed in making your personal investment decisions.

. . .

In most cases, relationships between buyers and sellers go smoothly. But, once in a while something goes wrong because of a misunderstanding, an error, or a failure to live up to promises made. When this happens, the company needs to hear from its customers. Both buyers and sellers stand to gain from this valuable feedback.

Companies recognize that correcting a mistake and mending a customer relationship can prevent the loss of a client and damage to the reputation of the firm. However, customers are often unsure

(Continued)

TEXT 5.2 (Continued)

about the right steps to take to let a company know that they've experienced a problem.

This booklet, part of The Royal Bank's *Your Money Matters* series, is aimed at helping you take appropriate steps to get things resolved when you have a problem.

. . .

I believe that most people would agree that personal money management is definitely more complex than it used to be. There are more ways to spend, save, invest or lose money and much more attention is needed to put and keep sound money management principles in place.

At the same time, each household is uniquely different, whether it be a single-parent unit, an average Canadian family or a one-person enterprise. While *Your Money Matters—Budgeting* does not offer a magic formula to suit all situations, it does offer basic budgeting techniques designed to aid you in finding your own way.

. . .

SOURCE: From the series of booklets titled "Your Money Matters," © copyright the Royal Bank of Canada. Permission for use of this material has been provided with the courtesy of Royal Bank of Canada.

beginning to second-person singular *you* in the remainder of the letter. This easy fusion of *they* with *you* implies that the addresser recognize similar characteristics and interests for *you* as for *they*. The letters are very democratic and inclusive in identifying addressees. The third-person participants that get conflated with *you* throughout name groups of people that are about as wide and encompassing as could be. These include *Many people, individuals, most people, each household, an average Canadian family, a good many Canadians, buyers and sellers, customers,* and *Canadians*. These personal pronoun forms add up to the following: *We* (Allan Taylor and you, the reader, presumably) address *you* and "everyone else" (e.g., *they*) whom we conflate with *you*.

A similar fusion takes place with possessive determiners. Clearly, the letters are about particular social activities that involve money—buying a house or a car, renovating, investing, and so on. In the construction of this field, we expect a number of concepts related to the field to be named. Grammatically, the pattern used in the letters is to name them in a **determiner + noun** construction that attributes—from the addresser's point of view—a **possessive** relation. We get, for example, *your dream, your present home, your finances, your personal short- and long-term goals, your personal investment decisions, your financial and vehicle requirements, your needs,* and so on. These selections frame the topic at hand as being one you will have a shared interest in because they are identified with reference to *you.* Note that these concepts would not be nearly so inclusive (of the reader) if they had been identified without the second-person possessive determiner. Compare simple third-person plural referents such as "dreams," "homes," "finances," "short- and long-term goals," "personal investment decisions," "financial and vehicle requirements," and "needs" with the second-person possessive referents actually in the texts.

The texts construct Inclusion by going as far as to vouchsafe for the mental states of their addressees. In **mental processes** realized by verbs such as "like," "hate," "feel" and "see," "hear," and "understand," there are two inherent participants: a **processor** and a **phenomenon** (see Chapter 2). In most registers, the most common pattern is to have either a first-person pronoun as **processor** (e.g., "I like beer") or a third-person pronoun or participant as **processor** (e.g., "John likes beer"). Ascribing mental processes to addressees is a definitely marked option (e.g., "You like beer," "You feel sad," etc.) unless they are tagged ("You like beer, don't you?")—essentially forming a question rather than making a statement. When mental processes of these types are ascribed to an addressee, they construct a particular orientation for that addressee (e.g., likes and dislikes, mental abilities, etc.). Two different meanings are constructed in the booklet letters with their pattern of attributing mental processes. First, the attributions perform the marked function of saying what "you" think and feel (e.g., *you always dreamed of, you're thinking, you'll prefer*). Second, it fuses second- and third-person pronouns as **processors** in these processes, thereby presupposing that what a general "they" thinks is identical to what "you" think (e.g., *most people prefer, most people would agree*). These structures exhibit the Inclusion pattern because they imply both that "we know what you think" and that "everyone else thinks the same." Ascribing mental states to addressees in this way is also an index of the addresser's assessment of the authority and expertise, because one presupposes a certain measure of authority when deigning to tell others what they think, prefer, dream of, and so on.

In Chapter 2, I outlined the role of **circumstantial** elements in the ideational structure of propositions. Circumstances "attach" to the main process, creating scope in terms of **time, place, manner, reason, purpose,** and so on (see Table 2.5). I note that circumstances can be realized by single words, phrases, and independent clauses. A ubiquitous structure instantiated in the letters (indeed, throughout each of the booklets as a whole) is the **circumstance** realized by conditional clauses headed by "whether" and "whatever." We have, for example, *most people still prefer to own their own "wheels" whether they choose a standard sedan, a station wagon or a camper; each household is uniquely different, whether it be a single-parent unit, an average Canadian family or a one-person enterprise; Whatever type of housing you choose, a sizable sum will go to pay for the roof over your head.* These circumstances contribute to the Inclusion pattern because they clearly are meant to have the material apply in almost any case regardless of the preferences involved.

A number of other **circumstantial** structures contribute to this pattern by constructing a world where financial matters are, by nature, both important and ubiquitous. Examples include *The house you've always dreamed of could be the one you have; At the same time, each household is uniquely different; In recent years there has been increased interest and concern about . . . retirement; In most cases, relationships between buyers and sellers go smoothly; most people still prefer. . . .* Here Inclusion is constructed along the lines that financial matters are usual, common, and timeless.

Modal verbs realize and produce addressers' positional assessment of the likelihood, possibility, desirability, and so on of the content of their propositions. The letters consistently use models of possibility ("can," "may," "could") to signal that the addresser considers certain events (related to finance, of course) possible (e.g., *The house you always dreamed of could be the one you have; turning your dream into reality may simply be a matter of renovating . . . ; Buying a home can be the beginning of an exciting adventure*). These modals contribute to the Inclusion pattern because, like the circumstantials, they make the content potentially applicable across myriad cases.

Each of these structures of Inclusion identifies addressees and situations in terms of the financial field related to the advice, so not only do the texts cast a wide net to include any readers, they also hail readers as participants in activities that are ceaselessly and invariably financial. It is not surprising that financial advice booklets would be marked by such concepts. What is significant is that each of the structures discussed functions to relate finance to *you* (and to *most people*) in *most cases* and *always*. The Inclusion pattern thus hails all subjects as financial ones: The homogeneous economic being is Royal Bank's ideal addressee.

Promotion

The second pattern, Promotion, performs two main functions with reference to expert advice and the gift. First, it constructs the subject matter of the texts as important and invaluable: What it has to offer is distinctive, important, and authoritative. Second, it works to create a felt need for readers by making the advice something they would naturally desire. The booklets as gift need to valorize the knowledge offered. A gift needs to be desirable, and what makes information/knowledge desirable is that it will be profitable (and therefore recognizably important) for its users.

In Chapter 2, I outlined the difference between **classifying** and **qualitative** adjectives in English. The former assign the nouns they modify to a class of things, and the latter signal **positional** meanings of the speaker's attitude toward the nouns they modify. For example, "electronic" is a classifying adjective in the nominal group "the electronic message." In the nominal group "the beautiful message," "beautiful" does not assign "message" to a class; rather, it signals the speaker's attitude toward the message. Halliday calls such adjectives "attitudinal epithets" (1994, p. 184). The letters contain a set of **qualitative** adjectives that we could group under the name "important." Of course, what is or is not "important" is a subjective matter. The **qualitative** adjectives are assigned uniformly to noun heads that name some aspect of the information provided in the rest of the booklet (e.g., *key points; vital role; basic investment strategies; sound money management; basic budgeting techniques; detailed information; important stage of life; valuable feedback; right steps; appropriate steps*). These **qualitative** adjectives contribute to the Promotion pattern by construing each topic—from the point of view of the addresser—as important. None of these concepts is by nature or by definition important—they are promoted as such from the speaking position created by the text.

Relational processes link things together in **classifying, identifying,** and **attributive** relations (see Table 2.4). For example, "Sheila is a professor" assigns "Sheila" to a class; "Sheila is the professor" or "The professor is Sheila" identifies her or her role, while "Sheila is successful" assigns an attribute to Sheila. The central participants in a **relational: attributive** process are **carrier** and **attribute.** The letters are marked by a recurring pattern of attributive relations. Consistently, some aspect of money management or an empty subject *It* is assigned an attribute that is synonymous with "important" or "essential." Examples from the letters include *the world of investment can be complex and the range of opportunities diverse, it's important to gain an understanding of the options available, it's important that the purchase be well planned, it's important to end up with a home that both meets your needs and is a good fit with your financial situation,* and *personal money management is definitely more complex than it used to be.* Each of these attributive processes has **attributes** that are headed by adjectives capable of projection. The head (e.g., *important, complex*) encodes the subjective stance (i.e., the matter is "important"), while the post-head complement contains specific, field-related information (*that the purchase be well-planned,* etc.). Each example fits the basic ideational frame: "It is IMPORTANT that X" where "X" is an embedded proposition concerning finances.

The texts construct Promotion by nominalizing the booklets' expert advice. A nominalization reduces a clause to a nominal group, thereby packing into a name a whole process marked for **participants, time,** and **perspective.** The middle paragraph of each of these letters contains a **relational:possessive** process linking the "Your Money Matters" title with a possessed feature (X *includes / provides / covers / offer*[s] / *aim*[s]). Buried in this possessed feature are two processes that subtly presuppose the expertise of the advice offered (*key points you should consider, investment information designed to encourage you, key points to evaluate your financial . . . requirements, basic budgeting techniques designed to aid you, detailed information about financing your new home, designed to prompt you to consider and investigate, aimed at helping you take appropriate steps*). A number of processes are contained within the long nominal group following *provides* in the following example:

Your Money Matters—Investments provides *basic investment information designed to encourage you to search out the advice and counsel needed in making your personal investment decisions.*

- [we/Royal Bank] **design** basic investment information
- basic investment information **encourages** you
- you **search out** advice and counsel needed
- you **need** advice and counsel
- you **make** personal investment decisions

Packed within one nominal group is the whole logic of expert advice. These nominalizations are verbal analogs to the structure and function of expert systems. They are "timeless": Just as an expert system must be applicable across time and space, these nominalized processes lack tense, aspect, and circumstantial marking. They are "exhaustive": Just as an expert system is designed to lay out definitive procedures for accomplishing a goal, the relationship between concepts in a nominalization is "frozen" in its syntagmatic structure. We should also note in these nominalized processes the recurrence of **concepts** that collocate with "planned expertise": "design," "aim," "detail," "key," "appropriate," and so on.

Finally, Promotion is constructed within a second modal pattern expressing high affinity (**positional** modality) for the importance of the advice. This pattern occurs in sentences concerning the importance of financial planning and the assumed efficacy of the booklet's advice. This high affinity is signaled by modal verbs of necessity and obligation: *Renovating Your Home includes key points you should consider; a sizable sum will go to pay for the roof over your head.* It is also signaled in **relational** processes that have a strong modal dimension: *Bringing ideas to life requires imagination and careful planning; much more attention is needed to put and keep sound money management principles in place.*

The linguistic structures and functions I have identified construct both the Inclusion and Promotion patterns in a dense manner. The letters are very short, but they carefully orchestrate both these functions. We may even recognize in their brevity a presupposition on the part of the addresser that is supported by the co-text (the rest of the booklet) and the context of its exchange (a financial institution gives the booklets away to bank customers); that is, the conciseness is possible because there is an assumption that receivers know they are being hailed as (potential) customers of the advice offered (which they can see at a glance in the titles, charts, and illustrations) and that they are being given a gift (they are not charged for the booklets).

PERFECTION, GUILT, AND EXPERT ADVICE

My discourse analysis of the Royal Bank booklets focused on linguistic patterns and their functions at the level of text. My rhetorical analysis focuses on the rhetorical acts initiated by exchanging such texts. I will still be making reference to actual material from the booklets, of course, but with particular emphasis on the rhetorical and logological conditions and consequences of such acts.

Beginning with addressivity, we can recognize that the booklets do not so much address an audience that will identify with the topics, concerns, and ethos of the expert advice as they actively construct a site of identification where the means to fashion oneself as an ideal economic subject are at one's disposal. Address, in such a conception, has more to do with supplying the discursive means with which readers can recognize or identify themselves than it has to do with creating text that is contrived to "speak to" a pre-existing audience. My analysis of the Inclusion pattern posits that the implied addressees of the booklets include "everyone," but with the Promotion pattern factored in, we recognize that it becomes an "everyone who would identify with the value and importance of the advice offered." Identification is contingent upon readers constituting themselves along the lines of the terms presented to them; addressivity initiates an exchange in which readers are "given" the substance with which to construct an identity, that is, actively define themselves in the terms provided by the booklets. In this instance, identification presupposes an initial division between parties: an "expert" addresses a "non-expert." The booklets, as expert system, are constructed as a systematic, exhaustive, and authoritative body of knowledge on a particular financial topic: By implication, the addresser is therefore "expert." The division between expert and non-expert is the principal social difference to be transcended by the exchange of the advice, but becoming an "expert" engages readers in identifying with more than the instrumentality of the advice: It engages them in taking on other socially constituted roles that are implied by the terministic screens of financial advice. "Educated consumers," for example, are also consumers who, in principle, are better able to be manipulated because they are constituted as compliant subjects by systems and structures using the same terms that constitute them as active agents.

A dramatistic grammatical analysis of the booklets demonstrates the texts' means of constructing a transformational process whereby the subject hailed by the texts (*you*) moves through three stages of identity as a particular type of **agent**. I will argue that the booklets, as a whole, construct three dominant ratios that include the addressee as **agent** and that the sequence of transformations from one ratio to another provides substantial means for readers to recognize themselves as having moved from non-expert to expert. As with any pentadic analysis, the ratios that function to provide motive and to construct attitude are contained within the language of the text itself. Each ratio depends upon definition *in terms of* particular types of substance that posit the ratios' terms as "real" by presupposing what inalienably "is."

The booklets begin by characterizing the **agent** (*you*) in a **scene:agent** ratio. In this ratio, the agent is the *average Canadian,* the *ordinary person* who lacks the kind of expertise/knowledge with which to make his or her financial situation secure, profitable, and positive. The **agent** is in this position because of the nature of the **scene** he or she is in. The scene is most often characterized as a financial one in which an abundance of options, products, strategies, time frames, and so on complicate the agent's decisions and abilities. Here are two examples from the beginning of the *Investments* and *Budgeting* booklets:

> If you're like most people, you spend a large part of your life working for money. By investing, you make money work for you. The trouble is, the range of investment opportunities may seem bewildering to anyone new to it. How can an ordinary person be expected to choose among stocks, bonds, mutual funds, debentures, bank deposits, short-term notes, registered retirement plans and what-have-you that crowd the investment scene? The problem is compounded by the number of institutions vying for your investment dollar by offering ingenious variations on investment packages. (*Investments,* p. 3)

> Most people get their first experience with money-handling at an early stage of their lives—looking after allowances, special-occasion gifts, earnings from part-time work. A great deal of this experience is based on ideas, examples and values learned at home and school and, good or bad, has a powerful effect on the formation of our money habits. (*Budgeting,* p. 3)

In each case, agents are characterized as financial neophytes who know what they know because of the real but unstructured (in terms of presenting clear direction for financial decision making) scene they are in. We are presented with definition in terms of **contextual** substance. One inalienably *is* what one is—a composite of desires, needs, tastes—as prescribed by one's context. This context is consistently characterized in financial terms in the texts—initially as a chaotic, "untutored," financial context where agents can be constructed as relatively helpless in terms of transforming their contextually determined desires, wants, and beliefs into a systematic procedure for fulfilling them. Two examples follow.

> To retire or not to retire? And when? For many years, people had these questions answered for them. You retired when you were 65, and that was that. . . . The choice of life styles in retirement has also expanded. With more years of leisure time to look forward to, retirees are no longer willing to settle for a life of sitting on the front porch. (*Retirement*, p. 3)

> Most people consider their home as their castle. They want it to look good, to be comfortable, to weather the seasons and operate properly. When they have the financial flexibility, they want extra luxuries and conveniences that make homes more comfortable. (*Renovating Your Home*, p. 3)

Here scene (*For many years, in retirement, on the front porch, When they have the financial flexibility*) determines the nature of the agents' "wants"—their characteristics as agents (*no longer willing to settle, they want extra luxuries*).

The **scene:agent** ratio transforms into an **agency:agent** ratio as the booklets proceed. In this ratio, the agents begin to be characterized as "smart" or competent consumers, investors, home-owners, and so on (i.e., different kinds of agents) as a result of being equipped with the expertise offered by the booklets (agency). We are in a medial stage between being a novice beset by chaotic contextual influences and being capable of expert financial/economic acts because we are expert agents. At this stage, the **agency:agent** characterizes *you* as a more informed agent because *you* have sound financial planning advice as your tool. This ratio appears in each booklet soon after some of the advice is laid out in the form of checklists, definitions, methods, and descriptions of common activities relevant to the financial topic of the booklet:

The object of this self-analysis is simply to bring a little thought to bear on something that was formerly done out of habit. With that thought may come a commitment to spend your money more effectively in the future. (*Budgeting*, p. 7)

You may need to keep a record of the dates on which you requested service. If your warranty runs out before the repairs are done, you'll be able to establish that the problem started while the warranty was in effect. (*Taking Action When Something Goes Wrong*, p. 7)

A good way to establish your transportation needs is to keep track of the use of the car for three or four weeks. You may find the checklist on page 6 helpful to do this. (*Buying a Car*, p. 5)

For some couples taking a comprehensive pre-retirement planning course together can help them reach a decision or, at least, get discussions underway. (*Retirement*, p. 5)

In each case, the agent is enabled by the agency of the advice. The characteristics and abilities of the agents (e.g., *commitment, able to establish, reach a decision*) are determined by what means they have at their disposal (e.g., *self-analysis, a record, keep track, the checklist, taking a . . . course*). With the transformation from a **scene:agent** ratio, where agents' abilities and characteristics were determined by their scene, to an **agency:agent** ratio, where agents are empowered by the advice in the booklets, readers are provided the means to see themselves as becoming active agents with tools rather than passive reactors shaped by contexts largely out of their control.

The **agency:agent** ratio undergoes transformation to an **agent:act** ratio by the end of the booklets. With this ratio, which asserts that *you* are capable of certain (financial) acts because of the (new) kind of agent *you* are, the evolution from non-expert to expert is consummated. Now that *you* are an agent with particular abilities and characteristics (which come directly from the expert advice in the booklets), you can initiate acts (*more effectively, benefit, rational plan, well on your way, more efficiently*) based on those abilities and characteristics.

There is obviously much to consider in the buying and maintenance of a car. Taking the "*before*" steps suggested in this booklet may help you to negotiate more effectively and thereby make a better spending decision. (*Buying a Car*, p. 32)

In the end, you, the customer, will ultimately decide which products and services will "make it." So, whether you're dealing with a bank, a department store, or a contractor, take the extra effort to keep the communication lines open. Understand your rights and responsibilities. The marketplace—and you—can only benefit. (*Taking Action When Something Goes Wrong*, p. 23)

After you've learned what the household spends and how it is prone to spend; what it owns and owes, you can move on to developing a rational plan to govern household spending. (*Budgeting*, p. 27)

Keep in mind that besides providing quality shelter, for most people owning their own home is also a satisfying investment. By ensuring in advance that it's what you want within the limits of what you can afford, you are well on your way to making it a happy home before you move in. (*Buying a Home*, p. 32)

Once you've worked out your financial situation and are confident you can manage borrowing for the renovations, take your financial information with you when you go for your loan. Being organized beforehand will help you and the lender negotiate more efficiently. (*Renovating Your Home*, p. 17)

At this point the texts have also changed from definition in terms of **contextual substance** to definition in terms of **directional substance**. Burke notes that definition in terms of **directional substance** is "strongly futuristic, positive" with its emphasis on where one is headed (1945/1969a, p. 31). It entitles "being" as founded upon the natural trajectory of actions; people and things are what they are because of where they are headed. Several **modal** verbs used in describing the acts express futurity by encoding possibility (i.e., possible acts are **after-now** in terms of **time**): *may help, can . . . benefit, can move on, will help.*

The pentadic analysis enables us to chart how the texts construe the addressee/agent as undergoing a transformation from novice to expert. It is, of course, in the best interest of advice givers to enable such a transformation to be inferred from their advice. We might posit that, by

scene:agent →	agency:agent →	agent:act
you are constrained by your context	*you* are a product of the tools you possess	*you* can act effectively because you are an informed agent
"novice," "untutored" →	"apprentice" →	"expert"

contextual substance →	directional substance
"you *are* where you are" →	"you *are* where you're going"

Figure 5.2. Summary of ratios and substance of "Your Money Matters" series.

definition, "experts" are capable of "expert" acts because they are a particular type of agent. The goal of expert advice is to enable users to identify themselves in this way. Figure 5.2 summarizes the transformations I have identified.

At the same time, however, this transformation is constrained by the meaning potentials of the terms of the texts themselves; that is, the texts themselves both instantiate and constitute a logonomic system of terms, rules, and procedures that determine what kind of agent and what kind of acts are sanctioned. The discourse of expert financial advice, as informative and implicitly regulative, fashions certain conditions and consequences for those who would "follow" it. "A given terminology contains various *implications*," Burke says, "and there is a corresponding 'perfectionist' tendency for men to attempt carrying out those implications" (1966, p. 19). If we identify with the subject position that is created for us by the text (and by the rules and procedures it lays out in the form of financial advice), we will have "progressed" from being an agent who has little or no direct control over finances to one who is in "full" control. Becoming consubstantial with the injunctions of expert advice shifts responsibility to the agent/subject. Expert advice, by definition, is construed as being *in principle* proper, correct, and widely applicable (i.e., applies to everyone), yet in this case, it is framed consistently with reference to *you*. The "order" created by the injunctions of the advice (e.g., its do's and don'ts, its checklists, its reminders, and so on) constitutes an exhaustive and comprehensive system to be followed. A tension exists between the exhaustiveness of the system and the construing of responsibility on the part of the addressee (the assumed "user" of the system). Despite the fact that it uses structures that include a variety of people and circumstances (see Inclusion and Promotion above)—seemingly providing the means for readers to find their own *particular* state of affairs within the strictures of the advice—taken *in toto,* the system of advice creates many opportunities for transgression, and consequently "guilt."

The advice implicitly constructs a double bind (Bateson, 1972) for its audience: To identify with being constructed as an "expert" (in the final **agent:act** ratio) implies that the reader is responsible for being able to practice the expert advice in its entirety. This is a negative option because any one person's financial activities could at best only approximate the perfection of the system. The alternative option of resisting identification with the subject position created for the reader—ignoring the advice— does not necessarily absolve one from the "guilt" of transgressing the system. In this case, one has transgressed the system as a whole, rather than in part. Even if we completely disagree with or contradict the advice, we are still made to recognize that it exists as valid, comprehensive, and important: We are hence "guilty" for not complying with common sense. The multi-valence of the series's title supports the injunction that one ought to at least entertain the possibilities offered in the booklets' content: "Your Money Matters." Interpreting "Matters" as a noun pre-supposes that there are such kind of matters (i.e., "Money" ones that are "Your[s]"); interpreting it as a verb presupposes that, whether you identify with the advice or not, you understand that it is important. To be able to understand the title, even, implicates readers in the perfection of the system offered. Double-bind situations always involve a "third injunction" (Bateson, 1972) that says, in effect, that you cannot leave the field: You must play by the (contradictory) rules presented to you. The "Your Money Matters" series is a part of a much larger system that presupposes that money is important, that growth (in capital) is always good, and that *you* are responsible for your place in such a system. To resist completely the role constructed for us in the booklets contradicts this ostensibly inviolable injunction.

The expert financial advice, as a kind of logonomic system in mini-ature, sets up some additional paradoxes for readers. On one hand, it implies that if one follows its rules, one will be an "expert" agent. I have argued that the language of the text culminates in constructing an **agent:act** ratio that implies that *you* are capable of expert financial acts because you are now an agent endowed with (our) expert advice. If expert advice was perfectly successful, however, there would be no need for further advice or contact between the adviser and the advisee, the teacher and the pupil. The exchange of the Royal Bank booklets nevertheless is a gift exchange in which contacting the bank, *Should you have any questions about bank services* (last page of each booklet), constitutes one form of appropriate or expected counter-gift. To fulfill their obligation in the gift exchange, readers paradoxically have to divest themselves of the identity mapped onto them by the gift in the first place.

Finally, the exchange of the expert advice as gift absolves Royal Bank of any culpability for readers' potential transgressions against the perfection of the advice in two ways. First, as both a constituent and product of expert systems, the advice is constructed as valid and applicable *in principle:* If readers cannot "live up" to it or cannot find a place for their own financial situations in it, this is not a fault of the system. Second, by giving a gift, the bank can disguise "self-interest" as "mere" generosity: If customers paid for the advice, the bank would have a responsibility (to make the advice "fit" and so on) that is apparently absent when it simply "gives away" advice.

Case 3: Speech Pathology Progress Report

The final text I will examine is a progress report concerning a 6-year-old boy's participation in a "fluency program for preschoolers" conducted at a university speech and hearing clinic. The report is signed by three authors (a student clinician, a speech language pathologist, and a psychologist/speech pathologist). The latter two are also clinical supervisors for the fluency program. For confidentiality, I have changed proper names and dates, and I have removed institutional names. Otherwise, the report is reproduced verbatim as Text 5.3 (pp. 172-178), which appears at the end of this chapter.

In addition to being kept on file at the institution, the report was sent to Ms. Carver, Francis's mother, on November 14, 1995. My analysis of the text is shaped partially by my involvement in the case: I know Ms. Carver and her son personally but have no professional involvement with them except to the extent that when Ms. Carver told me by telephone that Francis was attending the fluency program, I expressed an interest in the results. I asked for permission from her for me to request a copy of the clinicians' report. She consented and told me whom to contact. I wrote the clinicians and asked them to send me their report. After receiving it, I sought and was granted their permission to reproduce the report here. My investigation of this text is "from the outside" of the institution in which it originated. I do not read this report as a speech pathologist; I read it from the point of view of discourse analysis, rhetorical theory, and social theory as these have been defined and practiced throughout this book. My investigation cannot focus on how the text is exchanged within the clinic and what it can mean to the speech pathologists, psychologists, and student clinicians involved. These are important dimensions to the meaning potential of the text; however, they surely do not exhaust *all* the meaning potentials of the text or what it means to receive and read this text in other contexts and from the point of view of other social roles.

With the previous texts analyzed (Saturn advertisement and Royal Bank booklets), the vested interest on the part of their producers is quite clear: We are ultimately being interpellated as consumers and being persuaded—by identifying with the social roles constructed for us in the text and its contexts—to respond as consumers. Although it differs greatly in terms of the audience it addresses, the ways it is exchanged, the material resources drawn upon for its dissemination, and its overall "purpose," the speech pathology report is as much a rhetorical, social, and discursive act as "public" discourse like advertising.

The analysis focuses on issues of authority that are occasioned by the text and its exchange. Francis is the subject of a progress report written by speech pathologists who have observed his speech behavior in their clinical environment. The progress report is passed on to Francis's mother, who is encouraged to comply with its recommendations. The text arises out of a real context with real consequences. As professionals working in a designed research and observation context, the speech pathologists are endowed with the authority to describe Francis's "dys-fluency" and prescribe courses of action to address his "problem." By exercising their authority, the speech pathologists draw upon a variety of "authoritative resources" that Giddens defines as "Non-material resources involved in the generation of power, deriving from the capability of harnessing the activities of human beings; authoritative resources result from the dominion of some actors over others" (1984, p. 373). Among the specific resources that the authors of the progress report draw upon are linguistic/discursive (e.g., knowledge of technical terms of speech pathology, the generic and registerial expectations of report writing in speech pathology), rhetorical (e.g., the terministic screens of "scientific" and "empirical" discourse deflect attention from the inherently attitudinal and persuasive functions of their discourse), and social (e.g., they are endowed with institutional authority as doctors and researchers).

"Lay" readers of the report (such as Francis's mother) do not draw upon the same authoritative resources in interpreting the text, but this does not imply that "lay" readers are without authority. Having different linguistic, rhetorical, and social resources to draw upon authorizes different readings of the text. Different readings indicate the struggle inherent both in producing and in responding to assessment and diagnosis of problems such as "dysfluency." The power of authority is the power to have one's reading (or writing in the case of the report's authors) of a situation and the social agents involved recognized as legitimate and worthy of being acted upon. I will discuss the discursive, rhetorical, and social resources the text provides as resources for two different readings of the progress report. In the first, I discuss features of the text that could enable readers to produce a reading that complements the constructed authority of the report. This reading complies with the authority of the text by identifying the text's discursive, rhetorical, and social indices of authority and interpreting these as invitations to be reassured, comforted, and confident in the text's description of Francis's problem and the recommended course of action. The second reading of the text focuses on how the text itself creates the potential for resistant or antagonistic response.

AUTHORITY AND ASSURANCE

The progress report indexes an authority that can assure its intended audience of its diagnosis and recommendations. It offers an exhaustive and systematic description of the problem, it outlines the observational context and the procedures followed in it, it offers concrete indicators of progress, and it recommends a course of action. I will discuss some of the principal text patterns through which this authority is constructed discursively, rhetorically, and socially.

The text employs a technical vocabulary that, on one hand, accurately characterizes and assesses Francis's dysfluency and progress in the program, and on the other, characterizes the program itself and its methods as requisitely comprehensive and specialized. Terms used to identify speech characteristics form a specialist vocabulary that readers may assume names significant factors in dysfluency: *dysfluent speech, word and syllable repetitions, prolongations, hard starts, blocking, interjections, secondary behaviors, rate of speech, messages,* and *smooth messages.* What the average non-expert might characterize as a "stutter" or "talking funny" is here broken down into discrete terms that the reader may assume have specific (representational) meanings in the field of speech pathology. Statistical terms co-occur with these speech features and indicate that, by virtue of being quantifiable, these speech features have been established as empirical facts. They are discussed in terms of *assessment data, frequency, display, occurrence, sample, increase, decrease,* and *number.* Francis's speech patterns are the object of actions that are framed in terms of objective, empirical observation. They are *judged, noted, observed, recorded,* and *noticed.* Description of both the program's and the clinicians' actions frame the activities as effective, practical, and goal-oriented. The clinicians and the program *focused, conducted, obtained, scheduled, communicated, allowed, provided, encouraged, reinforced, elicited, facilitated, demonstrated, reported, stated, indicated,* and *recommended.* Finally, the program itself is labeled with terms that indicate expert and authoritative design: *assessment, direct reinforcement, intensive program, fluency enhancing activities, therapy, structured activities,* and *intensive fluency program.*

The text is structured as an instance of the progress report register, the form of which is in itself authoritative and persuasive because it allows content to be organized in sections and in a sequence that is indexical of comprehensive and exhaustive treatment. The sections "break down" the problem and the actions taken toward solving it (the situation that gives rise to the report), thereby imposing form and order on both. The progression from the Description of Problem and Background Information to Procedures & Progress (including an enumeration of goals) through to Summary & Recommendations imposes both a temporal order (past "condition" to proposed future "actions") and logical progression ("if" this is the condition, "then" this is a recommended course of action) on the situation that in effect guarantees that the situation has been authoritatively and expertly managed.

As a rhetorical act, the text reassuringly invites identification with an image of attainable perfection: It constructs the "problem" in a terministic screen where features are both identifiable and quantifiable. Being able to label the problem is reassuring because it at least enables differentiated access to the problem (i.e., we could, for example, focus on *prolongations* or on *repetitions* rather than simply on Francis's "speech"). Because the features of his dysfluency are quantifiable in this terministic screen, we can at least entertain the possibility of their decreasing. The concretizing of potential progress through labeling and quantifying creates an order that implicitly contains its own kind of perfection. Here *dysfluency* can be broken down into discrete components (*prolongations, hard starts, blocking,* and so on) and measured (*data, frequency, occurrence, sample, increase, decrease, number*), which implies that Francis is at least situated on a scale that culminates in near-zero frequency of features—"fluency" (this is reflected in the name for the program: *Fluency Program for Preschoolers*). The report authoritatively demystifies Francis's problem by creating a "frame of acceptance" (Burke, 1937/1984a). The vocabulary of speech pathology creates a boundary/frame around identifiable, observable, and statistically salient features that can be monitored, targeted, and improved. It demystifies by ruling out-of-court folk or naïve speculation about the nature, cause, or consequences of "dysfluency." Even though, at the end of the program, Francis's *number of dysfluencies* increased and he *produced similar dysfluencies as those seen initially,* the report's terministic screen (the discourse of speech pathology) is reassuringly positive because it implicates Francis in a process in which a transformation is both identifiable (labeled and counted) and possible (because the diagnosis has enabled both a *summary* and a *recommendation*).

Finally, we may assume that the report is reassuringly authoritative when the parties involved recognize the social and institutional power vested in the authors. Because the report is generated by authors who hold university positions, have appropriate advanced degrees, and have conducted research, teaching, and training in the field, readers can trust that what the authors say in their progress report is efficacious—that it will have effect, or "count." Bourdieu (1991) remarks,

The specificity of the discourse of authority (e.g., a lecture, sermon, etc.) consists in the fact that it is not enough for it to be *understood* (in certain cases it may even fail to be understood without losing its power), and that it exercises its specific effect only when it is *recognized* as such. This recognition—whether accompanied by understanding or not—is granted, in the manner of something taken for granted, only under certain conditions, namely, those which define legitimate usage: it must be uttered by the person legitimately licensed to do so, the holder of the *skeptron,* known and recognized as being able and enabled to produce this particular class of discourse: a priest, a teacher, a poet, etc.; it must be uttered in a legitimate situation, that is, in front of legitimate receivers . . . ; finally, it must be enunciated according to the legitimate forms (syntactic, phonetic, etc.). (pp. 111-113)

Regardless of whether readers of the progress report understand—or even agree or consent to—its content, they are compelled to recognize that the text fulfills the legitimacy conditions that would assign it its authority. Authority rests not in the accuracy or usefulness of the report, but in the fact that it is a product of a recognized authority who meets the textual (e.g., it uses appropriate register features) and situational (e.g., produced by trained professionals reporting on a properly designed research program) requirements licensing such an act. Readers may be assured that they "have it on good authority."

In this section, I have attempted to outline some of the discursive, rhetorical, and social indices of authority that the text occasions. This reading has pointed to the features of the text (and the participants involved in its exchange) that would likely be a part of the means through which readers would comply with the report, be reassured by it, and have grounds for trusting the soundness of its recommendations. This reading, however, presupposes a positive complementarity between the different vested interests of the parties involved (the report authors, the mother, Francis, and others who are asked to read and act on the report). The constructed authority of the text may presuppose a unity of interests—it may be structured and exchanged *as if* its authority was certain, unquestionable, and "natural"—but, I will argue, it also bears traces of discursive, rhetorical, and social practices that complicate its authoritative unity. The remainder of my analysis is aimed at explicating patterns in the text itself that enable a resistant, much less compliant, reading. I characterize these as "antinomies": They are contradictions indexed by the text's own representation of the subject of the report, the clinicians and the clinic, and the nature of linguistic communication.

ANTINOMIES OF AUTHORITY

Representing the "Patient"

The first antinomy I will discuss has to do with the way Francis's actions are represented by the ideational structure of **participant** and **process** types. Francis is represented in three recurring structures throughout the text:

(a) as **patient** or **phenomenon** acted on or observed:
- Francis was first referred
- Francis was asked to revise a dysfluent message
- This activity allowed Francis to pause between messages
- The clinicians observed Francis interacting with classmates
- Francis was required to discuss a weekend event
- Mrs. Winters reported that she had not noticed changes in Francis's fluency
- It was recommended that Francis receive individual fluency therapy

(b) as **carrier** in an **attributive** relation that assigns an attribute or a characteristic of his "dysfluency" to him and evaluates his ability:
- Francis was able to sing a song
- Francis was able to remain fluent when talking in unison
- Francis was successful in sending messages one at a time using the beads
- Francis was able to send one message at a time without the beads in a highly structured activity
- Francis was able to revise hard messages when the clinician initiated the message
- Francis was able to respond to Who? When? Where? and How did it end? without difficulty
- When the activity allowed for spontaneous conversation and interaction, Francis was able to remain fairly fluent
- Francis was able to attend well during the craft activity

(c) as **carrier** in an **attributive** relation in which Francis or characteristics of his speech patterns are tokens of some statistical value:

- Francis presents with dysfluent speech
- Francis produced similar dysfluencies
- Francis was displaying less tension and fewer interjections when speaking
- Francis's rate of speech decreased slightly
- Francis displayed considerable difficulty initiating messages
- Francis's contribution to the group increased significantly as the term progressed
- His messages contained some dysfluencies
- He displayed more dysfluencies when responding to questions
- The amount of Francis's dysfluencies have increased
- Francis displayed a significant improvement in his ability to attend and to sit still during the session

Francis and his speech characteristics are objectified in these representations. He is either the passive object of observation or the carrier of a "dysfluent" attribute. Despite the fact that speaking *is* an act, Francis is consistently represented in structures in which he is inactive. In very few of the main clause processes is Francis an **agent** in an **action** process or a **processor** in a **mental** process. The structures in (b), *Francis was able to . . .* , demonstrate that his capabilities as an agent are framed only in terms of his performance in response to activity criteria. Comparing *Francis was able to send one message at a time without the beads* with "Francis sent one message at a time without the beads" demonstrates the objectifying effect of framing his action as a relation. In the latter, Francis is an active **processor**—he is *doing* something. In the former, a structure endemic to the report, Francis is a "static" or "passive" **carrier** to be equated with some speech characteristic recognized by the field of speech pathology. I will demonstrate in a later section how these representations of Francis contrast with representations of the clinicians and the clinic, both of which are unwaveringly represented as active **agents** and **processors.**

The **concepts** used to describe Francis's speech characteristics manifest an additional antinomy. At points, they seem to be used in field-restricted ways (i.e., a common word has a specialized meaning in relation to other technical vocabulary). This would seem to be the case in the Assessment Data section in which the terms *dysfluent speech, flow of . . . speech,* *word and syllable repetitions, prolongations, hard starts, blocking, inter-jections,* and *secondary behaviors* occur. A listing (from the whole report), however, shows the terms recurring and often collocating with terms in contexts where there are no systematic means for understanding them as technical or not. The terms used in the text follow.

- dysfluent speech
- flow of . . . speech
- word and syllable
  repetitions
- prolongations
- hard starts
- blocking
- interjections
- secondary behaviors
- lip smacking
- eye blinking
- short and simple sentences
- statements
- questions
- messages
- tension
- spontaneous conversation
- rate of speech
- whole word repetitions
- typical "ums" and "likes"
- pitch
- intensity
- speech production
- staccotic
- smooth flowing
- speech sample
- fluency difficulties
- reduced rate of speech
- pauses
- less complex sentences
- the feel of fluency

- slower rate of speech
- chunked . . . words
- inappropriate pauses
- comment on a topic
- meaning
- fluent initiation of the
  message
- number of messages
  required
- verbal scaffolding
- smooth messages
- revisions
- hard or bumpy messages
- hard messages
- good messages
- messages that were
  coherent
- easy talking
- spontaneously produced
  messages
- increased fluency
- story chain questions
- question representations
- carrier phrase
- easy messages
- specific response
- fluency difficulties
- informal comments
- intensive fluency
- significant improvement
- direct treatment

We would be hard pressed to form clearly identifiable collocational sets of these terms. Our ability to do so is one of the means we have of making sense of the report: Knowing what goes with what is as crucial to understanding the functions of these terms as knowing what any individual term represents. The semantic range of and relations among these terms may be well understood by the authors of the report, but several factors complicate readers' potential to understand the terms: They are dispersed throughout the report with no clear indication of when they are being used technically or informally; technical (e.g., *carrier phrase*) and seemingly nontechnical terms (e.g., *easy messages*) often appear together; some terms seem to describe articulation problems (e.g., *blocking*), whereas others seem to describe "meaning" problems (e.g., *meaning, specific responses*); with some it is not clear whether the term *refers* to a particular speech phenomenon or *evaluates* it (e.g., *inappropriate pauses, messages that were coherent*). The only clear principles readers have to organize these terms with are **repetition** and **synonymy:** Certain terms are repeated and many, at least at the level of common sense, seem to be roughly synonymous (e.g., *easy, simple, less complex*). These certainly make the text **cohesive** in terms of its **textual** functions, but the lack of signals of their **taxonomic** arrangement (i.e., how the terms related to one another in an ordered system) frustrates a clear understanding of their **ideational** content (i.e., what they represent).

The terms also seem to presuppose some standard of evaluation, but the text does not explain it (e.g., *complex, simple, hard,* and *easy* presuppose some standard for comparison). Presupposing a standard is problematic in itself because the complexity of factors involved in determining a "standard" are relative to those who make it and why it is made. Readers are invited to identify with the terms (and to assess Francis in similar terms), but without sharing the same expertise of the authors and without being given clear signals as to how to organize and interpret the vocabulary, this identification can be made only on faith.

Representing Communication

A number of the terms used to describe Francis's speech treat language and communication as a strictly medium-centered phenomenon. That is, the vocabulary focuses on the production and transmission of messages that are judged as successful or not depending on the amount of "noise" present (in the sense of the term in information theory, where "noise" is any undesired distortion of a message). This sort of focus is reflected in terms such as *hard or bumpy messages, staccotic, smooth flowing, blocking,* and so on. It would also seem to be clearly reflected in the presupposition (which remains unexplained and unjustified) that speaking is "easier" when one is not engaged in nonverbal activity (e.g., moving a bead and sending *one message at a time* is a goal to be pursued; making a craft and speaking at the same time is presumed to be a *more challenging environment*). Whether or not this focus is legitimate (I would claim it is not—how could one accurately characterize speech by divorcing it from natural speaking contexts?), the report interprets Francis's speech patterns according to criteria that encompass more than problems of articulation. It does so without clearly signaling that a shift in terministic screens has taken place. Goal #5 is a good example of this:

> **Goal #5:** To retell a story with increased fluency by answering story chain questions.
>
> The clinician told a story and then had the children answer story chain questions (e.g., Who? Where? When? What happened?, and How did it end?) in order to retell the story to the group. The clinician verbally asked the questions while pointing to question representations and then provided a carrier phrase to facilitate the child's fluency. Francis was able to respond to Who? When? Where? and How did it end? without difficulty although his messages contained some dysfluencies. When responding to the question "What happened?," he often responded "I don't know." It was felt that this was an attempt to avoid answering the question, perhaps because he feared he would be dysfluent. Francis required the use of a carrier phrase provided by the clinician to facilitate the production of easy messages.

On one level, we seem to be being told about "fluency" as a descriptor of the "smoothness" of the child's response. On the other hand, the activity queries the children about the details of a story they have had read to them. This activity thus calls upon much more than the children's "fluency" capabilities in terms of producing *smooth messages* because their ability to comprehend the story, their experience of this type of social activity (with parents, teachers, and so on), their identification or misidentification of the details of the story, the clinician's ability as a reader, and many other factors are involved in their responses. Notice that Francis's response *I don't know* is perfectly "fluent" according to criteria the report sets up (it contains no *blocking,* etc.), yet it is never-theless both quantified (*he **often** responded*) and interpreted (*It was felt that this was an attempt to avoid answering the question, perhaps because he feared he would be dysfluent*). That the response is interpreted signals that matters other than speech production are being observed and evaluated. The interpretation—which amounts to an assumption con-cerning the social functions of his response—is embedded in a discussion of the flow of speech as more or less "fluent" (*to facilitate the production of easy messages*), yet no clear signal is given that both sorts of "fluency" (social-interpersonal-functional and "production" fluency) are at risk. The criteria for describing "fluency" of speech production are not commensurate with the criteria for assessing the social or pragmatic appropriateness of a response.

A similar antinomy occurs in the characterization of *spontaneous conversation* in the report:

> In unstructured situations which elicited spontaneous conversation, Francis sometimes required verbal scaffolding in order to send one message at a time.

> As the demands on the children increased from spontaneously produced messages to responding to questions, Francis started to avoid responding by saying "I don't know."

> When the activity allowed for spontaneous conversation and interaction, Francis was able to remain fairly fluent. However, when asked a question, he became more dysfluent.

If conversation is *elicited* and requires *verbal scaffolding,* it ceases to be *spontaneous conversation.* Similarly, if *spontaneously produced messages* are subject to *demands,* they are, by definition, not *spontaneously produced.* If we did consider the situation in the second example above as one that included spontaneous conversation (what the report invites us to do), we would have to allow that Francis's *responding by saying "I don't know"* constitutes a response. To claim that this is to *avoid responding,* as the report does, imposes restrictions upon a kind of talk that by definition does not follow such rules. Finally, in the third example, the report unwittingly creates another contradiction in terms by linking *activity* and *spontaneous conversation.* If *spontaneous conver-*

sation has to be authorized or *allowed* by an *activity* (which we can assume is a designed activity like all the others discussed), then it is again, by definition, not *spontaneous conversation*. It is as if the presumed efficacy of the terministic screen—which includes the apparently technical term *spontaneous conversation*—is enough to substantiate the "reality" of the concept. This in itself is specious enough, but the terms of the text—the means at the readers' disposal for making sense—are themselves contradictory.

Representing Clinicians and the Clinic

The representation of Francis and his speech characteristics vividly contrasts with representation of the clinicians. Three different structures in which the clinicians are a **participant** recur throughout the text, representing them (and the research setting they work in) as being capable of an active and rich mental life. They are represented as:

(a) **processors** in **mental:cognitive** process related to observation
   - The clinician noted that Francis was displaying less tension and fewer interjections when speaking
   - Whole word repetitions . . . and interjections (e.g., /ere/ with rising pitch) were noted
   - Whole word repetitions were judged to be the most prominent dysfluency
   - The high pitched /ere/ interjection noted in the first sample was not noticed at all in the second speech sample
   - It was also observed that Francis's speech production in the second sample was staccotic
   - Dysfluencies noted most often included hard starts and repetitions
   - It was noted that over the term the number of repetitions decreased in activities which incorporated the use of the beads
   - Such observations were also noticed in the therapy sessions
   - It was also noted that Francis was more fluent when engaging in spontaneous conversation
   - An increase in the use of hard starts at the beginning of words, prolongations especially for "I," and the interjection "actually" was also noted
   - It was noted that Francis was less attentive when the parents joined the group

- It was observed that he had difficulty sitting still and diverted his attention toward his mother
- The clinicians observed Francis interacting with classmates

(b) **processors** in "positive" and "encouraging" **mental:verbalization** processes

- Clinicians communicated using a reduced rate of speech with distinct pauses and shorter, less complex sentences
- Clinicians verbally reinforced the sending of one message at a time
- Smooth messages sent by the children during any activity were verbally reinforced for easy speech
- The clinician told a story and then had the children answer story chain questions
- The clinician verbally asked the questions while pointing to question representations
- Clinicians attempted to elicit conversation from the children while they were completing a craft
- Clinicians verbally reinforced easy messages sent by the children

(c) in processes where some (inanimate) aspect of the program or its design is capable of **mental** processes

- Group sessions focused on creating an environment that facilitated fluency
- Individual sessions focused more on modifying messages
- Singing a song in unison allowed the children to experience the feel of fluency
- This activity helped to clarify the meaning of sending one message at a time, as well as, encouraged the children to pause between their messages
- This activity allowed Francis to pause between messages
- This encouraged the children to think about the message they wanted to send
- Mottoes were used to facilitate the above goal
- The activities focused on requiring the children to interact with one another
- Individual therapy would provide more specific and direct treatment
- Therapy could focus on modifying messages

The structures in (a) are expected for this register, especially when they are realized in the passive voice (e.g., *Whole word repetitions were noted*) or in cleft constructions with a "dummy" *It* subject (*It was noted that Francis was less attentive when the parents joined the group*). Defenders of this structure point to its being necessary for an "objective" style and to the fact that it enables constituents other than the "doer" to be **thematized.** Critics of this style point to its depersonalizing function and its ability to "hide" agency. Both these interpretations ignore the fact that the structure still constructs the observers as being capable of the **mental** process—more than can be said of the person being observed. The text ironically attributes the majority of the **mental:verbalization** process to the clinicians even though it reports on how and what Francis speaks (e.g., the structures in [b]). The structures in (c) even represent some inanimate aspect of the program as being capable of **mental** processes. Again, this sharply contrasts with the way Francis is represented.

Although the report is framed in the terministic screen of empirical and objective observation in which the subject *presents with* symptoms that can be *observed* and *noted,* there are several instances in which Francis's speech patterns are interpreted subjectively. On one hand, readers are being asked to identify with an objective scientific authority that impartially identifies and classifies what is significant, observable, notable, and so on, with a purportedly explicit and comprehensive vocabulary. At the same time, however, the text contradicts its own "rules" (without clearly signaling that it is doing so) by interpreting phenomena inconsistently (i.e., only some phenomena are given interpretations) and according to terministic screens (concepts) whose relationship to the technical terms of "fluency" and speech production is unclear. A few examples:

> When responding to the question "What happened?" he often responded "I don't know." It was felt that this was an attempt to avoid answering the question, perhaps because he feared he would be dysfluent.

> When seated on the carpet with classmates, after Ms. Carver had left the room, Francis responded "I don't know" to a question posed to him by Mrs. Winters. This observation was consistent with what Mrs. Winters reported. She felt that Francis may be avoiding some talking situations because of his fluency difficulties.

> Individual therapy would provide more specific and direct treatment as Francis is becoming increasingly aware of his dysfluencies.

At other points in the text, the authors resist interpretation when it would seem that the reasoning used in the cases quoted above would apply just as legitimately. For example, Francis's responding *I don't know* and *Actually* are treated simply as *repetitions* rather than as responses that perform an **interpersonal** function, which they clearly do.

When a purportedly "objective" assessment is peppered with "subjective" interpretations and no rationale is given for the change in perspective, readers are presented with a contradictory message. The interpretations seem to occur at points where the validity of assessment of Francis as "dysfluent" would be supported—made more convincing and authoritative—by filling out *his* motivations. What could be more authoritative than to predict the subject's motivations, to do so in a way that does not draw attention to itself, and to identify those motivations in terms that are provided by the terministic screens of the language of observation rather than the subject's? The inconsistency apparent in the (unannounced) alternation between objective observation and subjective interpretation (i.e., interpretation for the "subject") literally presents readers with the "paradox of substance" (Burke, 1945/1969a, p. 21): The terms/substance through which we are invited to classify Francis are themselves paradoxical when, on one hand, they are used in a way that presupposes "objectivity" (i.e., his speech patterns can be described according to "objective" criteria), while on the other hand, the *same* terms are used "subjectively" in interpretation.

Rhetorical Antinomies

The ideational representations of Francis and his speech characteristics invite readers to identify with a particularly static view of a "patient" who is constructed in a **scene:agent** ratio. Francis is characterized as "dysfluent" because he *contains, displays, presents with,* and *produces* the speech markers deemed "dysfluent." The ratio implicitly proposes that "dysfluency" is a scene that characterizes Francis as an agent. The dysfluencies are *in* him, as it were: They are contained in his speech. We cannot really interpret these structures in a **scene:act** ratio that would imply that he *speaks* "dysfluently" because he is not actually portrayed as having spoken, he is only portrayed as being the phenomenon that is *observed, noted,* and *noticed.* An extrinsic, scenic element, Francis's speech is something to be perceived, not something considered an act itself. It is a product rather than a process. The speech characteristics (both type and frequency) that are attributed to Francis define him in terms of **familial substance:** He is represented as possessing the attributes that belong to a class of "markers of dysfluency." These are very nearly the only substantial terms used to represent Francis, so the reader is invited to identify with the perspective of the report in these terms—to be consubstantial with their characterization of Francis implies seeing him in similar terms.

The clinicians and their clinic, on the other hand, are framed by a **purpose:act** ratio. To *verbally reinforce*—as the clinicians do—is to act with the aim of "reinforcing," for example. Each of the enumerated goals identifies purposes for the acts undertaken at the clinic (e.g., *Goal #1: To create an environment that facilitates fluency* [**purpose**]; *Clinicians communicated using a reduced rate of speech* [**act**]).

Exploring the listed goals in greater detail reveals a series of contradictions and inconsistencies. The seven goals listed in the report are as follows:

Goal #1: To create an environment that facilitates fluency.

Goal #2: To facilitate sending one message at a time.

Goal #3: To facilitate easy speech through modification of hard messages.

Goal #4: To encourage positive attitudes and feelings about talking.

Goal #5: To retell a story with increased fluency by answering story chain questions.

Goal #6: To demonstrate the ability to use easy, more fluent speech while motorically involved in an activity.

Goal #7: To act as a liaison with Francis's school in order to coordinate program planning.

Each of these (framed in a **purpose:act** ratio) is a goal from the point of view of the clinicians: They cannot be construed as goals for Francis, which we might assume would be the case in a program designed to enhance *his* fluency. In each case, the goal is construed as the purpose and the following text outlines the acts taken to fulfill the purpose. A contradiction emerges, however, when we consider that the report states as goals the very acts that would presumably fulfill the goals. For example, in #6, how can *to demonstrate* be a goal? It is the act that (from the clinician's point of view) fulfills the goal. The real goal, one can only presume, is for the subject to "speak fluently while motorically involved in an activity." Similarly, in #7, the stated goal is *to act as liaison*, but this is not really a goal at all, but something that might be done to achieve the goal of "coordinating program planning."

Particular logological consequences result from this. The discursive rules of progress reports in this case seem to require a statement of "goals"; however, the goals here seem to be more a "spinning out" of the implications of the logonomic rules for research protocols and for writing progress reports than a statement of the ends desired for the subject/patient. As they appear here, the goals conflate the means for understanding the system of classification in speech pathology observation (a logological feature—"goals must be stated") with what the subject/patient actually does or can do as a result of the "therapy." As stated, the goals cannot but be fulfilled because they are derived internally from the design of the observational context and the discoursal regimes followed in writing research reports. It seems to work like this, for example: Francis will be asked to move a bead and *send a message* at the same time. We assume this will *facilitate sending one message at a time;* therefore, *to facilitate sending one message at a time* is our goal. "Creating," "facilitating," "encouraging," "retelling," "demonstrating," and "acting" (the acts stated in the goals) are *not* goals, they are practices involved in the observational context. Acts of research are elevated to being markers of the subject's progress. The "perfection" posited by the logonomic system of speech pathology (i.e., "fluency") is superseded by the "perfection" of the register of progress report writing (i.e., goals must be identified and enumerated). The "patient" gets lost in such a spinning out of the implications of the logonomic system, just as in Burke's (1966) comment:

> A given terminology contains various *implications,* and there is a corresponding "perfectionist" tendency for men to attempt carrying out those implications. (p. 19)

Social Antinomies

I begin this section with a point that Bourdieu (1991) makes about the divisions and struggles endemic to any social field:

> While the structure of the social field is defined at each moment by the structure of the distribution of capital and the profits characteristic of the

different particular fields, the fact remains that in each of these arenas, the very definition of the stakes and the trump cards can be called into question. Every field is the site of a more or less openly declared struggle for the definition of the legitimate principles of division of the field. (p. 242)

The progress report is an act of definition and classification of its subject made in terms of the "legitimate principles of division" of the field of speech pathology. Francis's mother is expected to comply with the diagnosis and the recommendation that she enroll Francis in *individual therapy* in the future. To not agree with the diagnosis or to not comply with the recommendation, for whatever reasons, calls into question the authority of the text and its producers: It implicates the participants in a struggle for legitimacy. Whose assessment of Francis, whose intervention, if any, will be assented to and therefore stand as legitimate? The authors would claim that their report and its recommendations are incisive, comprehensive, and necessary. Their "trump cards" are the strictures of speech pathology as a science, the "stakes" both Francis's "fluency" and recognition of their authority in assessing him. What resources are at the disposal of those who would resist "the very definition of the stakes and the trump cards" of the field? My resistant reading of the text pointed to a number of antinomies—contradictions between principles that seem equally necessary and reasonable—evidenced in the report that call into question the "legitimate principles of division of the field, its "trump cards" and its "stakes." I have demonstrated that the discursive principles of classification of speech pathology used in this instance manifest irresolvable antinomies that seriously complicate the rhetorical (its success at creating identification) and social (its ability to enact the authority of its diagnosis and recommendations) "stakes" of the report. I do not claim that the evidence I have presented in investigating these antinomies would be the same as the evidence someone like Francis's mother would produce if she were called upon to explain her reasons for resisting the report and its recommendations. Her response draws upon different resources for resistance and is formed by a social agent faced with other contextual exigencies—being a mother, dealing with the consequences of having her son diagnosed as "dysfluent," responding to Francis's needs and desires, replying to institutional authority, trying to "do the right thing" for a loved one, and so on. My analysis draws on the resources of discourse analysis and rhetorical and social theory. I can imagine a mother's resistant response, or at least the kind of feelings that might precipitate it, but I cannot explicate it in its own terms. A discursive, rhetorical, and social analysis, however, can present explicitly, systematically, and publicly the textual traces of the antinomies that would be implied by a resistant response to the text.

We can assume that ultimately the progress report is something to be acted on: Francis's mother is encouraged to comply with the recommendation that *Francis receive individual fluency therapy*. This is a recommendation that is based on "evidence" so vitiated by contradiction—at least in the way it is communicated—that anyone having to make a decision based on the report is faced with a difficult decision. On one hand, the report represents an authority to be reckoned with, heard, recognized, and obeyed. The institutional authority and its concomitant symbolic capital—what Bourdieu (1991, p. 106) calls their "socially recognized power to impose a certain vision of the social world" (in this case, their "vision" of Francis's speech characteristics and what should be done about them)—impose a strong injunction to comply on those who would respond to the report. In outlining a process through which his "fluency" can be enhanced, the report also implicitly warns that by *not* complying, Francis's mother could cause his "fluency" to deteriorate. This is a good example of what Burke means by being "goaded by the spirit of hierarchy" (1989, p. 263). Francis's speech is described and classified according to a graded and rank series of "fluency" features: To not comply with the report's recommendation amounts to taking on the responsibility of removing his chances of perfecting the hierarchy. The recommendations pass guilt, or potential guilt, on to his mother and others who are called upon to respond.

On the other hand, the authority to have antinomies (inadvertent or not) misrecognized (which I assume is at the heart of a "compliant" reading and response to the text) is challenged when different "frames of acceptance" (Burke, 1937/1984a), authoritative resources, contextual knowledge—different *motives*—are brought to a reading of the text. The report does not "ask" for resistant readings, no more than the Saturn advertisement asks to be read as an instance that reproduces corrosive stereotypes by classifying social agents with binary oppositions, no more than the Royal Bank booklets ask to be read as "gifts" that ostensibly allow their own motives to be misrecognized as "mere" benevolence and generosity.

I have tried to show in these analyses that, however mundane the texts are, the stakes are high for everyone involved. These texts are indicative

TEXT 5.3
Speech pathology progress report.

[institution name]
SPEECH AND HEARING CLINIC
[place]
FLUENCY PROGRAM FOR PRESCHOOLERS
PROGRESS REPORT

Name: Francis Carver   **Date:** November 4, 1995
Address: **D.O.B.:** November 6, 1989
Phone: **Age: 6**
Parent: Julie Carver   **School:**
                                             Grade:

DESCRIPTION OF PROBLEM

Francis presents with dysfluent speech. The flow of his speech is interrupted predominantly by word and syllable repetitions (e.g., "dog, dog, dog, dog" and "be . . . be . . . before"). Prolongations (e.g., "nnnno"), hard starts or blocking (e.g., ". . . I) and interjections (e.g., "um . . ."), as well as, secondary behaviours such as lip smacking and eye blinking are also noted but with less frequency.

BACKGROUND INFORMATION

Francis was first referred to XYZ's Speech and Hearing Clinic by school Language Pathologist Jane Smith. Following an assessment, he attended an intensive preschool fluency program for 3 weeks in October (Report on file: Jane Smith, Oct. 29, 1995). Group sessions focused on creating an environment that facilitated fluency by modelling slow speech, using short and simple sentences, and by making statements rather than asking questions. Individual sessions focused more on modifying messages and providing more direct reinforcement regarding Francis's messages. Group parent counselling sessions were also conducted. At the end of the intensive program, Francis produced similar dysfluencies as those seen initially. However, the clinician noted that Francis was displaying less tension and fewer interjections when speaking.

ASSESSMENT DATA

A three minute speech sample was obtained during spontaneous conversations with Francis at the beginning and end of term. At the beginning of the term, Francis's rate of speech was approximately 104 words per minute. Whole word repetitions (2-4 reps), especially of the word "and," sound and syllable repetitions (sounds were repeated on average of 2-3 times; e.g., w-w-well), prolongations (average of 1 second duration; e.g., nnnno) and interjections (e.g., /ere/ with rising pitch) were noted. Whole word repetitions were judged to be the most prominent dysfluency. Lip smacking and eye blinking were also present but to a lesser extent. At the end of term, Francis's rate of speech decreased slightly (94 words per minute). The types of dysfluencies observed remained essentially unchanged except for the additional use of hard starts or blocking. These were most evident on the first word of a message. Use of the word "actually" as an interjection, along with the typical "ums" and "likes" were also observed. The high pitched /ere/ interjection noted in the first sample was not noticed at all in the second speech sample. The word "I" was the most frequently prolonged and was increased in pitch and intensity. It was also observed that Francis's speech production in the second sample was staccotic rather than smooth flowing. Eye blinking was less prominent than evidenced in the initial speech sample, whereas lip smacking increased in occurrence.

THERAPY GOALS, PROCEDURES & PROGRESS

Francis attended 11/12 therapy sessions scheduled once weekly. Two other boys, aged 5 and 6, who also present with fluency difficulties made up the group. The parents observed sessions and participated in the last 15 minutes of the therapy session.

Goal #1: To create an environment that facilitates fluency.

Clinicians communicated using a reduced rate of speech with distinct pauses and shorter, less complex sentences. Fluency enhancing activities such as singing and talking in unison were used in therapy. Singing a song in unison allowed the children to expe-

(Continued)

rience the feel of fluency. In addition, stories were read containing a re-occurring line which the group repeated in unison. Francis was able to sing a song, both by himself and in unison with the group fluently. In structured activities, such as repeating a single line in a story book, Francis was able to remain fluent when talking in unison. When Francis was asked to revise a dysfluent message he sent the message easier, although dysfluencies continued to be present. Dysfluencies noted most often included hard starts and repetitions. In therapy, Francis followed the model of the clinician using a slower rate of speech with pauses and shorter, less complex sentences. However, at times, the flow of Francis's speech was staccotic where he chunked his words and added inappropriate pauses.

Goal #2: To facilitate sending one message at a time.

Beads were used with activities in which the children were required to provide more than one comment on a topic. One bead was moved along a string for each message the child sent. This activity helped to clarify the meaning of sending one message at a time, as well as, encouraged the children to pause between their messages. Clinicians verbally reinforced the sending of one message at a time (e.g., "You sent good messages, one at a time"). Francis was successful in sending messages one at a time using the beads. This activity allowed Francis to pause between messages. Part way through the term the children were instructed to move the bead before they sent their message. This encouraged the children to think about the message they wanted to send in order to facilitate fluent initiation of the message. It took Francis approximately 3 sessions to learn to move the bead before saying his message. By the end of the term, Francis was able to send one message at a time without the beads in a highly structured activity, such as "show & tell" where the children were told the number of messages they were required to send. In unstructured situations which elicited spontaneous conversation, Francis sometimes required verbal scaffolding in order to send one message at a time. Even when sending one message at a time, Francis was often dysfluent. However, it was noted that over the term the number of repetitions decreased in activities which incorporated the use of the beads.

Goal #3: To facilitate easy speech through modification of hard messages.

Smooth messages sent by the children during any activity were verbally reinforced for easy speech. Children were asked to revise hard or bumpy messages. Revisions involved the child repeating the message in unison with the clinician, following a model or on their own depending on their ability. Francis displayed considerable difficulty initiating messages as noted by the use of hard starts, prolongation of sounds and numerous interjections. Ms. Carver indicated, during the mid-term conference, that Francis was utilizing sound prolongations, as well as, the word "actually" as an interjection more frequently than noticed in the past. Such observations were also noticed in the therapy sessions. Francis was able to revise hard messages when the clinician initiated the message with him and continued to mouth the message rather than verbalizing it with him. Some dysfluencies continued to be present during revisions, though fewer in number. It was also noted that Francis was more fluent when engaging in spontaneous conversation than when responding to questions.

Goal #4: To encourage positive attitudes and feelings about talking.

Mottoes were used to facilitate the above goal and were reviewed in every session. The mottoes were: (1) "We like talking!", (2) "We send good messages!", and (3) "Easy does it!" These were used to reflect group participation and to remind the children that talking is important. The use of "good messages" in the second motto was to reemphasize the significance of the clinician's reinforcement, since "good message" was frequently used as reinforcement for messages that were coherent. The last motto was used to remind the children to make talking easy. Francis's contribution to the group increased significantly as the term progressed. For example, in the initial few sessions, Francis did not sing spontaneously with the group. However, by the end of the term, he sang both with the group and independently. Francis volunteered to say a motto independently in front of the group more frequently as the term

(Continued)

progressed. As the demands on the children increased from spontaneously produced messages to responding to questions, Francis started to avoid responding by saying "I don't know." An increase in the use of hard starts at the beginning of words, prolongations especially for "I," and the interjection "actually" was also noted.

Goal #5: To retell a story with increased fluency by answering story chain questions.

The clinician told a story and then had the children answer story chain questions (e.g., Who? Where? When? What happened? and How did it end?) in order to retell the story to the group. The clinician verbally asked the questions while pointing to question representations and then provided a carrier phrase to facilitate the child's fluency. Francis was able to respond to Who? When? Where? and How did it end? without difficulty although his messages contained some dysfluencies. When responding to the question "What happened?" he often responded "I don't know." It was felt that this was an attempt to avoid answering the question, perhaps because he feared he would be dysfluent. Francis required the use of a carrier phrase provided by the clinician to facilitate the production of easy messages.

Goal #6: To demonstrate the ability to use easy, more fluent speech while motorically involved in an activity.

Clinicians attempted to elicit conversation from the children while they were completing a craft. This was a more challenging speaking environment for the children since they were required to do two things at once (i.e., speak and make a craft). By the end of term, the activities focused on requiring the children to interact with one another, while involved in manipulating objects. Clinicians verbally reinforced easy messages sent by the children. When the activity allowed for spontaneous conversation and interaction, Francis was able to remain fairly fluent. However, when asked a question, he became more dysfluent. The dysfluencies consisted of hard starts, interjections, prolongations and/or repetitions. It was noted that Francis was less attentive when the parents joined the group. It was observed that he had difficulty sitting still and diverted his attention toward his mother relying on her to answer for him.

Goal #7: To act as a liaison with Francis's school in order to coordinate program planning.

A school visit was conducted on November 13, 1995. Upon arrival, the clinicians observed Francis interacting with classmates and Ms. Winters, the teacher, during "carpet time" and during an activity where students made a Santa Claus craft at their tables. The classroom environment was an open concept (i.e., there were 2 classes in one room) and there were a large number of students in each class; hence, the noise level was above average. Ms. Carver was present in the classroom for carpet time. Francis was required to discuss a weekend event and read from his journal in front of the class. Francis was fluent when reading with some assistance from his teacher. He displayed more dysfluencies when responding to questions posed by peers and, at this time, he tended to look to his mother for assistance in responding. Ms. Carver did not provide Francis with a specific response, although she did provide clues to facilitate the generation of a response. When seated on the carpet with classmates, after Ms. Carver had left the room, Francis responded "I don't know" to a question posed to him by Mrs. Winters. This observation was consistent with what Mrs. Winters reported. She felt that Francis may be avoiding some talking situations because of his fluency difficulties. During the craft, Francis spoke little with peers at his table, but spoke freely with clinicians. His speech, at this time, consisted of numerous hard starts and repetitions. Francis was able to attend well during the craft activity. Mrs. Winters reported that she had not noticed changes in Francis's fluency recently. She indicated that he seemed to be more dysfluent when responding to questions than when making informal comments and that she had not noticed more dysfluencies when speaking in front of the class compared to interacting with peers. Mrs. Winters stated that she often responds to Francis's dysfluencies by asking him to speak louder. She further indicated that his peers do not react to his dysfluencies.

(Continued)

SUMMARY & RECOMMENDATIONS

The amount of Francis's dysfluencies have increased since his attendance in the intensive fluency program in July, 1995. However, number of dysfluencies remained constant throughout this term. A slight increase in the following types of dysfluencies were observed: hard starts, prolongations and interjections. Francis was successful at modifying hard messages when speaking in unison with the clinician. He was also able to send one message at a time during structured situations. Francis interacted appropriately with group members during most activities, but had more difficulty when parents were present. By the end of term, Francis displayed a significant improvement in his ability to attend and to sit still during the session. It was recommended that Francis receive individual fluency therapy in January, 1996. Participation in some aspects of the fluency group could be incorporated in order to provide him with the opportunity to interact with same aged peers while continuing to work on facilitating fluency. Individual therapy would provide more specific and direct treatment as Francis is becoming increasingly aware of his dysfluencies. Therapy could focus on modifying messages to make them easier and improving Francis's ability to respond to questions with fewer dysfluencies. These recommendations were discussed with Ms. Carver on November 6, 1995, and she was in agreement with them.

[signature]
Jane Smith, HBSc
Student Clinician

[signature]
Diane Brown, Ph.D.
Psychologist/Speech Pathologist
CCC-SLP, Reg. OSLA, SLP(C)
Clinical Supervisor

[signature]
John Murray, MA CCC-SLP
Speech Language Pathologist
Reg. OSLA S-LP(C)

of the sorts of everyday (public and private) discursive practice that is both the medium and the outcome of the ways in which we are organized socially. Discourse, rhetorical, and social analysis provides a means for critiquing, participating in, and communicating the consequences of these practices. First, critique is based on an explicit analysis that is capable of identifying patterns in discursive practice; determining their linguistic, rhetorical, and social functions; and demonstrating the relationship between the patterns and between the discoursal, rhetorical, and social relevance of each. Second, analysis implies participation: No analysis operates "objectively" outside the practices it seeks to illuminate. A text can perform several different functions in the context of analysis: It can be an exemplar of a register; an object of criticism; a site for the discussion of power, authority, or ideology; a "puzzle" to be solved; and so on. Depending on what the purposes of analysis are, who is conducting it, and what tools are brought to bear in analysis, the text functions differently, but in every case, analysis participates "in" and "with" the text because it produces knowledge that becomes a part of the resources we have to draw on in responding to similar and related texts. Finally, the vocabularies of discourse analysis and of rhetorical and social theory provide a means for communicating analyses. Along the way, here, I have demonstrated that each perspective shares the substance of the text and each provides tools and vocabularies with which to identify and explain the significance of patterns in discursive practice.

Note

1. In 1989, the Canadian Federation for the Humanities (an academic society) established "The Corporate Humanist Awards" to "recognize exceptional examples of humanistic values in Canadian business life" (Canadian Federation for the Humanities, 1996, p. 9). One of the awards—the Text Award—is for the "best piece of writing by a corporation, bearing on business or related matters [in which] jurors look for the philosophical virtues of breadth of vision and clarity of thought, and the literary virtues of imagination and strength of expression." The 1995 award (for an English text) was given to Allan R. Taylor, Chair and CEO of Royal Bank, for an address he made to the Montreal Neurological Institute and Hospital. It was titled "The Company and Society; Investing in the Future."

6 Integrating Theoretical Resources and Critical Practices

In my introduction to this book, I quoted a statement by Burke—"The symbolic act is the dancing of an attitude"—to set the stage for the chapters that followed. We have seen how each of our three theories—discoursal, rhetorical, and social—is concerned with the symbolic. Discourse analysis interprets instances of text in relation to systems of meaning-making resources. Rhetorical analysis focuses on the role and nature of symbolic systems in enabling and constraining our means of identification and consubstantiation. Social theory recognizes the symbolic as both a constituent of social orders and a major means through which social orders are produced and reproduced.

Each of these perspectives also emphasizes the active nature of text—its "dance." Discourse analysis interprets linguistic patterns in text according to the social functions they perform in contexts of their use. Rhetorical analysis stresses that attitude itself (the product of rhetorical practices) is an incipient act that is analyzable in terms of drama. Social theory emphasizes that social systems and structures—including the distribution of symbolic capital—can be theorized adequately only through an understanding of the nature of practice, of acts.

Finally, each of these perspectives foregrounds the relationship between symbolic acts and attitude. Even when analyzing the ideational

179

and textual functions of text (as distinct from the interpersonal, which clearly involves the construction of attitude), I have stressed the attitudinal and orientational aspects of these meaning-making resources (e.g., characterizing the situation of handing in a late paper in terms of **mental** processes is an index of the student's attitude toward what counts as a "legitimate" explanation). Burke's grammar, rhetoric, and logology all focus on symbolic acts as the "constant striking of attitudes." Social theory assumes a fundamental link between social practices and the interests, orientations, and attitudes of agents: Even the most highly structured social practices (e.g., gift exchange) are meaningful for social agents exactly because they allow for interest, orientation, and attitude.

I also began this book with an instance of text—the student note. I did so because each of the perspectives' takes on the nature of the symbolic act as "the dancing of an attitude" can be borne out only with reference to the unique properties of an instance of text. The resources of systems (i.e., its structures) do not match up in a one-to-one correspondence with their functions: We cannot "read off" the instantial functions of structures like items on a checklist. Function is a product of situated, contextualized resources. This is particularly important when it comes to understanding the function of "attitude" in instances of text.

The linguistic resources for meaning-making are not in and of themselves attitudinal: Particular combinations of these resources in relation to particular situational contexts construct attitude. The point about the student's construction of the situation in terms of **mental** processes exemplifies this: **Mental** processes are not inherently attitudinal, but in instances of text they can be interpreted as partially constitutive of attitude (and interest, orientation, and so on) in relation to other resources instantiated in the text and in relation to the field, tenor, and mode characteristics of the situation.

The same goes for a rhetorical analysis: The pentad and ratios, substance, identification, addressivity, and consequences of symbolic action conducted in terms of particular logonomic systems are the resources of rhetorical acts. Only by identifying and interpreting particular ratios, particular substances, particular occasions of addressivity, and so on, in instances of text, can the local "logic" of attitude, orientation, and interest be gleaned. For example, the **agent:agency** ratio of the Royal Bank booklets projected readers as expert agents because they are armed with the bank's expert advice and characterized readers in terms of **directional** substance that declares that one unequivocally "is" what one is because of where one is headed. This ratio and substance have particular meanings in the context of the booklets that would not necessarily be relevant in different texts.

Likewise, social theory recognizes that what interests, attitudes, and orientations are at risk in a given situation are determinable only through careful attention to the distinctive characteristics of the particular field, habitus, and types of symbolic capital concerned. For example, my analysis of the speech pathology report recognizes that what types of symbolic capital are recognized as legitimate in the therapy situation depends upon how the field is constructed by participants (the clinicians, the mother, and so on). That is, when different types of symbolic capital are considered relevant to the field of diagnosis and therapy (for example, a different interpretation of what constitutes "spontaneous conversation"), the structure of the field changes—different attitudes, responses, and orientations result. We may move from an "assured" reading to a "resistant" one, for example, when we actively seek out contradictions and antinomies in the report, as I do in my analysis. Different readings imply different responses to the report, both of which affect the distribution and function of symbolic resources in the field.

In the remainder of this conclusion, I will pick up on these themes: the shared foci of the three perspectives, the relationship between resources and instances of symbolic action, and the purposes and results of close reading and critical analysis.

Systemic, Functional, and Social Characteristics

Chapters 2 to 4 outlined the theoretical resources for analyzing text. Chapter 5 put these resources into practice by analyzing several text instances. In both cases, I have characterized text as systemic, functional, and social. The three theoretical perspectives this book advocates share a concern for these characteristics. Each provides a framework for identifying and interpreting text patterns that index its systemic, functional, and social nature. In the following three sections, I will review how each of the perspectives addresses the systemic, functional, and social characteristics of text.

SYSTEMIC FEATURES

I have characterized systems, in general, as resources for meaning-making. Instances of text draw on (instantiate) the resources of a variety of systems: systems for linguistic meaning-making, for rhetorical acts, and for social practices. Systems characterize the potentials for meaning-making acts—the available choices, combinations, and relational values of meaningful elements.

From the point of view of discourse and linguistic meaning-making, we recognize that texts instantiate the resources of a language system (sounding, wording, and meaning resources), the particular registerial resources appropriate to the situation of which the text is a part (the typical ideational, interpersonal, and textual resources that pattern with the field, tenor, and mode of the situation), and the resources for linking one text to another and to the patterns of social activity typical of our communities (intertextual resources).

From a rhetorical perspective, we recognize that instances of symbolic acts draw on grammatical, rhetorical, and logonomic resources. The potentials associated with choices in the pentad, ratios, and substance are resources for a particular text's reflection, selection, and deflection of "reality" (Burke, 1966, p. 45). Hierarchy and division in the social order are a resource for the rhetorical forms of addressivity, transformation, and identification in instances of rhetorical acts: What kinds of consubstantiation are possible, and how these will be effected in text, depend upon the social systems at risk in the rhetorical act. Logonomic systems of all types (from "language" in general to specific, "local" logonomic systems initiated by individual texts) systematically enable particular "terministic screens," with their attendant entelechies for perfection, guilt, and hierarchy, to function in instances of text.

Our social perspective posited a dialectic between systems of resources and the practices they enable and constrain. The general social resources of habitus and field enable practices of distinction, taste, and the exercising of certain forms of capital. The specifically symbolic resources of linguistic habitus force recognition and misrecognition of forms of symbolic capital and power. Social systems and social practices are related by the duality of structure: Practices are both the medium of production and reproduction of social systems and the outcome of the structure of those systems.

FUNCTIONAL FEATURES

The features of discoursal, rhetorical, and social systems are interpreted as functional features: Forms and structures are identified and interpreted with reference to what they "do" in instances of text.

Discourse analysis organizes its description of linguistic resources in terms of functions by recognizing that language is called upon extrinsically (that is, in contexts of its use) to represent processes, participants, and circumstances; to construct social relations and indicate orientation; and to organize text as internally cohesive and externally (in relation to its context) coherent. Discourse analysis understands linguistic meaning as function in context. For example, the "meaning" of question speech function is that it assigns a particular speech role to the speaker and the hearer; the "meaning" of a sentence's theme is that it is the point of departure, the "what-I-want-to-tell-you-about-is," and some other element is not. The structures of instances of text exhibit the three types of functional meaning—ideational, interpersonal, and textual—simultaneously.

Rhetoric posits identification as the overall function of rhetorical acts. Rhetorical acts function to bring together what was formerly divided or divide what was formally united. To be united in identification is to share substance—to be consubstantial by construing "reality" in the same terms. The resources of grammar, rhetoric, and logology all conspire in rhetorical acts to realize identification and consubstantiation. Rhetoric does not reduce the symbolic act to a unifunctional act of "persuasion." Because the resources drawn upon in rhetorical acts are complex and diverse (e.g., ratios, substances, hierarchies, logonomic systems) and each performs unique functions in the act (e.g., ratios "give reason"; substances posit inalienable "being"; hierarchies structure mystery and division; logonomic systems graft perfection, guilt, and hierarchy onto their users; and so on), identification is realized through multiple functions.

The concept of function is central to social theory not as a mode of explanation positing that social systems and structures "exist" to fulfill the functional "needs" of social agents (e.g., institutions exist because we "need" to organize ourselves institutionally) but as a concept with which to recognize that social systems and structures—including habitus and linguistic habitus, and other resources—are best characterized in terms of how they function in particular social contexts. Habitus, for example, is functional because it *generates* practices; linguistic habitus *generates* certain discursive practices that, in relation to particular fields, may or may not function in such a way as to increase a speaker's symbolic capital. Similarly, "field" is not a static concept that identifies the organization of a social context in a gridlike fashion: Field performs social functions by organizing relations among social agents, distributing the volume and determining the nature of their economic and symbolic capital, and governing the relative value of their capital.

SOCIAL FEATURES

Throughout this book I have continually emphasized and illustrated that symbolic acts are social acts. In fact, it is because symbolic acts are social that we have any reason to inquire into their characteristics and functions in the first place. Texts index and construct power relations, forms of domination and authority; they produce, reproduce, and legitimate ideologies; they mark the ways in which different groups are classified and the way different groups classify themselves and others— they are the product of, and the medium for, our vision and division of social "reality."

Discourse analysis attends to the social characteristics of text in terms of its description of systems of linguistic resources and the functions they perform in context. Both resources and functions are considered social phenomena in origins, contexts, and effects. The origins of linguistic meaning-making systems are social because they have evolved in relation to and have been shaped by socially situated discoursal practice over time. The situational demands that are made upon language resources are social ones—the nature of the activity, the social relationships, and the demands upon the medium of communication in context. These demands shape what can be done with the resources of the system. The meaning potentials of the functions of language—what they can do in actual instances—also are bound by the real social conditions of the situation: "Meaning" is function in social context. At the same time, the functions of text in context always have social consequences. Discourse analysis therefore investigates the resources of linguistic meaning-making systems as socially constituted potentials (i.e., social origins), it recognizes that functional meaning is constrained by the structure of social situations (i.e., social contexts), and it analyzes how text constructs social activities and relations (i.e., social effects).

Rhetorical analysis assumes that every rhetorical act bears relations both to division and hierarchy in the social order and to the symbol systems that are a major means through which social orders are structured and coordinated. The divisions that identification and consubstantiation attend to are social divisions: A government legitimates its involvement in a war, a political party attempts to garner support from groups traditionally supportive of other parties, new expert testimony tips an indecisive jury toward a guilty verdict, a homosexual love story removes or confirms bigotry and prejudice, and so on. Instances of rhetorical acts therefore have social consequences because they contribute to the production and reproduction of social orders. Burke (1966) comments: "All terminologies must implicitly or explicitly embody choices between the principle of continuity and the principle of discontinuity" (p. 50). Ultimately, continuity and discontinuity—identification or division—are the principles underlying the demarcation of class, group, institution, tradition, category, denomination, and so on—all of which are social boundaries.

Social theory attends to the social characteristics of text practices by not bracketing off symbolic action from social action, that is, by not looking upon discourse as a mere representation of some pre-existing social reality. Two aspects of social theory are especially relevant here. First, symbolic action is both a product of, and a medium for, the production and reproduction of social orders. Linguistic habitus, for example, endows certain speakers with symbolic power in relation to certain fields. At the same time, the exercise of that power also reproduces and legitimates the organization of the field. In other words, symbolic action (for example, in the form of text and text exchange) is both a phenomenon of social orders and a major constituent of social orders. Second—and this is how social theory creates a special impetus for critical analysis—symbolic productions (e.g., texts, discourses) invite misrecognition; that is, they "euphemize" (to use Bourdieu's term) the very real, contested, and inequitable divisions of the social order. Bourdieu (1991) gives an example:

> The university system of classification [i.e., its discourses and discursive practices], which mobilizes in misrecognizable form the objective [i.e., "real"] divisions of the social structure and especially the division of labour, in both theory and practice, converts social properties into natural properties. The truly ideological effect consists precisely in the imposition of political systems of classification beneath the legitimate appearance of philosophical, religious, legal (etc.) taxonomies [i.e., discourses]. Symbolic systems owe their distinctive power to the fact that the relations of power expressed through them are manifested only in the misrecognizable form of relations of meaning (displacement). (pp. 169-170)

I have argued, especially in the analyses of Chapter 5, that the structure of social relations is homologous to the discoursal and rhetorical patterns of texts and that the task of critical analysis is to make the homologies explicit by mapping out the discoursal and rhetorical processes that correspond to and realize social divisions.

Resources and Practices of Theory

This section explores the whole framework for discoursal, rhetorical, and social analysis metatheoretically. My aim here is to present the reader with ways of thinking about the **resources** of the framework and the kinds of analytical and critical **practices** that it enables. I will discuss how each of the three theories addresses systemic, functional, and social analysis in special configurations that give unique emphasis to one of these general textual characteristics. I will argue that the complementarity among the three theories results in a framework that is more generative than one that consists of three theories simply added together. I then consider the framework as a resource of requisite **diversity, systematicity, and applicability** for attending to text and context relations. I end with recommendations concerning the kinds of practices that such a framework enables: **critical, participatory,** and **communicative** practices.

SIMILARITY AND DIFFERENCE

I have argued that all three theories are capable of systematically and explicitly identifying and interpreting the systemic, functional, and social characteristics of texts and text practices. Each theory, however, deals with these characteristics in different ways: Different emphasis is given to certain elements of text and text practices. I see these different points of emphasis as an opportunity to integrate the three theories into one complementary framework.

Discourse analysis focuses on the functional properties and social origins, contexts, and effects of instantiated linguistic resources through the lens of the systemic: Its vocabulary is best suited to identifying and interpreting text patterns with reference to how they instantiate system resources. For example, my analysis of the social meanings of Inclusion and Promotion in the Royal Bank booklets focused on the function of patterns of linguistic structures that realized these meanings. In each case, the interpretation of the linguistic structures depends upon reading the instantiated forms against the potentials of the system. For example, a part of the Inclusion pattern in the introductory letters involved ascribing

mental processes to the reader (e.g., *you always dreamed of, you're thinking, you'll prefer*). These can be interpreted as a part of Inclusion in the light of different systemic resources, namely, the system of differences among **mental, action,** and **relational** processes; the pronoun system (i.e., first-, second-, and third-person pronouns and subjective, objective, and possessive case); and the resources of register (i.e., the expectation that in most *other* registers one does not normally ascribe mental processes to the second person, e.g., *you'll prefer, you're thinking*). So, while attending to the social effects and the contextual functions of instantiated linguistic structures, discourse analysis is always attempting to relate the text (i.e., the instance) to the systems that enable it.

Rhetorical analysis focuses on the symbolic systems at risk in, and the social consequences that result from, rhetorical acts through the lens of the functional: Its vocabulary is best suited to identifying and interpreting text patterns with reference to how they function to initiate identification and consubstantiation through transformations in attitude, orientation, and perspective. Burke's rhetoric is a rhetoric of the *act*—the function of symbol-use by symbol-using animals. The act is always considered from the point of view of what resources are drawn upon to frame the act (i.e., what ratios and substances lead to what kind of *in terms of?*) and what social consequences result from the act (i.e., how do the logonomic systems involved structure hierarchy, guilt, and perfection?). Rhetorical analysis foregrounds the function of symbolic action in overcoming division. For example, my rhetorical analysis of the Saturn advertisement focused on the text's attempts to have readers identify with June—to construct themselves in similar, albeit contradictory, terms. My rhetorical analysis of the Royal Bank booklets focused on how the text functioned (a) to create a "new" identity for its readers—the "expert" financial agent, but also (b) to frame the possibilities for identification with such an agent in a system of rules and procedures (e.g., expert financial planning) with an entelechy of perfection impossible for any one individual's practice to satisfy. Similarly, my rhetorical analysis of the speech pathology report explored the function of its construction of "goals" in terms of a **purpose:act** ratio that actually, upon close analysis, created a circularity—the purpose turned out to not be a purpose at all, but another kind of act (e.g., *Goal #7: To act as a liaison with Francis's school in order to coordinate program planning*). The consequence of such a construction is that readers are being asked to identify with (see in similar terms) a goal that can be fulfilled only in a closed system concerning the design of the clinic and its reporting structure; that is, the goal has nothing to do with Francis's goals. In each of these three examples (Saturn, Royal Bank, speech pathology report), the function of the text has been to have readers become consubstantial with (i.e., identify with) paradoxical, contradictory, and antinomic terms.

Social analysis focuses on the functions of the instantiated (i.e., practiced) resources of social systems and structures through— evidently—the lens of the social: The vocabulary of social theory is less a vocabulary for interpreting the structures and patterns of text (it relies on discourse and rhetoric for this terminology) than it is a vocabulary for marking the social consequences of these structures and patterns *and* for being explicit about the homologies between social practices and symbolic practices. Bourdieu's terms for the types of social practice that habitus, field, and linguistic habitus (as resources) enable are terms that identify the consequences of the practices as well: distinction and taste, symbolic power (violence) and misrecognition. The resources and practices of the social are related dialectically in instances of social practice: Habitus and field structure the classificatory practices of social agents (i.e., their exercising of taste and distinction), while at the same time, those practices produce and reproduce specific types of habitus and the organization of specific fields. For example, the Saturn advertisement invites readers to classify social agents with a set of recognizable binary oppositions (e.g., white/black, rational/emotional, male/female, able-bodied/disabled, and so on). It relies on, and appeals to, the reader's practical sense of these oppositions in its efforts to "recoup" or "valorize" the traditionally dominated and pejorative second term of each of the binaries. By doing so, the advertisement reproduces these oppositions (i.e., it instantiates them) but also implicitly attempts to restructure them (i.e., by valorizing the dominated term); hence, the text is a site of production and reproduction of classificatory schemes that mark the social order. Social theory quite rightly also emphasizes that such a practice trades on misrecognition; that is, the binary oppositions are treated *as if* they were simple representational alternatives that make the advertisement communicative (i.e., "Do you understand? June is rational *and* emotional. Saturn cars let you have both!"), rather than principles of division that are homologous to real, inequitable oppositions and divisions in the social (i.e., "In general, black, disabled, and heavyset women are an unfairly disadvantaged and stigmatized group").

Each of the three theories of analysis (discoursal, rhetorical, and social) uniquely focuses on one of the text's general characteristics (systemic, functional, and social)—not to the exclusion of the other characteristics, but with one characteristic made most salient in relation to the other two. Focusing on the social consequences of text practices, for example, still involves looking at the functions of text patterns in context (the social is all about "doing") and looking at the systems of resources that are drawn upon (because the resources are systemic, they have value and meaning-potential with reference to other resources). At the same time, the three theories themselves are integrated. I have argued for and demonstrated that text analysis profits from being able to link the insights of discoursal, rhetorical, and social analysis. The three share in the substance of the text but are also integrated in analysis. For example, my analysis of the speech pathology report drew connections between antinomies that had a discoursal, rhetorical, and social dimension. At the level of discourse, I showed how the report used the technical vocabulary of speech pathology inconsistently (i.e., without clearly signaled taxonomic arrangement of terms or obvious collocational sets). This was interpreted rhetorically as a part of the report's invitation to identify with an antinomic image of perfection (i.e., the terms functioned contradictorily in characterizing Francis as "dysfluent"), and these patterns were interpreted in social terms as indicative of the symbolic struggle endemic to the field of speech pathology and expert diagnosis of "dysfluency" (i.e., a part of speech pathologists' symbolic power is the power to have these antinomies recognized as "natural" and legitimate whether they are contradictory or not).

I present this example of how the three theories are integrated not so much to suggest that they be related in ways that are determined by the theories themselves (i.e., that the theories contain axioms that determine their relations to other theories) but to suggest that they *can* be related in these ways depending on the texts being analyzed and the purposes of analysis. I take up this issue in a discussion of the resources of an integrated discoursal, rhetorical, and social theory in the next section.

RESOURCES: DIVERSITY, SYSTEMATICITY, AND APPLICABILITY

An integrated theory for the close analysis of everyday written texts must have certain properties to produce relevant analyses. It must be

diverse to respond to the complexity of text, text types, and situations of text exchange; it must be **systematic** to enable the statements produced by analysis to be related to one another consistently; and it must be **applicable** in that it enable analysts to produce insights about texts that go beyond a mere labeling of the text. Taken together, discoursal, rhetorical, and social analysis, and their attendant special foci on the systemic, functional, and social characteristics of text and text practices, present a diverse, systematic, and applicable framework for analyzing text in context.

The framework responds to the **diversity** and complexity of text first of all by attending to it as a discoursal, rhetorical, and social practice. Second, the shared substance of text (i.e., a common object of analysis) is identified and interpreted from three different, but related (or relatable), points of view. For example, the binary oppositions of the Saturn advertisement are analyzed as products of a discoursal practice: June is represented predominantly through **mental** and **relational** processes—she does not act much; hence, the ideational patterns of the text help construct the "dynamism" versus "stasis" opposition. The binary oppositions are also analyzed in rhetorical terms that extend their interpretation into the realm of their symbolic functions; for example, readers are asked to identify with a figure (a social "type") who is defined in terms of "divided" **substance** (i.e., June is *both* "rational" *and* "emotional," and this is construed as ironic because one could not be both); hence, the choice of substance in the text helps construct the text's central fantasy, in which one can take on the characteristics of both terms of an opposition (i.e., one can "be" *both* A *and* B in a situation and with a structure that normally characterizes people as *either* A *or* B). The binary oppositions were also analyzed as a form of symbolic power that extends their analysis into the realm of social consequence. For example, the advertisement controls representation of types of social agents through binary oppositions but also operates as if the binaries could cease to be oppositional. It is a prime example of what Bourdieu (1991) means by "concealing the function of division beneath the function of communication" (p. 167). The oppositions are "real"—they do operate in the divisions of agents in the social order. By suggesting, however, that one can champion the depreciated term of the opposition or, better yet, be represented by both of the terms, a real division is turned into a set of nonconsequential communicative alternatives (i.e., "mere" labels for distinction). I think that these discoursal, rhetorical, and social observations show that the resources of the theories can both (a) identify and interpret text patterns from the point of view of the individual theories—that is, they interpret diversely—and (b) complement one another by interpreting the same phenomena, but not repeating or simply relabeling them; that is, the efficacy of observations of the same phenomena comes in the ability to show different, but related, consequences.

Each of the three theories is **systematic;** that is, each consistently and explicitly identifies and interprets text patterns and practices. Each theory presents well-worked-out vocabularies for marking (identifying) text patterns. The terms of each individual theory have specific relations between them. I have also attempted to be explicit about the relations among the vocabularies of the three theories by showing how each responds to particular shared features of texts and text practices. I have used two organizing principles for outlining the theories individually and in relation to one another: The vocabularies of each theory are organized in terms of (a) **resources** (including "systems" and "structures") and **functions** (including "practices"), and (b) their application to the **systemic, functional,** and **social** characteristics of texts and text practices. These organizing principles cannot guarantee that an analysis is "right" or "wrong," but it may be used to decide (in some context of analysis) whether or not the analysis is useful or valid or interesting with reference to these criteria. Theories are (or ought to be) open and flexible systems, not deterministic regimes. This is especially the case when it comes to trying to theorize such a dynamic process as symbolic action.

The combination of discoursal, rhetorical, and social theory presented here offers, I hope, increased opportunities for **applicability.** An applicable theory enables analysts to provide evidence for their insights about text; it enables them to engage the theory with a variety of text phenomena (i.e., different aspects of texts and different types of texts); and it creates opportunities for applications that are relevant to more than one approach to text (i.e., different critical purposes, different disciplines, and so on). In each of my extended analyses in Chapter 5, I provided evidence and arguments for my critical interpretations of the texts. I have analyzed a variety of written texts, but this is not a book about any specific type of text. The principles and tools of analysis, I believe, can be extended to a variety of text types, text practices, and situations. Applying the three theories together offers different opportunities for creating salience in analysis because the points of entry are increased when we approach text from three perspectives. Because there are more questions that can be asked with three related approaches than with any one single approach, the points of connection for analysts coming from diverse disciplines increase.

PRACTICES: CRITIQUE, PARTICIPATION, AND COMMUNICATION

I have outlined the resources of an integrated discoursal, rhetorical, and social framework for analysis, and I have given examples of it in practice by analyzing several texts. My hope is that readers will be able to use the framework I have outlined in ways that enrich their own critical practice. I will conclude with some general remarks that may help orient readers to critical practice. The framework, as a resource, enables practices of **critique, participation,** and **communication.**

By identifying and interpreting text patterns with a diverse, systematic, and applicable theory, analysts are able to make critical judgments concerning the conditions and consequences of textual practice. Each of the three theories provides a foundation upon which an explicit **critique** can be built.

Discourse analysis recognizes text making, exchanging, and understanding as "choice"—that is, as a selection from systems of resources for making meaning. This conception allows analysts to ask questions not only about why certain resources are chosen and with what effect, but also about why certain resources were *not* chosen. Discourse analysis is largely a comparative practice: We interpret instantiated resources with reference to the wider, more encompassing systems of resources. In other words, choice can be understood as initiating difference: What is chosen is different from what could be chosen. A critical impetus is created when we ask about the effects and consequences of difference: How would the text mean if it used other resources? What are the differences between what is chosen and what could be chosen in similar contexts?

Rhetorical theory posits that every text, while attempting to represent "reality," selects and deflects "reality" (Burke, 1945/1969a, p. 59). Rhetoric provides us with a system for recognizing that text is always framed *in terms of;* that is, it relies on selected ratios and substances, both of which demonstrate that there is no *one* way to represent reality and orient ourselves and our audiences to it. Again, the critical impetus arises with the recognition of difference: One substance is different from another; one ratio is different from other ratios. The opportunity for critique resides in explicating these differences, in recognizing that particular substances and ratios, for example, slant perspective one way and not another, that particular motives are the product of one vision of the social and not another.

Social analysis stresses the homologies between social and symbolic practice. Text cannot be treated as an "arbitrary" representation of the social, that is, unmotivated by it. Neither can it be simply passed off as "natural," that is, as simply a mirror representation of "how things really are" and not a motivated legitimation of existing divisions in the social order. Text representation is both a product of and a site for the reproduction of the divisions of power, capital, and distinction in social life. Critique involves identifying those instances where text functions *as if* it were "mere" representation ("natural" or "arbitrary"), explicating the conditions under which this misrecognition occurs, and exploring its social consequences for the social agents involved.

The integrated theory for discoursal, social, and rhetorical analysis also enables forms of **participation** with the texts being analyzed and the contexts of which they are a part. My point here is a simple and hopeful one: Critical analysis produces new perspectives on the kinds of everyday texts we all make and exchange as a routine part of our day-to-day lives. When we create new knowledge about text, we create new ways to be involved with text—as readers, writers, teachers, students, and critics. I purposefully do not lay out schemes for what form that new knowledge will take or how it should be used: These are the concerns of those who would undertake analysis, in particular contexts, for particular purposes.

Finally, the integrated framework presents us with a means for **communicating** analyses—for constructing an audience with vested interest in understanding the discoursal, rhetorical, and social characteristics of text. I have laid out the vocabularies of the individual theories and the points of connection among them; together these constitute a register (a sublanguage) for the analysis of the rhetoric of discourse as social practice. It is subject to the same conditions of any language: Its resources are combined in typical and recurring ways, its resources are open to being recombined in response to new exigencies, it is a generative system, it is an open system that will continually evolve, and it is also a language that is subject to critical analysis itself.

Postscript

This book—the theoretical resources it outlines, the analytical practices it instantiates, and the integration of theories it proposes—is itself a reflection, selection, and (consequentially) a deflection of a "reality" of everyday texts. It speaks about the analysis and critique of everyday texts *in terms of* discoursal, rhetorical, and social functions. The way I lay out the three perspectives, show connections among them, and practice analysis with them represents—necessarily—only one way of going about analyzing everyday texts. So much more needs to be done—not only within the constraints of the integrated theory presented here but also with reference to other crucial features of everyday texts: investigating other modes (e.g., *spoken* everyday texts); developing other perspectives on the reception and production of texts (e.g., how particular readers respond to particular texts); theorizing the interaction of different semiotic modalities in text production, exchange, and reception (e.g., the interaction of visual, verbal, gestural, and material semiosis); exploring the diachronic developments within and between certain registers (e.g., variation in advertising registers); and so on.

Even the selections I make within the fields of discourse analysis, rhetorical theory, and social theory stand as a deflection of other concerns, inventories, and methods that have been pursued in these disciplines. It can only be so. Deflection—in this case, drawing attention to this approach rather than that approach—need not be read as an attempt to suppress an "other." Although I have not touched on narrative theory, poetics, conversational analysis, pragmatics, sociolinguistics, other types of discourse analysis, classical rhetoric, or other types of social theory, I acknowledge their relevance to this project and keep all doors open. By systematically outlining the inventories of the theories I do use, however, and showing how they may be applied (roughly, Chapters 2 to 4), by presenting extended applications (the three cases in Chapter 5), and by presenting a model for both evaluating and understanding their complementarity (Chapter 6), I am attempting to give you at least one explicit way to mark differences that make a difference in text and text practices. This book is as much a logonomic system as any it investigates. It practices its attitudes—it is a locus of motives that indicate my orientation. An orientation marks a potential division—you may disagree with me, you may not share my interest, or you may go about analysis differently. I hope so. I don't stand where you stand. Nor are the reasons we do analysis necessarily the same. The way we do analysis also indexes our politics—it is unlikely that we share totally symmetrical perspectives. And your approach to text analysis, which presupposes a theory or theories, is no more "true" or "correct" than mine. What we do share, however—what makes us consubstantial—is everyday texts. We share them as social agents practicing in our communities: We make and exchange "mundane" texts daily. I am going to end by exploring a few important characteristics of everyday texts that indicate—to me, at least—both how and why we should be attentive to them not just as participants but also as analysts and critics.

Everyday texts are, by definition, quotidian, yet this does not make them trivial. Because they both reflect and shape our attitudes toward our worlds and one another, the consequences that attend everyday texts are serious, complex, and often far-reaching.

We tend to have a more or less practical knowledge of the everyday texts we engage with daily; that is, they are familiar to us because they are such a common component of our living. We embody them and they embody us. Given that the very "local" exigencies of the everyday text—the situations in which they unfold and that help make sense of—are immediate, practical, and real, the conditions and consequences of everyday texts are not hidden to us. The sheer substantiality, the materiality of text and context—from the intonation contours of our sarcastic tones to "gut" feelings about who gets to speak first around the dinner table—constitute, as habitus, a knowledge without concepts. Conditions and consequences may not be explicitly acknowledged or intended, but we nevertheless *feel* and *act* on them accordingly. Analysis and critique must recognize that the "meanings" of everyday texts are not "hidden" to participants. "Ideology," for example, does not have some hidden determinant that analysis uncovers; analysis does not magically produce power where there was none before; critique engages symbolic and material violence that have already harmed and may be continuing to harm. When it is doing its job, analysis and critique use a metalanguage to make arguments and gather evidence to speak about what is already initiated, felt, and experienced by text-makers and text-receivers. It does not replace text and the strategies of text production and reception—it reframes them in a language suited to the purposes of examination, comparison, classification, appreciation, and so on. Critique can occasionally contest the seemingly incontestable (i.e., "natural") only because there is already contest or struggle in the very objects and processes it analyzes—everyday texts.

References

Bateson, G. (1972). *Steps to an ecology of mind.* Toronto: Random House.

Bateson, G. (1979). *Mind and nature: A necessary unity.* New York: Dutton.

Bertelsen, D. (1993). Kenneth Burke's conception of reality: The process of transformation and its implications for rhetorical criticism. In J. W. Chesebro (Ed.), *Extensions of the Burkeian system.* Tuscaloosa: University of Alabama Press.

Bourdieu, P. (1984). *Distinction: A social critique of the judgement of taste.* Cambridge, MA: Harvard University Press.

Bourdieu, P. (1990a). *In other words: Essays towards a reflexive sociology.* Stanford, CA: Stanford University Press.

Bourdieu, P. (1990b). *The logic of practice.* Stanford, CA: Stanford University Press.

Bourdieu, P. (1991). *Language & symbolic power.* Cambridge, MA: Harvard University Press.

Burke, K. (1952). Mysticism as a solution to the poets' dilemma: Addendum. In S. R. Hopper (Ed.), *Spiritual problems in contemporary literature: A series of addresses and discussions.* New York: Institute for Religious and Social Studies.

Burke, K. (1966). *Language as symbolic action: Essays on life, literature, and method.* Berkeley and Los Angeles: University of California Press.

Burke, K. (1968a). *Counter statement* (3rd ed.). Berkeley and Los Angeles, CA: University of California Press. (Original work published 1931)

197

Burke, K. (1968b). Dramatism. In D. Sills (Ed.), *The international encyclopedia of the social sciences* (Vol. 7). New York: Macmillan.

Burke, K. (1969a). *A grammar of motives* (California edition). Berkeley and Los Angeles: University of California Press. (Original work published 1945)

Burke, K. (1969b). *A rhetoric of motives* (California edition). Berkeley and Los Angeles: University of California Press. (Original work published 1950)

Burke, K. (1970). *The rhetoric of religion: Studies in logology.* Berkeley and Los Angeles: University of California Press. (Original work published 1961)

Burke, K. (1972). *Dramatism and development.* Worcester, MA: Clark University Press.

Burke, K. (1973). *The philosophy of literary form: Studies in symbolic action* (3rd ed.). Berkeley and Los Angeles: University of California Press. (Original work published 1941)

Burke, K. (1984a). *Attitudes towards history* (3rd ed.). Berkeley and Los Angeles: University of California Press. (Original work published 1937)

Burke, K. (1984b). *Permanence and change: An anatomy of purpose* (4th ed.). Berkeley and Los Angeles: University of California Press. (Original work published 1935)

Burke, K. (1989). Poem. In H. W. Simons & T. Melia (Eds.), *The legacy of Kenneth Burke.* Madison: The University of Wisconsin Press.

Canadian Federation for the Humanities. (1996). 1995 Corporate Humanist Award. *Bulletin, 17*(2), 9.

Collins Cobuild English Grammar. (1990). London: Collins.

Cook, G. (1992). *The discourse of advertising.* London: Routledge.

DiYanni, P., & Hoy, C. (1995). *The Scribner handbook for writers.* Toronto: Allyn and Bacon.

Fairclough, N. (1989). *Language and power.* London: Longman.

Fairclough, N. (1992). *Discourse and social change.* Cambridge, UK: Polity Press.

Firth, J. R. (1964). *The tongues of men and speech.* London: Oxford University Press. (Original work published 1937)

Firth, J. R. (1968). *Selected papers of J. R. Firth 1952-1959* (F. R. Palmer, Ed.). Bloomington: Indiana University Press.

Gefvert, C. (1988). *The confident writer* (2nd ed.). New York: Norton.

Giddens, A. (1984). *The constitution of society: Outline of the theory of structuration.* Berkeley and Los Angeles: University of California Press.

Giddens, A. (1991). *Modernity and self-identity: Self and society in the late modern age.* Stanford, CA: Stanford University Press.

Gregory, M. (1985). Towards communication linguistics: A framework. In J. Benson & W. Greaves (Eds.), *Systemic perspectives on discourse.* Norwood, NJ: Ablex.

Gregory, M. (1988). Generic situation and register: A functional view of communication. In J. Benson & W. Greaves (Eds.), *Linguistics in a systemic perspective.* Philadelphia: John Benjamin.

Gregory, M. (1995). *Before and towards communication linguistics: Essays by Michael Gregory and associates* (J. S. Cha, Ed.). Seoul: Sookmyung Women's University.

Guffey, M., Rhodes, K., & Rogin, P. (1996). *Business communication: Process and product*. Scarborough, Ontario, Canada: Nelson Canada.

Halliday, M. A. K. (1978). *Language as social semiotic: The social interpretation of language and meaning*. London: Edward Arnold.

Halliday, M. A. K. (1989). Part A. In M. A. K. Halliday & R. Hasan, *Language, context, and text: Aspects of language in a social-semiotic perspective*. London: Oxford University Press.

Halliday, M. A. K. (1994). *An introduction to functional grammar* (2nd ed.). London: Edward Arnold.

Halliday, M. A. K., & Hasan, R. (1976). *Cohesion in English*. London: Longman.

Hinton, D. (Producer and Director). (1985). *Francis Bacon* (Video, London Weekend Television with RM Arts). Concord, MA: Home Vision.

Hodge, R., & Kress, G. (1988). *Social semiotics*. Ithaca, NY: Cornell University Press.

Lemke, J. L. (1985). Ideology, intertextuality, and the notion of register. In J. Benson & W. Greaves (Eds.), *Systemic perspectives on discourse*. Norwood, NJ: Ablex.

Lemke, J. L. (1992). Interpersonal meaning in discourse: Value orientations. In M. Davies & L. Ravelli (Eds.), *Advances in systemic linguistics: Recent theory and practice*. London: Pinter.

Lemke, J. L. (1995). *Textual politics: Discourse and social dynamics*. Bristol, PA: Taylor & Francis.

Martin, J. R. (1985). Process and text: Two aspects of human semiosis. In J. Benson & W. Greaves (Eds.), *Systemic perspectives on discourse*. Norwood, NJ: Ablex.

Schiffrin, D. (1994). *Approaches to discourse*. Oxford, UK: Blackwell.

Taylor, A. R. (1996). The company and society: Investing in the future. *Bulletin* [of the Canadian Federation for the Humanities], *17*(2), 17-22.

Thibault, P. (1991). *Social semiotics as praxis: Text, social meaning making, and Nabokov's Ada*. Minneapolis: University of Minnesota Press.

Wilden, A. (1987). *The rules are no game: The strategy of communication*. New York: Routledge & Kegan Paul.

Index

Act. *See* Pentad; Ratios
Action processes. *See* Process types and participant roles.
Addressivity, 73-77
  in Royal Bank financial advice booklets, 144-145
  in Saturn advertisement, 123-124
Advertising. *See* Saturn automobile advertisement
Agency. *See* Pentad; Ratios
Agent. *See* Pentad; Ratios
Anticipation of profits, 103. *See* also Bourdieu, P.
Antinomy. *See* Speech pathology report
Aspect. *See* Time and perspective
Attitude. *See* Orientation
Attitudinal lexis, 35-38
  illustrated, 44-45
  in Royal Bank financial advice booklets, 141-142
Authority. *See* Speech pathology report

Bacon, F., 40-45

Bateson, G., 4, 50
  double binds, 150-151
Bertelsen, D., 6
Binary oppositions, 109-124
  and ideational representation, 109-112
  and interpersonal orientation, 111
  and intertextuality, 117
  and social classification, 116-121
  discursive construction of, 112-116
Bourdieu, P., vii, ix, 91, 109, 170, 189, 191
  authoritative discourse, 156
  capital, 100
  classification, 98, 118, 186
  consumption, 11
  dialectic of social and symbolic, 95
  distinction, 101
  dominant culture, 120-121
  duality of structure, 94
  field, 100
  formal oppositions, 119
  gift exchange, 133
  habitus, 10, 95-100
  perceptual schemes, 119

production and reception, 103
representation, 105
structure of social field, 169
symbolic capital, 100, 104-105
symbolic power, 102, 104
symbolic violence, 84
the logic of stigma, 120
Burke, K., vii, ix, 6, 10, 88, 115, 123,
149, 155, 170-171, 183, 186, 193
action and motion, 81
attitude, 62, 180-181
consubstantiation, 6, 73
definition of man, 80-89. *See* also
Logology
directional substance, 69
dramatism, 63
familial substance, 68
function of rhetoric, 5, 59
geometric substance, 68
guilt, 79-80
identification and division, 74-75
logology, 79
mystery and hiearchy, 75, 85-87
nutritive substance, 68-69
order, 87
paradox of substance, 67, 69-70, 167
pentad, 63
perfection, 87-88
reflection, selection, and deflection, 64
semantic ideal, 111
substance, 66
symbolic acts, 3-5
symbolic communication, 61
symbol-using animals, 73
terministic screens, 61
the negative, 82-83
transformation, 6

Capital, 99-100. *See* also Symbolic
capital; Linguistic habitus
Circumstances, 26
illustrated, 28-30
in Royal Bank financial advice
booklets, 139-141
in Saturn advertisement, 114-115
Circumstantial functions. *See*
Circumstances
Classifying adjectives. *See* Attitudinal lexis
Cohesion, 48-52
Collocation, 51

Communication linguistics, 20, 22
Concept taxonomies, 27-28
as related to lexical cohesion, 52
illustrated, 31-32
in Saturn advertisement, 115-116
in speech pathology report, 154,
158-161
Conjunction. *See* Cohesion
Consubstantiation. *See* Identification
Context of situation. *See* Context
Context:
and field, tenor, and mode, 53-54
and text functions, 52
Cook, G., 112

Directional substance. *See* Substance
Discourse analysis:
and diversity, systematicity, and
applicability, 190-193
as critique, participation, and
communication, 193-194
as systemic, functional, and social,
107, 183-187
sources of, 9-11
special focus of, 187-188
Discourse, 5-6
defined, 11-12
Distinction, 99, 101
and binary opposition, 117-121
Division. *See* Identification
Dramatistic grammar. *See* Grammar
Dramatistism. *See* Grammar
Duality of structure, 93-94. *See* also
Giddens, A.

Ellipsis. *See* Cohesion
Emphasizing adjectives. *See* Attitudinal
lexis
Everyday texts, 1-5
as symbolic act, 2-4
role of, 1, 195-196
Expert advice, 124-151
as gift, 129-144
See also Royal Bank financial advice
booklets
Expert systems. *See* Expert advice; Royal
Bank financial advice booklets

Fairclough, N., 12, 56
Familial substance. *See* Substance
Field (social theory), 99-100
Field (discourse analysis):
    as social activity, 53
    defined, 53
    in relation to register, 54-55
Firth, J. R., 9, 92

Geometric substance. *See* Substance
Giddens, A., vii, ix, 6, 91
    duality of structure, 10, 94
    expert systems, 125, 129-130
    reflexivity, 131
    resources, 152-153
Gift. *See* Royal Bank financial advice
    booklets
Grammar, 62-73
Gregory, M., 22, 56

Habitus, 95-100.
    as embodied by social agents, 97
    as generative, 97-98
    as objective, 98
    as structured, 97
    as structuring, 97
    defined, 96
    in relation to classification, 98-99
    in relation to practice, 96
    See also Linguistic habitus
Halliday, M. A. K., and Hasan, R., 48
Halliday, M. A. K., vii, 10, 58
    circumstances, 26
    field, tenor, and mode, 52-53
    functions of language, 20-22
    ideational function, 22
    interpersonal function, 32
    meaning as choice, 15
    textual function, 45
Hierarchy, 85-87.
    in Saturn advertisement, 124
    See also Order
Hodge, R., and Kress, G., 12, 56
    logonomic systems, 78

Ideational function:
    defined, 20
    in relation to pentad and ratios, 64-66
    in relation to social discourse analysis,
        91-92
    resources of, 22-28
Identification, 6, 59, 62, 73-75
    in relation to social rhetorical analysis,
        92-93
    in relation to substance, 73
    in Royal Bank financial advice
        booklets, 144-145
    in Saturn advertisement, 123-124
Inclusion. *See* Royal Bank financial advice
    booklets
Interacting, 19-20. *See* also Interpersonal
    function
Interpersonal function:
    as positional meaning, 32-39.
    as relational meaning, 32-39.
    defined, 20, 32
    in relation to pentad and ratios, 64-66
    in relation to social discourse analysis,
        91-92
    in Royal Bank financial advice
        booklets, 135-139
    in Saturn advertisement, 113-114
    resources of, 34-39
    See also Positional value; Relational
        value

Korzybski, A., 82

Lemke, J. L., 5, 12, 56
    interpersonal function, 33
    register, 54-55
    social practice and semiosis, 81
Lexical cohesion. *See* Cohesion
    as related to Concept taxonomies, 52
Lexical relations. *See* Concept taxonomies
Linguistic capital. *See* Linguistic habitus;
    Symbolic captial
Linguistic habitus, 100-106
Logology, 59, 62, 77-89
    in relation to social rhetorical analysis,
        92-93
    in Royal Bank financial advice
        booklets, 149-151
    in Saturn advertisement, 123-124
    in speech pathology report, 168-169
Logonomic systems.
    and alienation, 84

defined, 78
See also Logology

Marked theme. See Theme
Market. See Field
Martin, J. R., 55
Mental processes. See Process types and
    participant roles.
Misrecognition. See Recognition
Modality, 35
    illustrated, 44
    in Royal Bank financial advice
        booklets, 140-141, 143
Mode, 17
    as social role, 53,
    defined, 53,
    in relation to register, 54-55
    in speech pathology report, 161-163
Mood. See Speech function
Multiple theme, 47-48. See also Theme
Mystery. See Hierarchy

Negative, 82-83. See also Logology
Nominalization, 25
    in Royal Bank financial advice
        booklets, 142-143
Nutritive substance. See Substance

Order, 73, 75-77
    in Saturn advertisement, 124
Organizing, 16-18. See also Textual
    function
Orientation, 4, 61
    and attitude, 180-182
    in relation to ratios, 64

Participants. See Process types and
    participant roles.
Pentad, 63-66.
    illustrated, 70-73
    in relation to functions of language,
        64-66
    in relation to identification, 74
    in relation to social rhetorical analysis,
        92-93
    See also Ratios
Positional value, 32-39

in Saturn advertisement, 113-114
Process types and participant roles:
    as attitude, 181
    defined, 22-25
    illustrated, 28-32
    in Royal Bank financial advice
        booklets, 139-142
    in Saturn advertisement, 114-116
    in speech pathology report, 157-158,
        163-166
Promotion. See Royal Bank financial
    advice booklets
Purpose. See Pentad; Ratios

Qualitative adjectives. See Attitudinal lexis

Ratios, 59, 63-66.
    as attitude, 181-182
    illustrated, 70-73
    in relation to identification, 74
    in Royal Bank financial advice
        booklets, 145-149
    in Saturn advertisement, 121-123
    in speech pathology report, 167-169
    See also Pentad
Recognition, 104-106
    and symbolic power, 104
    as impetus for criticism, 106
    in relation to paradox of substance,
        106
Reference. See Cohesion
Register, 15
    defined, 54
    in relation to function, 54-56
    in speech pathology report, 154-155
Relational processes. See Process types
    and participant roles.
Relational value, 32-39
    in Saturn advertisement, 113-114
Representing, 18. See also Ideational
    function
Resistant readings. See Speech pathology
    report
Rhetoric, 62, 73-77
Rhetorical analysis:
    and diversity, systematicity, and
        applicability, 190-193
    as critique, participation, and
        communication, 193-194

as systemic, functional, and social, 108, 183-187
sources of, 9-11
special focus of, 188-189
Royal Bank financial advice booklets, 124-151

Saturn automobile advertisement, 109-124
Scene. *See* Pentad; Ratios
Schiffrin, D., 20
Sentence adjuncts, 38-39
Situation. *See* Context
Social discourse analysis, 91-92
Social rhetorical analysis, 92-93
Social semiotics, 20, 32
Social theory:
    and attitude, 182
    and diversity, systematicity, and applicability, 190-193
    as critique, participation, and communication, 193-194
    as systemic, functional, and social, 108, 183-187
    sources of, 9-11
    special focus of, 189-190
Speech function, 34
    illustrated, 41-44
Speech pathology report, 151-178
Substance, 59, 66-70
    as attitude, 181-182
    illustrated, 70-73
    in Royal Bank financial advice booklets, 145-149
    in Saturn advertisement, 121-124
    in speech pathology report 167-169
    paradox of, 67
Substitution. *See* Cohesion
Symbolic capital, 100
Symbolic power, 102-106
Symbol-using animal. *See* Logology
Systems, 7-8
    as meaning making resource, 14
    in relation to function, 90, 182-185

Taste. *See* Distinction
Taylor, A. R., 131-132, 135-138
Tenor:
    as social role, 53,
    defined, 53
    in relation to register, 54-55
Tense. *See* Time and perspective
Terministic screens, 61, 81-82, 84
    in speech pathology report, 155, 165-167
Text, 5-6.
    as discourse, 5
    as rhetorical action, 5
    as social practice, 6
    as systemic, functional, and social, 7, 14-15, 182-187
    defined, 11-12
    See also Discourse
Textual function:
    defined, 21
    in relation to pentad and ratios, 64-66
    in relation to social discourse analysis, 91-92
    resources of, 45-52
Thematic development. *See* Theme
Theme, 17
    defined, 46-47
    in Saturn advertisement, 116
Thibault, P., 12, 56
Thompson, J.:
    linguistic capital, 100
    linguistic habitus, 101
Time and perspective, 26-27
    illustrated, 30-31
Transformation, 6, 74-75
    in relation to social rhetorical analysis, 92-93
    in Saturn advertisement, 123-124

Unmarked theme. *See* Theme

Wilden, A., 111

About the Author

Glenn F. Stillar, PhD, is Assistant Professor in the Department of English at the University of Waterloo (Waterloo, Ontario). He teaches undergraduate and graduate courses in discourse analysis, linguistics, rhetoric, stylistics, and semiotics. He has published articles in journals such as *Social Semiotics, Language and Style, Language and Literature,* and *Occasional Papers in Systemic Linguistics.*